Dedication

To Mitch (the mountain goat),
and
to Ariel and René—
you *are* Spartacus.

Hot Showers, Soft Beds, and Dayhikes in

The CENTRAL CASCADES

SALLY O'NEAL COATES

WILDERNESS PRESS
BERKELEY

Photos and maps by the author except as noted
Design by Margaret Copeland
Cover design by Larry Van Dyke
Front cover photos:
    top: Mt. Hood from Lost Lake (see Section 5—Mt. Hood) ©1998 by Larry Ulrich
    bottom: Timberline Lodge on Mt. Hood (see Section 5—Mt. Hood)
        © 1998 by Ed Cooper
Back cover photos:
    top: Mt. Rainier viewed from Naches Peak Loop Hike (see Section 1—Mt. Rainier)
    bottom: St. Helens Manorhouse (see Section 2—Mt. St. Helens)
Frontispiece photo: Mt. Rainier viewed from Naches Peak Loop Hike (see Section 1—Mt. Rainier)

Library of Congress Card Number 98-16134
ISBN 0-89997-218-7

Manufactured in the United States of America
Published by   Wilderness Press
                 2440 Bancroft Way
                 Berkeley, CA 94704
                 (800) 443-7227
                 FAX (510) 548-1355
                 wpress@ix.netcom.com

                 Visit our website www.wildernesspress.com
                 Contact us for a free catalog

Library of Congress Cataloging-in-Publication Data

Coates, Sally O'Neal
    Hot showers, soft beds, & dayhikes in fthe Central Cascades/
Sally O'Neal Coates. -- 1st ed.
    p.   cm.
    Includes bibliographical references and index.
    ISBN 0–89997–218–7
    1. Hiking--Cascade Range--Guidebooks. 2. Hiking--Washington
(State)--Guidebooks. 3. Hiking--Oregon--Guidebooks. 4. Cascade
range--Guidebooks. 5. Washington (State)--Guidebooks. 6. Oregon
--Guidebooks. I. Title.
GV199.42.C37C63 1998
917.97'73–dc21   98–16134
                                        CIP

Table of Contents

Acknowledgements

Thanks to my husband, Doug, who, as always, carries more than his share of the load, both literally and metaphorically. Your unflagging belief in me is one of the things that keeps me going when the writing life seems ridiculous. And on the days when all the hiking and writing seems too good to be true, you remind me that I deserve it.

Thanks to Shirley and Norm and Stan Miller, my employers and extended family at The Book Place. Only an independent bookseller would understand how important my books are to me. You give me the time off I need for research, and keep my job for me when I return—the best job in the world. Thanks for all your support. *And* for the spirited book signing parties. Thanks to Phyllis Bowersock, too, for hiring me in the first place.

Thanks to Geri and Keith Leonard, Ben and Nick Massey, Mitchell Coates, Eric Petersen, and B.J. Woodruff, for helping with the field work at Mt. Rainier. Your stalwart hiking was exceeded only by your repertoire of bad jokes. To Lizann Powers-Hammond, my new hiking buddy, who is entirely too cheerful in the morning, but otherwise the perfect companion. I think we were separated at birth. To Dottie and Bob Carrell, my rock-and-roll partners, for always being ready for anything—including hiking and impromptu swimming. Your support means more to me than you know. Thanks to Tyler and Kelsey, too—just for being you. You kids teach me a lot.

Thanks to Ariel and René O'Neal, strong hikers, brilliant girls, chips off the old block. I love you. And thanks to Melody O'Neal, my sister-in-law, for letting them hike with Crazy Aunt Sally.

Thanks to my family and friends for watching my house and livestock in my absence: Dick and Kay, Julie and Rob, Mandy and Melissa, Mitch, Mom (Jeanne O'Neal). And Mike Rumsey—I know you would rather have been hiking, but someone has to keep the home fires burning. You're a pal.

Thanks to Marilyn Morford and Diane Molleson, who help me remember that I'm a writer first, a hiker second (or third, or fourth…)

Thanks to Katie Sanborn, who not only climbed to the summit of Mount St. Helens with me, but continually reassures me, through her presence in my life, that I'm a contender. Remember who you are and what you represent.

Thanks to Wilderness Press and the mighty Winnetts: Tom, for discovering me, giving me a chance, and encouraging me to continue; Jason, for being a gracious host at Breitenbush, and letting me play my first didjeridoo; and especially Caroline, my publisher, editor, friend, Finder of Lost Commas, and Fixer of Wounded Egos—and one hell of a dancer.

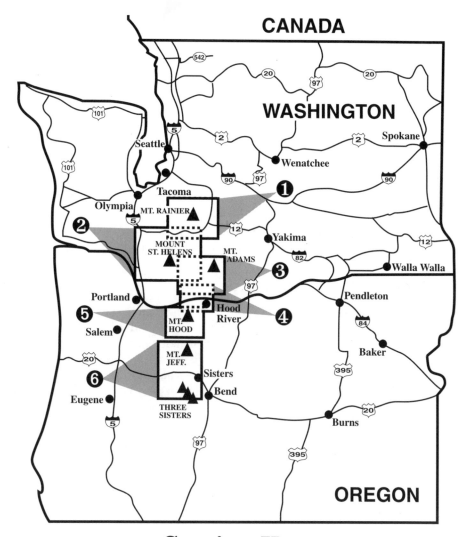

Section Key

❶ Mt. Rainier
dayhikes inside and outside the national park boundaries; lodgings in Ashford, Packwood & White Pass

❷ Mount St. Helens
hikes in and near the national volcanic monument; lodgings on the east, west, and south approaches

❸ Mt. Adams
dayhikes south and west of Washington's "forgotten" Cascade peak; lodgings in nearby Trout Lake and Glenwood

❹ Columbia Gorge
a sampling of features along the Columbia River Gorge corridor between Washington and Oregon

❺ Mt. Hood
dayhikes and lodgings along Highway 26 and along the Hood River Valley corridor east of the mountain

❻ Central Oregon
Mt. Jefferson, Mt. Washington, Black Butte, the Sisters, Belknap Crater, Metolius and Breitenbush river areas

Preface

In the summer of my fifth year, my parents abandoned me at the base of Mt. Rainier.

Okay—to be fair, they didn't leave me behind on purpose. Through a comedy of errors, they thought I was in the truck-mounted camper with my brothers and sister; my siblings thought I was in the cab with Mom and Dad. (Or so they say. I can picture them now, giggling and poking one another in mischievous complicity and full knowledge of my absence.)

My parents remember this as The Big Error, a source of shame that, although joked about in years to follow, still produces a guilty, embarrassed flush when mentioned. I, on the other hand, remember it as The Big Adventure. Having toddled off to the restroom while my family was breaking camp, I returned to find the spot that had been our campsite swept bare. I reacted by wandering up the road to the visitor center, not to mention my predicament to anyone, but simply to enjoy the time I now had to peruse the lighted display panels of native flora and fauna at my leisure.

I loved the Ohanapecosh Ranger Station. I loved the push-a-button-and-light-me-up panels, and I loved trying to pronounce the mellifluous names of the flowers ("pip-sis-se-wa, pip-sis-se-wa..."). I loved standing next to the giant tree-trunk cross-section, pondering its rings and wondering how it looked as a sapling when Columbus was crossing the sea. I loved wandering the path through the outdoor displays trying to distinguish deer fern from sword fern.

Not much has changed in thirty years.

This summer, standing at the tree-trunk cross-section at the Ohanapecosh visitor center at Mt. Rainier National Park, I grinned as I recalled my mother, in a teary-eyed panic, bursting from the cab of the pick-up truck to "save" me. I remembered how, just last spring, my father regaled relatives with the old story over pizza: "If we hadn't stopped to gas up in Packwood, she'd have still been there today."

I asked a fellow tourist to take my picture by the tree trunk. Then I strapped on my pack, grabbed my notepad and mini-cassette recorder, and headed up the old trail, past deer fern and pipsissewa, to Silver Falls.

Introduction

WHAT THIS BOOK IS

The *Hot Showers, Soft Beds* series is written for the tens of thousands of us who love the wilderness but also appreciate life's creature comforts. We enjoy the sounds of a burbling brook, but we also appreciate the *whoosh* of a cappuccino machine. We might not mind pitching a tent in an alpine meadow, but we also understand the joy of waking up between clean sheets under a down comforter, well-rested and refreshed, with the smell of French toast and sausage wafting down the hall. We are true wilderness lovers, who appreciate nothing more than a day of leisure in the mountains, where miles of trails beckon, wildflowers bloom, and the air is crisp and clean. But we also like the idea of ending the day with a hot shower, a decent meal, and a comfortable bed.

To serve people like us, this book is a sampling of some of the best short- to mid-range dayhikes near the peaks of the central Cascades, and a sampling of some of the comfortable lodgings in various price ranges near those hikes. It also provides descriptions of some of the restaurants near each set of hikes and lodgings.

The walks and hikes in this book range from flat, wheelchair-accessible strolls of less than a mile to an 11-mile round-trip climb to the rim of a volcano. Each is within an easy walk or drive of a comfortable lodge, cabin, motel, or bed & breakfast. The lodgings range from rustic cabins and simple motels to luxurious resorts and historic lodges.

WHAT THIS BOOK ISN'T

Hot Showers, Soft Beds, and Dayhikes in the Central Cascades is not an exhaustive list of hikes or of lodgings. It is a sample, a cross-section, a "best-of-the-best" selection according to the author and editors of the book. It is not meant to list every hike, lodging, or restaurant in the area. Instead, it provides detailed descriptions of a number of selected trails and lodgings, with photos, to help you plan your trip to the central Cascades with a bit more stimulation of the imagination than a mere list of statistics could offer. For more information on a specific area, addresses and telephone numbers are provided at the end of each section.

As this book emphasizes hiking from lodgings, information about camping is not provided. Ranger districts, listed at the back of the book under *Contact Information*, can help if you plan to camp.

This is not a wilderness survival text. If you plan to venture beyond the recommended routes, please check with local rangers and arm yourself with the appropriate topographic maps and backcountry equipment.

IS THIS BOOK FOR YOU?

Maybe you haven't hiked in years. *Hot Showers, Soft Beds, and Dayhikes in the Central Cascades* can be a gentle way to "get back in the saddle" and try a few trails, all within driving distance of a comfortable overnight lodging.

Maybe you have children, or a spouse or a friend, who are new to hiking. This book will help you choose trails appropriate to their level of ambition and conditioning, and provide everyone in your party with an enjoyable outdoor experience.

Maybe you're an experienced hiker—a backpacker, even—whose idea of heaven is a week-long trudge in backcountry isolation. But you don't *have* a full week to kill every time you get the urge to hike. This book is for you—it will let you get out on the trail for a day or two when you have the chance.

Maybe you're new to the Pacific Northwest, or just visiting. In the pages that follow, you'll find an introduction to the various parts of the central Cascades. Choose the historic, topographic, and scenic features that appeal to you, and head out with confidence. Each region described has easy, moderate, and more challenging dayhike trails.

Or maybe you're like me, a Pacific Northwest native who knows a few trails and has already discovered the joy of hiking from a comfortable lodging. You need this book for its lodging and trail descriptions, to help you make informed choices before you head out, and to avoid nasty surprises.

Hiking from lodgings, as opposed to backpacking or dayhiking from a campsite, is practical as well as comfortable. Not everyone owns a collection of camping gear; such equipment can be expensive to acquire and maintain, and is difficult to justify if you hike infrequently. It doesn't require as much preparation time to pack for dayhiking as it does to pack for backpacking or camping out. And hiking from lodgings is a nice foul-weather alternative. Few things are more depressing than a leaky tent in a downpour. Even if you don't mind hiking in the rain, it's nice to come back to a warm, dry refuge at day's end. I would rather exercise on the trail, then relax in front of a fireplace, than get my workout packing and unpacking wet camping gear, making a mad dash to the car, and heading home early because of a storm.

WHAT ARE THE "CENTRAL CASCADES?"

The Cascade mountain range runs north-south from British Columbia, Canada, through Washington and Oregon, into northern California. This book defines "central Cascades" as the area from Mt. Rainier, in central Washington state, south to the Sisters, in central Oregon. (Those seeking dayhikes and lodgings north of Mt. Rainier should read *Hot Showers, Soft Beds, and Dayhikes in the North Cascades,* which covers Washington's Cascades from the Interstate 90 corridor to the Canadian border.) The areas covered in this book are as follows:

Section 1 - Mt. Rainier
Dayhikes in the national park and surrounding Gifford Pinchot National Forest and Goat Rocks Wilderness; lodgings in Ashford, Packwood, and White Pass.

Section 2 - Mount St. Helens
Dayhikes and lodgings divided into three subsections: the west approach (Highway 504); the east approach (Highway 12 and Road 99); and the south approach (Highway 503 and Road 90).

Section 3 - Mt. Adams
Dayhikes south and west of the mountain, including Mt. Adams Wilderness, Indian Heaven Wilderness, and the Yakama Nation Recreational Area; lodgings in Trout Lake and Glenwood.

Section 4 - Columbia Gorge
A few dayhikes and a number of lodgings along the Columbia River Gorge National Scenic Area corridor between Washington and Oregon; lodgings and restaurants in this section also serve Sections 2, 3, and 5.

Section 5 - Mt. Hood
Dayhikes and lodgings along the Highway 35 (Hood River Valley) corridor east of the mountain and along the Highway 26 corridor south of the mountain, including Lolo Pass Road 18.

Section 6 - Central Oregon
Dayhikes near Mt. Jefferson, Mt. Washington, and the Sisters; lodgings near Sisters, Camp Sherman, and Detroit.

ABOUT THE HIKES

The walks and hikes included in this book range from short strolls of less than a mile to full-day adventures up to 11 miles. Most are 5 miles or less. All are considered "dayhikes," hikes that the moderately fit individual without mobility impairment could drive to, hike, and then return to one of several nearby lodgings before dark.

Each hike begins with a listing of distance (usually round-trip), elevation gain or loss, and estimated time.

Elevation gain is provided to help you get an idea of the steepness and relative difficulty of the hike. Experienced hikers will find this more useful than novices. For those of you new to hiking, bear in mind Sally's Elevation Rule Of Thumb: 1000 feet per mile = butt-kicker. The difficulty increases geometrically if this pitch continues for a number of miles. (Example: *Section 4*, Dog Mountain: 7.0 miles, 2900′ elevation gain. 7.0 miles round trip = 3.5 miles each way. 2900 ÷ 3.5 = 829 vertical feet per mile, extended over 3.5 miles, or a couple of hours. In other words, this is a borderline butt-kicker to the moderately fit dayhiker.)

Elevation figures in this text are sometimes rounded off, using a combination of topo map review, US Forest Service information, and altimeter measurement.

Regarding estimated time for hiking, I start with 2.0 miles per hour as a basis, and take several factors into consideration. The elevation gain and terrain, of course, affect the length of time—a mile that gains 1000′ or one that requires rock scrambling may take an hour, while a mile that is flat and well-graded may take only 20 minutes. Most guidebooks factor in such conditions. I also tried to take other intangibles into consideration, such as scenic viewpoint stops, ideal picnic areas, and natural features worth pausing for. The result is that a 5.8-mile hike such as Bird Creek Meadows Loop (*Section 3*, "Mt. Adams") may take four hours, because it's so full of whizbang views, whereas Patjens Lakes Loop (*Section 6*, "Central Oregon"), similar in length at 5.6 miles, may take only 2 hours, 45 minutes, because much of the trail is viewless and featureless—it's more of a "walk for the sake of walking."

At the end of each section, *Other Hike Notes* is a listing of hikes which did not merit a complete write-up, either because I did not personally review them or because I do not recommend them. The descriptions of these hikes are shorter and less detailed. If a hike is not recommended, the brief description explains why.

Recommended maps are listed at the beginning of each hike. I favor Green Trails maps and US Forest Service maps because they are easy to read and are readily obtainable at outdoor stores. Their scale is large enough to show detail, but the maps are small enough to be conveniently carried. USGS topographic maps can also be useful, but they are bulky and hard to read, and often outdated. Some trails, particularly the very short ones and the very new ones, do not show on existing maps; in these cases, I will list a map of the area, and say "access only," meaning that the map shows how to get to the trail, but not the trail itself. The hikes in this book follow well-defined trails, and the directions given in the text provide complete instructions to find your way. In a few instances, where many trails cross one another, or where the written directions may require some visual clarification, I have provided a rudimentary map. It's always a good idea to purchase and use a current map when hiking any but the shortest nature trail. Maps can be purchased from ORIC (Outdoor Recreation Information Center), MapLink, or the US Forest Service; these phone numbers and addresses are listed under *Contact Information* near the end of the book.

The hikes in this book are not rated for beauty or for difficulty; each hike included is extremely scenic or unique. Difficulty is in the eye of the beholder (or the thighs of the hiker…)—a flat 10-mile round-trip might feel easier than a steep 4-miler to one hiker, but harder to another. In general, hikes in each section are listed in their approximate order of difficulty, with easy strolls and walks first, followed by easy hikes, followed by moderate hikes, and ending with the section's most challenging hike. To determine the best hikes for you, read the descriptions thoroughly.

While I have attempted to classify certain hikes as especially appropriate or especially inappropriate for children, it should be noted that a wilderness experience always carries with it certain dangers. Children should be mindful of the dangers posed by slippery rocks, talus surfaces, wildlife seen and unseen, rivers and streams, and drop-offs—nature does not provide hand rails and warning signs.

Be aware that hiking trails and access roads are subject to change over time: forks appear and disappear from use and disuse; washouts and other phenomena—natural and man-made—necessitate re-routing. Also note that mileage calculations vary from one source to another. Various hiking guides may differ on mileage for the same hike. Official Forest Service mileage often differs from that shown on recreation maps. Posted mileage often differs from printed information. Mileage in this book was based on a combination of Forest Service information, time/distance calculation, and use of a pedometer.

ABOUT THE LODGINGS

A wide variety of lodging styles were included: four-star resorts, humble cabins, charming B&B's, basic motels. Their common criteria were (1) they were located within easy access distance to the hikes in their section, (2) they were clean and comfortable, with hot showers and soft beds, and (3) they were a good value for their type of lodging in their geographic area. A $40 motel room will obviously offer a different experience than a $175 resort suite, but both can be good values.

Lodgings are not rated. If a lodging is listed under *Lodgings* and a full description is given, that lodging has been reviewed and it is recommended. Please read the descriptions and understand, while all accommodations detailed are recommended, that "rustic" is different than "elegant." In some cases, a brief listing of *Additional Lodgings* follows the detailed descriptions of recommended lodgings; these establishments were visited, but not reviewed in detail and are not endorsed by the author.

At the end of each section, I have provided a grid comparing the basic features of the recommended lodgings at a glance. For a more complete explanation of prices and amenities, refer to the individual lodging description. The cells within the grid can be interpreted as follows:

Price This is the rate for two persons during peak season (July/August) of 1997. Tax may be added to this rate.

Extra Person This is the extra charge, if any, for each person beyond the two persons staying in the same room or unit.

Payment Methods Lists which credit cards (VISA, Mastercard, American Express, or Discover) the establishment accepts, and whether they accept personal checks or cash.

# of Units Total number of rental units available at the property.

Private Bath How many units have private baths, how many have shared baths.

Breakfast Included Whether a full breakfast is included in the price of your room. If "yes," it's a full breakfast. "Continental" breakfasts are so designated.

Cooking Facilities If some rooms have kitchens, or if a kitchen is available for guest use, this will say "yes." If a few appliances, such as a microwave and/or a toaster, are offered, this space may say "kitchenette."

Pool Whether a swimming pool is available for guest use during the summer months.

Hot Tub "Yes" means one or more of the rooms has a private hot tub or that one or more shared hot tubs is available for guest use. If some rooms have jetted spa tubs, these may be mentioned here.

Children This says "OK," "No," or lists the ages over which children are accepted by the establishment. "By Arrangement" means call ahead and discuss your needs. This often applies to B&B's and other intimate arrangements, where it depends upon the nature of the other guests the night(s) you plan to stay.

Pets "OK" means pets are allowed in at least one room of the premises. If a deposit or fee is collected, it will be listed here. As with children, "By Arrangement" means to call ahead and discuss your situation.

Handicapped Accessible Means that one or more rooms or units are considered barrier-free. It does not imply ADA standards, nor does it mean that the entire premises and all amenities are accessible.

All prices and features are subject to change. Many properties have lower rates during the off-season, which may be winter if they aren't a skiing destination, or spring/fall if they have a large winter trade. Some also offer discounts for midweek guests, for multiple-room bookings, and for multiple-night stays; be sure to inquire. Advance reservations are strongly encouraged at all lodgings.

TRAIL PARK PASS SYSTEM AND OTHER TRAIL USE FEES

The national forests of Washington and Oregon began implementing the Trail Park Pass System in 1997. By 1998, all national forests covered in this book— Gifford Pinchot, Mt. Hood, Deschutes, and Willamette, plus the Columbia Gorge National Scenic Area—were participating in this fee system. In the wake of crisis-level funding cuts for our national forests, this system was devised to enable users of the parks to participate in trail and facilities maintenance.

Trail Park Passes cost $25 per vehicle per calendar year. The same pass is valid throughout all of the forests and the Columbia Gorge National Scenic Area. The pass itself is a static-cling windshield label bearing your vehicle's license plate number. (A second pass, for another vehicle driven by the same family, can be purchased at the same time for $5.) Passes can be purchased at ranger stations and selected locations including sporting goods stores, supermarkets, and visitor centers. A single-day pass can be purchased for $3. For up-to-date information on pass outlets, contact the ranger district or information center in the area you plan to visit first. Contact telephone numbers are given at the end of each section.

Mt. Rainier National Park charges an entrance fee of $10 per carload, valid for 7 days. Mount St. Helens National Volcanic Monument requires that all adults purchase and wear a Monument Pass for access to visitor centers and some trails; at $8, it is valid for 3 days. Full details regarding these fee areas are provided in the relevant chapters.

SAFETY AND SENSE

Even short dayhikes are wilderness experiences, and should be approached with caution, respect, and common sense.

Always tell someone where you're going and approximately when you expect to be back. This is another advantage to staying in a lodging: you can tell your hosts. If someone is expecting you, you won't have as long to wait should something unexpected happen along the trail. Self-registry at many trailheads is another safeguard. If you have an opportunity to sign in, do so.

Always set out with a full tank of gas and a topped-off radiator. Very few of the hikes in the book involve lengthy drives, but many are on unpaved, somewhat difficult roads, and some require your vehicle to climb steep stretches of road. Check with the local rangers as to access road conditions before you start out. Note that all hikes included in this book can be reached with a normal passenger car under normal circumstances; a 4-wheel-drive vehicle is not required.

Don't leave valuables in your car at the trailhead. Better yet, don't drive a valuable car to the trailhead. And don't assume that your trunk or your glove compartment are safe from trailhead thugs.

Anytime you venture away from town or your vehicle, you are subject to the vicissitudes of wilderness and weather. For that reason, stock your daypack with:

- Water—more than you think you need—and extra food.
- Extra clothing, including rain gear, dry socks, hat, and gloves.
- Map and compass (and the knowledge to use them).
- First aid kit, including treatment for cuts, snake bites, and bee stings (and the knowledge to use it).
- Flashlight.
- Sunscreen and sunglasses.
- Matches (waterproof) and fire-starter (such as a candle).
- Whistle and signal mirror.
- Pocket knife.
- Insect repellent.
- Trowel or small shovel (see Leave No Trace, below).

Dayhikers often underpack water. It's heavy, but running out is a nuisance, and dehydration can be very dangerous, leading to disorientation even on a dayhike, and organ damage over a prolonged period. You shouldn't drink from sources along the trail. Giardia and other dangerous bacteria and microorganisms are odorless, tasteless, and everywhere; the only safe water is that which you pack along or purify. For dayhikes, why not just pack it in?

It's a good idea for *each* hiker in your party—child and adult—to have a basic "survival" kit on their person; often, a fanny pack will do. This provides an extra measure of safety, should you become separated. The personal kit should contain some nutrient-dense food (such as Power Bars), a whistle, and a small flashlight. Those with the knowledge to use them should have a knife, a compass, waterproof matches, and a fire-starter candle as well. And everyone should carry his or her water. Instruct children to STAY PUT if lost, to signal for help if they're able, and not to resist or hide from rescuers.

Extra clothing may seem an excessive precaution for the dayhiker. It's probably not necessary on short strolls a mile or less from the car, but for longer hikes, it's really a good idea to be prepared for the unexpected. A shift in weather (common in the mountains) or a change in terrain can change the climate of your hike. You can be on a hot, open, rocky ridge at 9 A.M., in a moist, cool, shady creekbed at 10, and crossing the remainder of a chilly, late-season snowfield at 11. And raingear is always in order.

Mosquitoes and flies can be thick in some locations, especially in midsummer, and especially near water. While insect repellent is useful, your best defense is a sense of humor and acceptance. Expose as little skin as possible, or bring a bandanna to brush across your legs and arms as you walk. A few areas, most notoriously *Section 4*, "Columbia Gorge," are also home to ticks, which don't seem to be affected by insect repellent. Check your skin and scalp thoroughly after hiking in an area with ticks.

Another item I recommend is pepper spray—and make sure you get one that is rated for bear attack, with adequate quantity and spray range (preferably 30 feet). It should have a locking device to prevent accidental spraying, and some sort of holster with a quick-release mechanism for immediate access. Using a thumb or index finger trigger, you simply aim and shoot. Black bears are common in the Cascades, and grizzlies have been sighted. Of course, the wilderness is the bears' home, not yours, so I hope you never have to use it. Your best defense against bears is to avoid startling them. Make a bit of noise as you travel (a bell on your shoe or walking stick is helpful), and keep an eye peeled.

A major pepper spray manufacturer suggests the following three-step approach:

1. If a bear approaches, shoot a cloud of pepper spray toward it when it is about 30 feet from you.

2. If it continues to advance, aim another 2 short blasts at its face when it is about 20 feet from you.

3. If it advances within 10 feet of you, spray continuously, aiming directly at the bear's face and eyes.

Pepper spray is also a good idea for women hikers, or anyone concerned about personal defense against the human element.

Rattlesnakes are another wilderness bugaboo. I have tried to indicate hikes on which these reptilian friends are particularly common. Be alert on sun-warmed, south-facing slopes. If you see one, let it pass. As with bears, the best defense is to avoid startling them. Thump a walking stick on the ground as you travel, carry on a quiet conversation, hum a little tune. In other words, be yourself. *They* don't like *you* much, either.

A walking stick, in addition to warning snakes, comes in handy for stream fording. For longer hikes, or if you want to maintain a brisk pace, consider "trekking poles." These poles, singly or in pairs, are like short ski poles, and are said to save wear and tear on the knees.

If you plan to do more than a few quarter-mile nature strolls, consider purchasing and wearing hiking boots. Tennis shoes are OK for pavement and short distances on level surfaces; running shoes offer support for forward motion, but have insufficient lateral support or midsole stability for hiking. If a trail has any elevation gain, or surfaces described as "rocky" or "rooty," wear hiking boots—they have tread and ankle support for a reason. If you're new to hiking, by all means break them in by wearing them around the house, then around town, before using them on the trail.

LEAVE NO TRACE

Things have changed in the past several decades. Some of us may remember tramping through the woods as children, our parents picking the occasional flower or grabbing a handful of fragrant cedar or interesting leaves. As 20th- and 21st-century stewards of the wilderness, we don't molest nature for our own curiosity's sake anymore. We don't build fires wherever we feel like it; we don't drink from streams if we're wise. Today, we carry tiny stoves and bottled water, we take photographs rather than samples.

We certainly don't litter. Fortunately, most hikers seem to understand and respect this most basic of trail courtesies. You might want to carry an extra plastic bag for the trash you find on the trail as well as your own. Plan to pack out every scrap you pack in, including orange peels, apple cores, and nut shells, which don't "return to the soil" as fast as we would like to think. Most trailheads don't have trash cans, so plan to take your garbage and scraps with you. Never put garbage in a pit toilet.

Please don't feed wildlife. It teaches them dependence and is not healthy for them.

Stay on the developed trail. Cutting switchbacks and trampling meadows cause erosion and flora damage that will only worsen with time.

Dispose of human waste properly. When toilets aren't available, urinate on rocks or bare soil, not on foliage. Bury feces 4–6 inches deep (here's where that trowel comes in), and use only biodegradable toilet paper (available in RV or camping stores). Always choose spots at least 100 yards from water sources.

Do not collect rocks, flowers, mushrooms, or anything else without checking beforehand with the ranger or administrative jurisdiction responsible for the area in which you are hiking.

Generally speaking, do not build fires. If your dayhike picnic plans call for something hot, consider bringing it in a thermos or packing along a camp stove. Fires in designated campsites can be an exception, but these should generally be left to the backpackers and campers.

Many Cascade trails are for hikers only: closed to stock and/or bicycles. Be sure to check before hitting the trail with anything but your feet.

Pets are not allowed on some trails, and are required to be leashed on others. Such regulations change all the time; please check before bringing your pet.

WHEN CAN I HIKE?

Hiking in the Central Cascades is generally a summer and early fall activity. The trails at the highest elevations may be open only mid-July (or even late-July) through mid-September; other trails may be open as early as May and remain open until late October. Some very low-elevation trails, such as those in the Columbia Gorge, may be open all but a few snowy mid-winter months. Conditions vary dramatically from year to year; always check with the local ranger district or other authorities before visiting an area with hiking plans.

Early- and late-season hiking can be rewarding; you avoid the summertime crowds and see a different set of foliage. When the snow first melts, little fairy clumps of mushrooms remain untrammeled, and the tiniest, most delicate and palest flowers reach out to catch the sun's first rays. But trails are often wet and mucky in the early season, and you may have to pick your way over winter's deadfall debris if you hike before a trail has been cleared. Wear long pants if you hike at the beginning of the season, as you'll likely be breaking trail, and things may be wet.

Late-season hiking presents its own challenges, mostly in terms of unpredictable weather. No one knows for sure when snow will fall, so late-season hikes are hard to plan. If conditions are right, September and October can be beautiful hiking months in the Cascades, rewarding you with fall colors and ripe huckleberries.

If you hike during the high season, try to hike early and late in the day, and on weekdays if you can, to avoid the crowds.

No matter when you choose to hike, or which of the six areas in this book you choose, the Central Cascades offer a wealth of scenic opportunity and a variety of trails sure to please and challenge walkers and hikers of all levels of ability.

Now, let's hit the trail.

Happy hikers on the trail

Section 1—Mt. Rainier

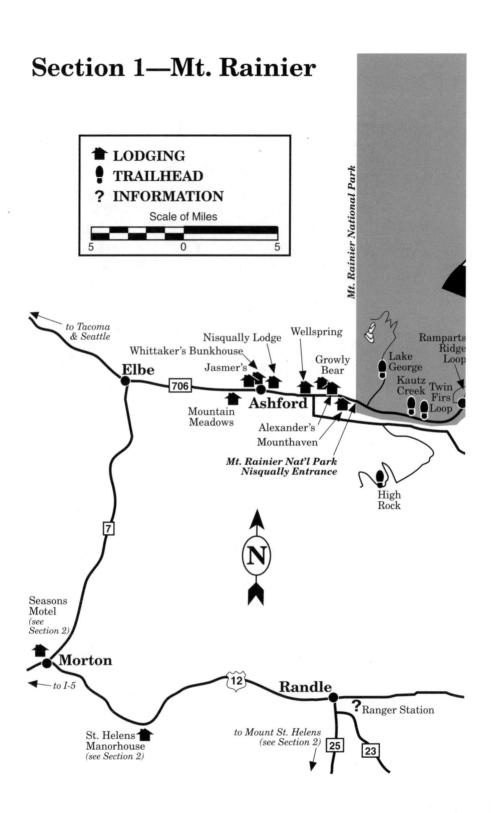

LODGING

TRAILHEAD

? INFORMATION

Scale of Miles

5　　　0　　　5

Mt. Rainier National Park

to Tacoma & Seattle

Nisqually Lodge　Wellspring

Whittaker's Bunkhouse

Elbe　706　Jasmer's　Growly Bear

Ramparts Ridge Loop

Lake George

Kautz Creek　Twin Firs Loop

Mountain Meadows

Ashford

Alexander's

Mounthaven

Mt. Rainier Nat'l Park Nisqually Entrance

High Rock

N

Seasons Motel *(see Section 2)*

Morton

to I-5

7

12　**Randle**

? Ranger Station

St. Helens Manorhouse *(see Section 2)*

to Mount St. Helens (see Section 2)　25　23

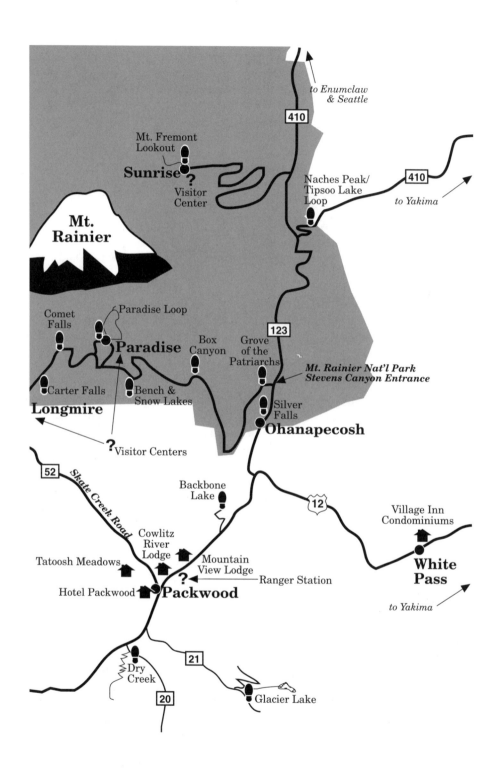

Mt. Rainier

OVERVIEW

King of the Cascades, Mt. Rainier is the tallest of the great volcanic peaks of the Cascade Range. Native Americans abandoned metaphor in the face of this mighty peak and called it what it was: *Tahoma*, "The Mountain." Once you stand at its base and gaze up its glaciered flanks, you will understand why. This imposing monarch of a mountain, made accessible for all by the national park system, defines Mountain.

In 1792, British explorer George Vancouver named the mountain in honor of fellow navigator Peter Rainier. The first documented ascent to Mt. Rainier's summit was made by Hazard Stevens and Philemon Van Trump in 1870. The mountain remains a climbers' paradise today. With the largest single-peak glacier system in the US, it offers a variety of technical challenges and is used by climbers from all over the world to prepare for other summit climbs such as Mt. Everest.

The roughly square national park surrounding Mt. Rainier has four main access points: Nisqually entrance, on Highway 706 at the park's southwest corner; Highway 123 near Ohanapecosh at the park's southeast corner; Highway 410 at Chinook Pass, midway up the park's east side; and Highway 410 at the park's northeast corner. Two other entrances, Carbon River and Mowich Lake Road, both at the park's northwest corner, are less-used, due in part to flood damage of the roads, trails, and campgrounds in that part of the park. The Mt. Rainier National Park dayhikes featured in Section 1 are located along the more accessible south and east corridors of the park.

The road from the Nisqually entrance to Longmire is open year-round, but other park roads are open seasonally only, depending upon snow levels. (Even at summer's end, 34 square miles of snow remain on Mt. Rainier—more than on all the other Cascade volcanoes combined.)

Two million people visit Mt. Rainier National Park annually. The first—and sometimes the only—place they go is Paradise. With its spectacular wildflowers and full view of the mountain, it's easy to see how Paradise earned its name, and why it's so popular. It's less clear why so many dazed tourists jam inside the incongruous, spaceship-like Henry M. Jackson Memorial Visitor Center, a disappointing structure that houses a book store, a café, a few interpretive displays, a gift shop, and pay showers. I suppose everyone must stop here, but I'd recommend against it on a midsummer weekend, when it seems that all 2 million visitors are here at once. In fact, even on a drizzly June day, when such easy and lovely trails as Carter Falls and Silver Falls were virtually empty, I found the visitor center packed, especially the gift shop, which isn't even particularly well-stocked (the one just up the hill at Paradise Inn is better).

Many Mt. Rainier National Park trails are hikeable only from mid-July through early October. When in doubt, use the contact telephone numbers provided at the end of this section. No pets, bicycles, or weapons are allowed on the trails within the park. Stock use is permitted on some trails. Do not pick or cut flowers, plants, or trees; do not make fires except in designated drive-in campgrounds; and pack out everything you pack in.

As with many of our national parks, Mt. Rainier is going through a certain amount of administrative turmoil in terms of budget and providing services to the public. Overuse and underfunding is not unique to Mt. Rainier National Park. Access and fees may change in the future; services may be added or cut back. Some roads are in need of repair. Visitors to the Sunrise area (northeast corner of the park) may experience delays due to road maintenance in the coming few years—sections of Highway 410 are scheduled for work.

The basic Mt. Rainier National Park access fee is $10 per carload, and is valid for 7 days. An annual pass can be purchased for $20. Senior citizens (age 62+) can purchase the Golden Age Passport, valid for life, for $10. Mt. Rainier also accepts the Golden Eagle Passport (available to senior citizens for $50, valid for one year at most federal recreation sites) and the Golden Access Passport (available free of charge to individuals with permanent disabilities).

Many excellent hiking trails are located outside of the national park in the Gifford Pinchot National Forest. Unlike the national park trails, some of the national forest trails allow leashed pets, mountain bikes, and even motorized vehicles. Designated wilderness areas, including Goat Rocks, Tatoosh, Glacier View, and William O. Douglas, have their own regulations, including: permits required (self-issuing at trailheads); group size limited to 12, including pack and saddle stock; no mountain bikes or motorcycles; no chain saws; no shortcutting of trail switchbacks; pack-it-in-pack-it-out. Regulations specific to an individual trail may be listed in its detailed description under *Walks and Hikes,* below. When in doubt, contact the Forest Service.

Gifford Pinchot National Forest participates in the Trail Park Pass system. To park at a trailhead, you must display a Trail Park Pass decal in the window of your vehicle. See *Trail Park Pass System* in the Introduction.

The towns of Ashford and Packwood are the two primary service communities outside the park, and the ones in which this section's featured lodgings are concentrated.

Ashford, located just outside the Nisqually (southwest) entrance to the park, is a charming, remote, serene woodland community of about 600 year-round residents and 300 tourist beds. As of this writing, it is a community almost completely without pretense: no tacky tourist shops, no boardwalk attractions. Its serene and soulful collection of almost exclusively owner-operated properties is tucked unobtrusively along or just off Highway 706, which bisects town.

As early as 1998, construction may be underway for a behemoth resort complex just west of Ashford that could eclipse the eclectic, small-town atmosphere visitors now enjoy. The controversial resort was conceived as a year-round vacation and convention facility with a golf course, three restaurants, a shopping center, and over 500 total rooms in mixed lodge and condo units. The property would appropriate 400 acres of elk pasture, and is being contested by environmental groups and local businesses, which would like to see the scope of the project downsized to be more compatible with the traffic flow and atmosphere of the national park.

Packwood, 7 miles from the park's southeast entrance on Highway 123, near Ohanapecosh, is a bit more in-your-face touristy than Ashford, with its two-block "main drag," its ice cream and pizza shops, its craft and gift stores, and its small-town, high-country festivals. With ample amenities for kids, including boating and fishing at nearby Packwood Lake, Packwood is a good base for families visiting Mt. Rainier.

East of Packwood on Highway 12 is White Pass, a ski destination that offers a few lodging options in the summer, one of which is featured in this section. West on Highway 12 is Randle, then Morton. Lodgings in these communities are featured in Section 2, Mount St. Helens, but are also close enough to visit Mt. Rainier and do the dayhikes listed in this section.

LODGINGS
Listed in alphabetical order under two subsections "Ashford Lodgings" and "Packwood/White Pass Lodgings"

Ashford Lodgings:

ALEXANDER'S INN
37515 SR 706 East • Ashford, WA 98304
(800) 654-7615 • (360) 569-2300

Most folks who've driven into Mt. Rainier National Park from the west have driven past a curious and beautiful old inn a mile from the park's Nisqually entrance. They might remember its quaint turret and its water wheel. That's Alexander's Inn.

The inn is named for Alexander Mesler, an important local historic figure, whose original 1890 homestead still stands today as the Growly Bear B&B (see below). But Alexander liked visitors, so he built an inn next to his home and mill. That inn, originally called "Mesler Inn," survives today as the restored and gracious Alexander's Inn.

The historic architecture of the inn has been beautifully restored, with decorative woodwork and stained glass touches throughout. Rooms are on the small

ALEXANDER'S INN
Historic inn with charming ambience

side, in keeping with the period of construction, but the lounge is marvelously roomy and inviting. Located on the second floor (away from the non-guest traffic of the first floor restaurant), the lounge is full of elegant yet comfortable furnishings, and is decorated in tones of rose and seafoam green. A large fireplace warms the room both literally and figuratively. Games are provided for your amusement, and complimentary wine is served at

5 P.M. daily. As there are no telephones in the rooms, the lounge area has a pay phone for guest use.

Each of Alexander's 12 rooms is unique. Each has its own bathroom, but some are across the hall from the room. All rooms have queen beds, and some have balconies or decks. While modest in size, they are airy and well-appointed, with fresh, pale-tone decor and comfy quilts. "Petite Suites" include a sitting area with couch. Two of the most popular rooms are located in the tower. The Lower Tower Suite has its own porch. The Upper Tower Suite is a 2-level affair. A many-windowed sitting room and small bathroom are on the lower level, and a steep staircase leads up to a cute little round bedroom on the top level. Room rates vary by season, but a basic room runs $89–$95 during hiking season, and suites $115–$135.

Guests have use of a shared hot tub that overlooks the trout pond (from which fresh trout are pulled daily for breakfast—kids can catch their own).

Also on the property are two houses available for rent, each of which sleeps up to 8 people in 3 bedrooms (one with king bed). The Forest House, with its piano and sound system, is a great place for a small group to relax. Or choose The Chalet, a quaint, 2-story home.

All guests at Alexander's Inn, including those in the houses, receive a complimentary breakfast in the restaurant. Picnic lunches can be arranged. See Alexander's Inn Restaurant under *Dining*, below.

Alexander's Inn and Restaurant—an Ashford landmark

Getting There

From the west, take Highway 706 east through Elbe, then through Ashford. Alexander's is on the north side of the road, 12.1 miles east of the Highway 7/Highway 706 junction in Elbe. Coming from from the east (through the national park), Alexander's is 1.0 mile outside the Nisqually entrance.

Hikes and Walks Nearby: High Rock, Lake George, Kautz Creek, Twin Firs Loop, Ramparts Ridge Loop, Carter Falls, Comet Falls, Paradise Loop.

GROWLY BEAR B&B
P.O. Box 103 • 37311 SR 706 East • Ashford, WA 98304
(800) 700-2339 • (360) 569-2339

Susan Jenny Johnson's Growly Bear B&B has been a Mt. Rainier staple since 1986. She offers 4 guest rooms in a once-rustic 1890 homestead built by the pioneer Mesler family, to whom so much of this area's history is connected. Located alongside Goat Creek, the property is just over a mile from the Nisqually entrance to Mt. Rainier National Park, just west of Alexander's Inn.

GROWLY BEAR B&B
Established B&B in an 1890's homestead

Two of the Growly Bear's rooms have private baths and rent for $105 per night for 2 people (extra persons $30). The Rainier Room, on the main level, has a queen bed, a futon, a full and a half bath, and a spacious sitting area. The Mesler Room, a sunny upstairs unit, has a queen sleigh bed, a futon, a pullout couch, and a bathroom with shower, plus a

Growly Bear B&B

little deck overlooking the yard and garden. Both are large, more like suites than rooms.

The Beljica and Nisqually rooms are cozy, hip-roofed rooms that share a bath. Beljica is cheerfully decorated in blue and yellow, and has nice light; Nisqually features earth tones and a gorgeous autumn-leaf quilt. Each is $80/night.

Growly Bear guests can relax in a common sunroom on the main floor. There, they'll find coffee/tea service, reading material, and games. Outside, 15 wooded acres beckon you to stroll. "Sure," says Susan, "walk around…or weed my garden!" You'll feel right at home—I did.

The price of your room includes a full mountain breakfast—fruit, juice, pastries, and an entrée—served family-style in a building adjacent to the main house. Children are welcome at the Growly Bear, but no pets are allowed.

Getting There

From the west, take Highway 706 east through Elbe, then through Ashford. Watch for the Growly Bear's driveway on the north side of the road 12.0 miles east of the Highway 7/Highway 706 junction in Elbe. Coming from from the east (through the national park), the Growly Bear is 1.1 miles outside the Nisqually entrance.

Hikes and Walks Nearby: High Rock, Lake George, Kautz Creek, Twin Firs Loop, Ramparts Ridge Loop, Carter Falls, Comet Falls, Paradise Loop.

JASMER'S B&B AND CABINS
P.O. Box 347 • 30005 SR 706 • Ashford, WA 98304
(360) 569-2682
www.telcomplus.com/~oster/jas.html • e-mail osterhaus1@juno.com

Relaxing with a cup of tea in your private retreat, you gaze out the bay window at the arbor, lush with climbing roses. A rhododendron, heavy with lavender-and-burgundy blooms, screens your refuge. Tiny birds flutter by, gathering nesting materials. The romantic sounds of a flute sonata emanate from your CD player, and you ponder your next move: a private soak in the hot tub, just outside, or a little snack from the continental breakfast waiting in your refrigerator? You have discovered The Songbird, one of two delightful rooms at Jasmer's B&B.

JASMER'S B&B AND CABINS
Romantic B&B and nice cabins near Mt. Rainier

Jasmer's is a two-unit B&B and headquarters for a selection of exceptional private vacation rental cabins. Retaining the name of former owners for the sake of history, current proprietors Tanna and Luke Osterhaus have owned and operated the facility since 1990. Along with their delightful daughter, Alexi, they live in a house adjacent to the B&B. The house serves as the registration office, and is where you pick up keys and maps for the cabins.

The main property combines the charms of a rambling country inn with the sophisticated amenities of a properly-run contemporary bed and breakfast establishment. The two units, The Songbird and The Bird's Nest, each include a queen bed, private bath with double shower, TV/VCR, mini-stereo (romantic CD's provided), mini-fridge, coffee maker, and mini-microwave. Your hosts provide a generous continental breakfast in advance in the refrigerator, plus ground coffee, an assortment of teas, and all the utensils you need to serve it up in romantic style. A hot tub sits on the attractive grounds just outside the units; an "even/odd hour" schedule ensures privacy. The Songbird, the larger of the two rooms, includes a fireplace and rents for $65–$95/night; The Bird's Nest is $45–$75.

Tanna and Luke also manage a number of private cabins, each within 5 miles of the national park. Rates range from $75 to $145/night, double occupancy, and the cabins require a 2-night minimum stay. Each has its own amenities and features, and sleeping capacities vary, up to 7 persons. All have fully-equipped kitchens, fireplaces/wood stoves, and electric heat. Some have hot tubs, barbecues, TV/VCRs, and other features.

Jasmer's is a class act, with a fine selection of properties and a service-oriented attitude that is a credit to the Ashford area.

Getting There: From the west, take Highway 706 east through Elbe. From the Highway 7/Highway 706 junction in Elbe, drive 7.2 miles east; watch for the Jasmer's sign and main house on the north side of the highway. Coming from the east (through the national park), Jasmer's is 5.9 miles outside the Nisqually entrance.

Hikes and Walks Nearby: High Rock, Lake George, Kautz Creek, Twin Firs Loop, Ramparts Ridge Loop, Carter Falls, Comet Falls, Paradise Loop.

Jasmer's B&B

MOUNTAIN MEADOWS INN
P.O. Box 291 • 28912 SR 706 East • Ashford, WA 98304
(360) 569-2788
www.innsandouts.com/property/the_mountain_meadows_inn.html

A stately old home with wrap-around porch…a sprawling lawn with its own pond…spacious rooms filled with antiques, each with a private bath…now *this* is what a B&B should be! Add the exceptional cuisine and knowledgeable proprietors Harry and Michelle Latimer, and you have the ingredients for a memorable stay at the gateway to Mt. Rainier's Nisqually entrance.

> **MOUNTAIN MEADOWS INN**
>
> Picture-perfect historic B&B with outstanding naturalist library

As soon as you walk into Mountain Meadows Inn, you know you've entered a special place. Delicate fragrances fill the air. Soft music plays from unseen speakers. Decor in the entry parlor mingles Native American and wilderness themes, and the adjacent sitting room holds a library-quality collection of natural history texts. Amateur historians and naturalists, the Latimers are excellent hosts. Their John Muir library, assembled over 30 years, is one of the nation's best.

Next to the sitting room is the Sunnybrook Room, with its white wicker furniture, brass double featherbed, and antique Hudson's Bay camphor chest. This sunny room has windows on three sides, affording views of lush rhododendrons and the steady traffic of hummingbirds at a feeder. Sunnybrook's private bath is spacious, with tub and shower.

Mountain Meadows Inn

Or choose the Chief Seattle Room, a very spacious guest room with king bed and Native American decor. Its private bath has a double shower, and the room includes a day bed and trundle.

The Mountain Berry Room features a clawfoot tub in its spacious private bathroom, and a queen 4-poster plus a single bed in the sleeping room. The decor artfully mixes early American and Native American under a canopy of clouds painted subtly on the ceiling.

Also on the property is a 3-unit guest house. This separate facility offers a different style of lodging, perfect for families. Two of the rooms are studio units; like the rooms inside the inn, these rent for $75–$110/night for two (extra persons $15 apiece). The other unit is a 2-bedroom suite, with a separate dining and kitchen area. Appropriate for parties of 3–4, it runs $125–$165.

Outside, Mountain Meadows' 10-acre grounds invite strolling, or just sitting and watching the pond. In the evening, sounds of crickets fill the air. If you keep an eye out, you might see elk wander through the park-like yard.

After a restful night in your private retreat, awaken to the smells of the fabulous breakfast Harry and Michelle are busy preparing on their 1880-vintage stove. Emphasizing Northwest cuisine, breakfast is an important part of the Mountain Meadows Inn experience. Your hosts have 35 years of foodservice experience between them, and it shows in their delicate entrées, which may include a salmon-cream cheese omelette or an artichoke quiche. Breakfast is always accompanied by plenty of fresh fruit and robust coffee or choice of tea.

Built in 1910, Mountain Meadows' main house was once the superintendent's quarters for the Pacific National Lumber Company, in its day the largest lumber mill west of the Mississippi. The mill, and most of the town of National, was destroyed or moved in the 1960s and 1970s; Mountain Meadows is one of the few surviving remnants of this rich piece of Pierce County history.

Getting There
To find the Mountain Meadows property, watch for the sign on the south side of Highway 706 at the west end of Ashford, 6.5 miles east of Elbe and 6.5 miles west of the national park entrance.

Hikes and Walks Nearby: High Rock, Lake George, Kautz Creek, Twin Firs Loop, Ramparts Ridge Loop, Carter Falls, Comet Falls, Paradise Loop.

MOUNTHAVEN
38210 SR 706 East • Ashford, WA 98304
(800) 456-9380 • (360) 569-2594

Half a mile from Mt. Rainier National Park's Nisqually entrance is a rustic little collection of cabins along Tenas Creek called Mounthaven. Your hosts, Dick and Diane Gamache, purchased the property and cabins in 1995, and have been working hard to offer their guests a clean, cheerful, affordable woodland lodging experience.

MOUNTHAVEN

Cute cabins, half a mile from the park.

The history of this property as a lodging site dates back to the late 1800s, when a wealthy Tacoma woman named Mrs. Ann Billing purchased it. Taking hammer in hand,

One of Mounthaven's comfortable cabins

this odd, headstrong woman set about building a series of cabins, performing a then-surprising amount of the labor herself. As a result, they became known as Ann Carpenter's Cottages.

Mounthaven offers 12 rental units, most of which are named for trees. Each has its own bathroom and a fireplace; all but two have a kitchen or kitchenette. Coffee makers (with coffee) are provided, as is wood for the fireplace or outdoor firepit. The units range in size from 2-person Willow, a rustic, kitchenless single room with double bed ($54), to 10-person Ski Lodge, with full kitchen, living room, bedroom, and loft ($149). In between, Hemlock and Spruce sleep 2 for $69; Birch, also known as "the honeymoon cabin," sleeps 2 in a secluded location for $74. Cedar (a mobile home), Fir, Pine, and Alder each sleep 4, with prices ranging from $74 to $89. Style, layout, and "degree of rustic" varies in each unit.

The newest, most modern units, Oak and Homestead, were added in 1997. Both have private bathrooms with tub and shower. Oak is wheelchair-accessible, with two queen beds, brick fireplace, and kitchenette. It sleeps 4 and rents for $88. Homestead has a large living room, massive stone fireplace, and kitchen. Its couch and queen bed sleep 3, and it rents for $74.

Mounthaven is a wonderful place to relive memories of childhood cabin camping with your family or sweetheart. Each unit has a porch and outdoor firepit, for pleasant summer evenings. The park-like 6.5 acres also offer RV hook-ups and a coin-operated laundry facility.

Mounthaven is perfect for children of all ages. A playground is provided, and they'll enjoy fishing for brown trout or panning for gold in Tenas Creek. Your pet is welcome for an additional $10/night.

Getting There

From the west, take Highway 706 east through Elbe, then through Ashford. Mounthaven's driveway is on the right side of the road 12.6 miles east of the Highway 7/Highway 706 junction in Elbe. Coming from from the east (through the national park), Mounthaven is on the left, 0.5 mile outside the Nisqually entrance

Hikes and Walks Nearby: High Rock, Lake George, Kautz Creek, Twin Firs Loop, Ramparts Ridge Loop, Carter Falls, Comet Falls, Paradise Loop.

NISQUALLY LODGE
P.O. Box 381 • 31609 SR 706 East • Ashford, WA 98304
(888) 674-3554 • (360) 569-8804

Affiliated with the Cowlitz River Lodge in Packwood (below), Ashford's Nisqually Lodge offers 24 modern, motel-style rooms with air-conditioning, telephone, and cable TV. Rooms with one queen bed are $67 for one or two peo-

ple; rooms with 2 queen beds or 1 king are $77 for two. Extra persons sharing the room are $10 extra. No pets allowed. Rooms are spacious and clean, and continental breakfast is provided in the lobby. Outdoor hot tub available for guest use.

Getting There

The lodge is located on the north side of Highway 706, 4.8 miles from the national park entrance (8.3 miles east of the Highway 7/Highway 706 junction in Elbe).

Hikes and Walks Nearby: High Rock, Lake George, Kautz Creek, Twin Firs Loop, Ramparts Ridge Loop, Carter Falls, Comet Falls, Paradise Loop.

WELLSPRING
54922 Kernahan Road • Ashford, WA 98304
(360) 569-2514

Sunny Thompson-Ward is somewhat of a legend in the Ashford valley. As a young single mother with the gift of therapeutic touch, she began offering lodgings and massage therapy in the valley in the early 1970s. Using her training in interior design, her love of nature, and her desire to perform meaningful work, she began Wellspring, a woodland spa and labor of love.

In the more than two decades that followed, Sunny raised her children, expanded her lodgings, and her woodland spa became an Ashford mainstay. Wellspring has two private hot tubs (available for guest use on a reservation basis), wood-fired saunas, charming cabins, unique rooms, and a stunning retreat lodge suitable for groups of all types. Sunny, a licensed massage therapist, offers bodywork by appointment. What could be more rewarding after a day of hiking?

Lodgings at Wellspring include $85 rooms, $95 log cabins, a $110 cottage, and a $300 lodge. Other configurations are available at varying prices; depending upon how you look at it, about 8 units are offered, with sleeping capacities from

2 to 14. All have private baths. A continental breakfast basket is provided to guests in all units except those with kitchens.

Wellspring is not for everyone. There are no televisions or telephones to detract from the woodland retreat atmosphere, and the lodgings themselves are so unique they almost defy description. The Grace West Room, for example, requires sharing

The hanging bed at Wellspring

a bath with an adjoining massage therapy studio until 9 P.M.; your compensation is unrestricted use of a hot tub after 9. The Greenhouse, a less-frequently rented unit, is available for occupancy only after 9 P.M., but is a bargain at $75. Another unit, whimsically dubbed The Nest, has a hanging bed. Yes, hanging. It's suspended from the ceiling. Devotees say it has the effect of rocking you to sleep. "Better than a waterbed," they say. Other unique features include a shower constructed to emulate a waterfall in the Tatoosh Room.

The hot tubs and wood-fired sauna at Wellspring are available to guests for $5/person/hour, and to non-guests at $10/person/hour. Massage therapy, by appointment, is $45/hour. Longer and shorter appointments available.

If you like the sounds of such an unusual, connected-to-the-earth place, you'll probably love Wellspring. It exerts a certain magic over those who are open to it. Even the staff loves it here. A housekeeper, standing with an armload of fresh linens under a veil of light rain, offered this comment: "it's a place to be proud of—I tell everybody to come here."

Getting There

You'll find the gravel drive to Wellspring on the north side of Highway 706, 9.9 miles east of the Highway 7/Highway 706 junction at Elbe and 3.2 miles west of the Nisqually entrance to the national park. The northbound driveway is directly across from the junction of southbound Kernahan Road.

Hikes and Walks Nearby: High Rock, Lake George, Kautz Creek, Twin Firs Loop, Ramparts Ridge Loop, Carter Falls, Comet Falls, Paradise Loop.

WHITTAKER'S BUNKHOUSE
30205 SR 706 East • Ashford, WA 98304
(360) 569-2439

Owned by mountaineering legend Lou Whittaker and his wife, Ingrid, Whittaker's Bunkhouse is an 18-room motel and 10-person bunkhouse for climbers, hikers, and skiers. Billing itself as "The Place to Stop on the Way to the Top," these lodgings were designed to accommodate both budget-conscious travelers (including mountaineers) and tourists seeking a clean, comfortable motel room.

The bunkhouse is a rudimentary (but fresh, new, and clean) 10-bunk hostel-style accommodation. For $20/night, bunkers bring their own bedding and share a co-ed bunkroom and bathroom.

The motel rooms each have a private bath with tub. Thirteen of the units have two twin beds or one double bed, and rent for $60 for 2 people. The other 5 units are larger, with newer carpets and vinyls. On the upper level, they have beamed ceilings and each has at least two beds. These units are $80 for 2 persons; $5 each extra person. One unit is handicapped-accessible.

The original building around which the premises were designed was built in 1908 in the nearby town of National. Used for logger and millworker housing, its now-refinished floors still bear the traces of their boot marks. When the town of National began to be dismantled in the 1960s, this building was moved to its present location. It subsequently housed several business-es, but fell into disrepair before the Whittakers purchased it in 1991. Their initial renovations included putting in a foundation, re-roofing, re-plumbing, and re-wiring. Remodeling and decorating is ongoing.

WHITTAKER'S BUNKHOUSE

Motel, bunkhouse, and espresso bar

Today's comfortable, low-frills lodging includes a 300-foot wrap-around porch, lawn with picnic tables, guest hot tub, and on-premises espresso café.

Getting There

You'll find Whittaker's Bunkhouse by looking for the colorful, hand-carved sign with the mountaineer on it on the north side of Highway 706 just west of Jasmer's—that's 7.3 miles east of the Highway 7/Highway 706 junction in Elbe, and 5.8 miles west of the national park entrance.

Hikes and Walks Nearby: High Rock, Lake George, Kautz Creek, Twin Firs Loop, Ramparts Ridge Loop, Carter Falls, Comet Falls, Paradise Loop.

Mountaineering legend Lou Whittaker's Bunkhouse

Packwood/White Pass Lodgings:

See also Randle and Morton lodgings in Section 2, Mount St. Helens. These offer good access to Mt. Rainier and the Gifford Pinchot hikes near Packwood as well.

COWLITZ RIVER LODGE
P.O. Box 488 • 13069 US Highway 12 • Packwood, WA 98361
(888) 881-0379 • (360) 494-4444

The Cowlitz River Lodge offers 32 AAA-approved, modern, motel-style rooms with air-conditioning, telephone, and cable TV. Rooms with one queen bed are $50 for two people; rooms with two queen beds are $60 for two (extra persons over the age of six, $5). No pets allowed. Rooms are spacious and clean, and continental breakfast is provided in the lobby. Hot tub available for guest use. As with all Packwood lodgings, the Cowlitz River Lodge offers good access to all the hikes in this section, as well as the hikes on the east approach to Mount St. Helens.

> **COWLITZ RIVER LODGE**
>
> Modern AAA-approved motel rooms

Getting There

The Cowlitz River Lodge is located toward the east side of Packwood, on the northeast corner of the junction of Highway 12 and Skate Creek Road (Road 52).

Hikes and Walks Nearby: Dry Creek, Glacier Lake, High Rock, Backbone Lake, Silver Falls, Grove of the Patriarchs, Box Canyon, Bench & Snow Lakes, Paradise Loop, Naches Peak/Tipsoo Lake Loop, Mt. Fremont Lookout.

HOTEL PACKWOOD
104 Main St. • Packwood, WA 98361
(360) 494-5431

Established in 1912, the Hotel Packwood is a historic landmark recently refurbished as a budget lodging in the heart of Packwood. Two of its nine rooms have private baths, and the other 7 share two spacious baths. The rooms are small, but clean, tidy, and freshly-renovated; each includes cable TV. If you need a little more elbow room, relax in the lobby (a cozy, old-fashioned parlor with a brick fireplace, an old piano, and coffee/tea service), on the wrap-around porch, on the lawn/picnic area, or in the 24-hour outdoor hot tub. The property has a view of Mt. Rainier.

> **HOTEL PACKWOOD**
>
> Historic landmark; budget prices

The town of Packwood is just outside the door. The city park and community library are immediately adjacent to the hotel, and the shops and restaurants are all within easy walking distance.

The cheapest room at Hotel Packwood is a mere $20; with its twin bed and shared bath, it is appropriate for one person. Rooms for two persons start at $25, with twin bunkbeds or a double bed and a shared bath. The two rooms with private baths, both sunny corner units with double beds, are $38. Two of the shared-bath rooms are appropriate for up to 4 people—they each have a double bed, a twin bed, and a twin pull-out. For 2 people, these rooms are $35; for 4, they are $40.

The Hotel Packwood is not for everyone. The young, energetic proprietors have done a great job in repainting and refurbishing the simple, quaint interior. Expect the quirks of an older building and the inconsistencies of a work-in-progress. For the price, it's a great deal.

Getting There

The Packwood Hotel is located one short block north of Highway 12 as it passes through Packwood. It sits at the west end of "downtown," across from the city park.

Hikes and Walks Nearby:

Dry Creek, Glacier Lake, High Rock, Backbone Lake,

Historic Hotel Packwood

Silver Falls, Grove of the Patriarchs, Box Canyon, Bench & Snow Lakes, Paradise Loop, Naches Peak/Tipsoo Lake Loop, Mt. Fremont Lookout.

MOUNTAIN VIEW LODGE
P.O. Box 525 • 13163 US Highway 12 • Packwood, WA 98361
(360) 494-5555

Less than 7 miles from Mt. Rainier National Park's southeast entrance, the

> **MOUNTAIN VIEW LODGE**
>
> Comfortable, older rooms; great location

Mountain View Lodge Motel is situated in an ideal location for anyone hiking the park. It also provides excellent access to Goat Rocks Wilderness and any of the other hiking destinations along the Highway 12 corridor of the Gifford Pinchot National Forest.

The locally-owned hotel is a Packwood area institution, with portions of the facilities dating back to the 1940s. It consists of 7 motel-style rooms over the main office (5 of these are double beds with showers, 2 are queen beds with full baths), and 15 larger units housed in a collection of duplex, triplex, and fourplexes on the park-like grounds.

A wide variety of room configurations are available, some with multiple beds, others with hideabeds and/or rollaways, making this a great location for

Mountain View Lodge motel and cabins

families and groups. Eight units have kitchens, and 3 have fireplaces. Rates for two persons range from $34 in a motel-style unit with double bed to $73 for a unit with two queen beds, full kitchen, and a fireplace. Extra persons are $3, as are pets (pets allowed in the 15 ground-level units only).

"Comfortable" is the best way to describe Mountain View Lodge. Buildings and furnishings are a bit worn and dated (although nothing looks 50 years old), but everything is clean and cheerful, designed with the casual, laid-back traveler in mind. Even the grounds (behind which the Cowlitz River flows) invite a game of horseshoes or a family picnic.

The AAA-approved property includes a swimming pool and a hot tub, and all units have cable TV, telephones, air conditioning and baseboard heat. All have full baths with tub, except the 5 motel units mentioned above, which have only a shower.

Getting There

Located just east of Packwood proper, Mountain View Lodge is situated on the north side of Highway 12.

Hikes and Walks Nearby: Dry Creek, Glacier Lake, High Rock, Backbone Lake, Silver Falls, Grove of the Patriarchs, Box Canyon, Bench & Snow Lakes, Paradise Loop, Naches Peak/Tipsoo Lake Loop, Mt. Fremont Lookout.

TATOOSH MEADOWS
P.O. Box 487 • Packwood, WA 98361
(800) 294-2311 • (360) 494-2311
wwte.com/tatoosh.htm • e-mail tmcprop@i-link-2.net

Tatoosh Meadows is a collection of lodgings on a 32-acre parcel just outside of Packwood, where Skate Creek meets the Cowlitz River. Nine units, each with private hot tub, offer a range of lodging choices. (One cabin unit also has a 2-unit bunkhouse adjacent, for a total of 11 units.) The property is ideal for business or private retreats, with beds sufficient to sleep over 30 people, a commons building that seats 50 (plus another 50 under cover outdoors), and catering available. Owners Tom and Maree Lerchen also manage a number of cabins and condos throughout the Packwood and Randle area (ask for a list of prices and features); these properties raise the total number of available beds to about 100.

Tom and Maree began their enterprise in 1981 with a 3-room B&B. They expanded, adding a restaurant and another guest room. When a fire consumed the building in 1987, they rebuilt without the restaurant, and have gradually added other buildings to bring the campus to its current state. While there is no

TATOOSH MEADOWS
Sprawling campus with comfortable lodgings on Cowlitz River

restaurant on the premises, a commercial kitchen enables catering for groups, and an optional "Dinner en Suite" is available. When you reserve your room, you can also arrange for this service: a complete dinner, with salad, herb bread, and dessert, will be waiting in your refrigerator. Microwaves are available in all units, and disposable tableware "makes clean-up a non-event." Choices may include boeuf bourguignon, prawns sauté sec, coq au vin, and penne primavera; prices range from $15 to $18.25 for the complete meal. A selection of Northwest wines is also available. Since Tatoosh Meadows is such a lovely place, why leave for the (albeit short) drive into Packwood for mediocre café-style food? The Dinner en Suite program is a nice alternative.

Lodgings at Tatoosh Meadows begin with four studio units, each renting for $110/night. The Dean and Wallace rooms are lovely new units with contemporary decor in the main house. Each has a gas fireplace and two twin beds that can convert to kings. The Red Room and Green Room are in a building called The Annex, right above the river. These units are handicapped accessible, have queen beds, wrap-around verandas, and stone fireplaces. Luxuriously appointed, these are the only two units on the property that allow neither children nor pets, for a low-noise, allergen-free environment. Each of the four studio units has a private bath and private outdoor hot tub, a microwave kitchenette, and a barbecue.

Near The Annex, The Orchard House is a flexible building that offers two rooms. The Peach Room can rent as a studio like the above units (also for $110), or as a suite, with adjoining full kitchen and living room with queen hideabed, for $165. The Plum Room, with a kitchenette, rents for $135. Both have private hot tubs and fireplaces. The entire Orchard House rents for $250.

The Cottage is a 400-square-foot one-bedroom cabin with gas fireplace, full kitchen, and private hot tub with view of the orchard and river valley. It rents for $145/night.

The May House is a roomy two-bedroom cabin with optional adjacent bunkhouses. The main cabin includes a great room (living/dining/kitchen for 20), brick fireplace, 2 bathrooms, and covered porch. The yard has a hot tub and private river access. With a hideabed and several folding twin beds, the house sleeps up to 8, and rents for $220. If you need more room, each of the two adjacent bunkhouses sleeps 4—one with 2 queen beds, one with 4 bunkbeds. Each has its own bathroom, and rents for $55 with rental of the May House.

The Plum Room at Tatoosh Meadows

Children and pets are welcome at Tatoosh Meadows, except in the Red and Green rooms. They are especially appropriate in the May House and The Cottage, and pets are only allowed in The Orchard House when the entire house (Plum Room and Peach Suite) are being rented by the same party. A $25 fee is charged for pets.

While the lodgings are nice, you'll also appreciate the grounds, especially for longer stays. A sense of isolation and privacy surrounds you. Walk to the river's edge or organize a game of volleyball or croquet—there's plenty of room.

Packwood is just a couple of miles down the road, so you are within 10 miles of the Ohanapecosh entrance to Mt. Rainier when you stay at Tatoosh Meadows. Alternately, you can go north on Skate Creek Road, and approach the park from the Nisqually entrance.

Getting There

From Highway 12 in Packwood, take Skate Creek Road north (the Skate Creek Road junction is just east of downtown, at the large gas station/convenience store). Go north 1.1 miles, crossing over the Cowlitz River and passing a sign for the country club. Turn left on Craig Road and go 1.4 miles to its end.

Hikes and Walks Nearby: Dry Creek, Glacier Lake, High Rock, Backbone Lake, Silver Falls, Grove of the Patriarchs, Box Canyon, Bench & Snow Lakes, Paradise Loop, Naches Peak/Tipsoo Lake Loop, Mt. Fremont Lookout.

THE VILLAGE INN CONDOMINIUMS
P.O. Box 3035 • U.S. Highway 12 • White Pass, WA 98937
(509) 672-3131

White Pass is just 12 miles east of Highway 12's junction with Mt. Rainier National Park access highway 123. Predominantly a winter recreation area, with alpine lifts and cross-country trails, the area is sleepy during the summer.

Dayhikers can take advantage of the slow season at White Pass by staying at the summit's Village Inn Condominiums for their low summer rates.

The Village Inn's 56 condominium units are individually owned but centrally managed as rentals. They range in size from motel-like studio units with small kitchens to deluxe units with bedroom, sleeping loft, living area, and full kitchen. The smallest units sleep 2 to 4 people for $48; the largest sleep up to 8 people for $98. In between are various larger studio units, units with bedrooms, and units with lofts. Hideabed couches or Murphy beds in some units expand the sleeping capacity. Some units have fireplaces; some, but not all, have TV's (no local reception) and VCR's. Some smoking units are available.

> **THE VILLAGE INN CONDOMINIUMS**
>
> Private condos offer flexible lodging option

All units have kitchens, most of which are fully and reliably stocked with cooking and eating utensils, microwaves, and coffee makers. Decor and specific amenities throughout the units vary, as each unit is individually owned. If possible, view the units in advance and select the one that best suits your needs.

If your room feels small after a day of hiking, take advantage of the elbow room at the heated outdoor swimming pool or the impromptu campfire get-togethers on the grounds. If you don't feel like cooking, a restaurant on the premises is likely to be open (call ahead to be sure). Other dining options are Packwood, 20 miles west, or a café at the Silver Beach Motel, 8 miles east. A convenience store, complete with espresso, is adjacent to the Village Inn on the highway.

Getting There

The Village Inn Condominiums are on the north side of Highway 12 at White Pass. (The ski lifts are on the south side, right across the road.) From Packwood, take Highway 12 east 20 miles. From Yakima, take Highway 12 north through Naches. When the highway forks, and Highway 410 goes straight ahead to

The Village Inn Condominiums at White Pass

Chinook Pass, you bear left, continuing on Highway 12. Pass Rimrock Lake and continue about 9.0 more miles to White Pass.

Hikes and Walks Nearby: Backbone Lake, Silver Falls, Grove of the Patriarchs, Box Canyon, Bench & Snow Lakes, Paradise Loop, Naches Peak/Tipsoo Lake Loop, Mt. Fremont Lookout.

ADDITIONAL LODGINGS

The recommended lodgings above are located in the Ashford or Packwood/White Pass areas. Additional options are available within the national park and at other locations near the park, including the following. See also the Highway 12/East Approach lodgings in *Section 2*, "Mount St. Helens."

HOBO INN   **(360) 569-2500**
P.O. Box 20, Elbe, WA 98330

You gotta love railroad cabooses turned into motel rooms. A bit stuffy and rough around the edges, but the kids will get a kick out of staying here. The 7 converted rail cars rent for $70–$85 per night, and sleep up to 4. Restaurant adjacent.

MT. TAHOMA TRAILS ASSOCIATION HUTS
P.O. Box 206, Ashford, WA, 98304

Four exceptionally nice hike-in "huts" (actually, cabins) designed primarily for use by cross-country skiers. Situated at 4200´ and 4700´, along the 90+ miles of trails on the MTTA system. Each sleeps 6–12. Woodburning stove, propane stove, pots & pans, sleeping pads. BYO sleeping bag, mess kit, and garbage bags to haul out trash. Outstanding views.

NATIONAL PARK INN   **(360) 569-2275**
P.O. Box 108, Ashford, WA 98304-0108
(located in Longmire)
www.mashell.com/Rainier.guest/guestsv.html

This historic 25-unit National Park Service lodging was renovated in 1990. Rates from $64 for room with shared bath to $119 for two-room family unit. Most rooms $88. Children are allowed (cribs available, $10), pets are not. Two rooms are handicapped accessible. Restaurant on premises; adjacent to general store, museum and information center. Reservations highly recommended June–September.

PARADISE INN   **(360) 569-2275**
P.O. Box 108, Ashford, WA 98304-0108
(located in Paradise)
www.mashell.com/Rainier.guest/guestsv.html

Built in 1917, the historic lodge at Paradise has 126 rooms, starting at $68 with shared bath. Rooms with bath range from $95 to $127. Restaurant and gift shop on premises. Famous rustic lobby has 2 oversized stone fireplaces and is usually swarming with tourists. Children are allowed (cribs available, $10), pets are not. Open May–October only; reservations highly recommended.

WHISTLING JACK'S   (800) 827-2299
20800 SR 410, Chinook Pass   (509) 658-2433
Naches, WA 98937

This family-owned lodge is "the" choice when approaching the mountain from the east side, along Highway 410/Chinook Pass. Its 8 riverfront motel units rent for $90, and its cottages and bungalows, some with hot tubs, for $140–$220 for 2 to 4 persons (some units sleep up to 10; extra persons over age 12, $10). Children are welcome; no pets. The self-contained resort includes a restaurant, lounge, gas station, and convenience store/deli.

DINING

It's probably safe to say that, for the most part, gourmet dining is not a priority in the gateway towns to Mt. Rainier. The Ashford B&B's do a pretty good job on breakfast, but your choices for dinner are filling but uninspired on the whole. If your lodging has cooking facilities, consider using them. Otherwise, here are a few reliable choices and local favorites.

ALEXANDER'S INN RESTAURANT
37515 SR 706 East • Ashford, WA 98304
(800) 654-7615 • (360) 569-2323

On the first floor of Alexander's Inn (the one with the water wheel, one mile from the national park's Nisqually entrance, see *Lodgings*, above) is a full-service restaurant, and the Ashford area's answer to fine dining.

Alexander's specializes in Northwest cuisine, offering an upscale dining experience while still catering to the outdoor crowd. Their wine cellar includes the best of the region, as well as Californian and European wines.

At dinnertime, a demi-loaf of fresh-baked bread comes to your table with a decanter of herbed olive oil and a ramekin of shredded asiago—a pleasantly hearty appetizer and accompaniment to your salad. If you're extra hungry, split a meal-sized Caesar. It's not a classic Caesar, but it's a great salad, and, at $10.95 for two, beats the $2.95 dinner salad by a mile.

Entrée choices nod to nouvelle cuisine, but portions reflect patrons who enjoy an active lifestyle. The rotini primavera, at $13.95 a la carte, is a lush mountain of seasonal vegetables over spiral pasta. Other a la carte entrées include oven-roasted pork ribs ($12.95) and homemade Italian sausage lasagna ($10.95). Complete dinners, with soup or salad, bread, and vegetable, begin at $15.95. The rainbow trout is caught fresh in the on-premises pond and pan-fried; the Long Island duckling is served with brandied cherry sauce, on rice (both $16.95).

Alexander's also serves breakfast and lunch.

COPPER CREEK
35707 SR 706 E • Ashford, WA 98304
(360) 569-2326

For a reliable, if heavy, meal on the way into or out of Mt. Rainier National Park's Nisqually entrance, look for the log cabin signed Copper Creek 2.2 miles west of the park entrance and 10.9 miles east of Elbe. With a menu printed on a brown paper bag and featuring items like Country Fried chicken, the Log Dip sandwich, and the Paul Bunyan burger, you know you're in for a stick-to-your-ribs repast. It's definitely not a fern bar; what they do at Copper Creek, they do well. The beef stew is fresh and tasty (served, as are most entrées, with a hot, homemade mini-loaf of bread), the soups and salad dressings are homemade, and the wild blackberry pie—"pulled fresh from the oven every 45 minutes"—is out-of-this-world. Sandwiches and burgers run $3.50–$7.25, and complete dinners (with all the trimmings, from soup to dessert) run from $12.75 for country cured ham to $17.95 for a 14-ounce T-bone steak.

NATIONAL PARK INN RESTAURANT
Mt. Rainier National Park • Longmire, WA 98397
(360) 569-2411

Located inside the National Park Inn at Longmire, this restaurant serves three semi-fancy meals a day in a relaxed, family atmosphere. Prices are a bit on the spendy side, but, hey—you're at the base of the greatest peak in the Cascades.

Breakfast includes the standard eggs and griddle fare, plus novelties like dollar-sized blueberry or chocolate chip pancakes. Full breakfasts start around $5.00.

Lunchtime offerings include burgers (regular, cheese, and meatless) from $5.65, a red snapper sandwich, and a mesquite chicken sandwich, each with fries, and meal-sized salads. My pick is a bowl of their 3-bean chili and a mound of homemade blackberry cobbler. Even with a scoop of ice cream (hike hard), the whole thing's about ten bucks.

Dinner entrées range from pasta marinara at $7.95 to a charbroiled New York steak with merlot sauce at $15.95. Pacific Northwest signature dishes include chicken breast in a maple-hazelnut crust ($14.25) and pan-fried rainbow trout ($13.95). Beer and wine are available.

A restaurant and snack bar is also available farther up the hill at Paradise Inn.

National Park Inn and Restaurant

PACKWOOD PIZZA PARLOR
Packwood, WA 98361 • (360) 494-5400

This family-oriented pizza parlor is a downtown Packwood staple. Large pizzas start at $11, with a Parlor Combo $17.95. Spaghetti, lasagna, calzones, and burgers are also available, as well as draft and bottled beer. Take your pie to the park or back to your lodging for an extra 75¢. At the end of a day of hiking, it's an option.

WALKS AND HIKES
Listed in approximate order of difficulty

The walks and hikes in this section are either in Mt. Rainier National Park or Gifford Pinchot National Forest. Trails within the national park—especially the very short walks—are best previewed on the Mt. Rainier National Park Official Map & Guide, which is given to you upon entering the park during daytime hours, or can be obtained through the park superintendent's office at (360) 569-2211.

KAUTZ CREEK VIEWPOINT
Short, barrier-free stroll to a scenic creek basin.

Map:	Mt. Rainier National Park Official Map & Guide; Green Trail #301, "Randle"
Distance:	500 feet round trip
Elevation Gain:	None
Estimated Time:	20 minutes

This short, barrier-free stroll is the first leg-stretching point inside Mt. Rainier National Park's southwest entrance.

Getting There
Three and a half miles inside the park's Nisqually (southwest) entrance, watch for the large Kautz Creek picnic and restroom parking area on the right (south) side of the road.

Cross the road to a wide, well-delineated trail, which is the access point for this walk and also for Kautz Creek Trail, which backpackers can use to connect with the Wonderland Trail at an area known as Indian Henry's Hunting Ground, 5.7 miles to the north.

The Walk
This wide boardwalk path was the park's first fully handicapped-accessible trail, constructed in 1994 by park staff and student volunteers from Waseda University of Tokyo, Japan. The project was part of the university's North American Philanthropy Program. The result is a pleasant, sturdy path constructed of recycled plastic lumber.

A gravel landing at the end of the boardwalk affords a view of the Kautz Creek basin. An interpretive plaque explains how this draw was carved out in a 1947 mud and debris slide off Kautz Glacier.

Nearest Lodgings: Any Ashford lodgings.

BOX CANYON
Short, paved walk with great views.

Map:	Mt. Rainier National Park Official Map & Guide, Green Trails #270, "Mt. Rainier East"
Distance:	0.3 mile round trip to bridge, or 0.4 mile loop
Elevation Loss:	Negligible
Estimated Time:	30 minutes

From a roadside trailhead, stroll a comfortable, partially-paved path to see awesome views of Mt. Rainier above you and Box Canyon below you. Bring everyone; non-hikers will have a visual feast at the trailhead. The trail is handicapped-accessible to the bridge. Great leg-stretcher for the whole family.

Getting There
About halfway between Ohanapecosh and Paradise, watch for a large parking area signed BOX CANYON OF THE COWLITZ on the south side of the road. Coming from the east (Ohanapecosh), the parking lot will be on your left, just before a bridge crossing the Cowlitz River, and just before a tunnel. Coming from the west (Paradise), the parking lot will be on your right after the second tunnel and the crossing of the Cowlitz.

A viewing area just off the parking lot offers a look at the Cowlitz River, as well as Mt. Adams to the southeast and Mt. Rainier to the north.

The Walk
Crossing the road from the parking lot, you will head north on a paved path paralleling the Cowlitz River, along its east bank. Follow the split rail fence, passing an interpretive plaque entitled A TOUGH PLACE TO BLOOM, which discusses the hardy pioneer plants that establish themselves in the wake of a retreating glacier.

Double split rail fences keep you on the wide asphalt path and off the fragile soil, guiding you unerringly toward a bridged crossing of Box Canyon of the Cowlitz, so named for its steep vertical sides. A fascinating spectacle, the canyon is 115 feet deep, with sides so close you feel as though you could jump across (but please don't!).

Individuals with mobility impairment may want to turn around at the bridge. The path on the other side is paved, but is narrower and not recommended for wheelchairs. Those wishing to cross the bridge can return via this path up the west bank of the Cowlitz. At its junction with the road, turn left and cross the automobile bridge to return to the parking lot.

Nearest Lodgings: Any Packwood or White Pass lodging.

TWIN FIRS LOOP
Sweet-smelling, deep-forest experience.

Map:	Mt. Rainier National Park Official Map & Guide; Green Trails #301, "Randle"
Distance:	0.4 mile loop
Elevation Gain:	Approx. 80´
Estimated Time:	30 minutes

This short loop through Douglas-fir, Western hemlock, and Western red cedar provides a bona-fide deep-woods experience, and an excellent look at a low-elevation Cascade forest. Suitable for children, this is one "wilderness" hike that doesn't require hiking boots and shouldn't be missed. As with all Mt. Rainier National Park trails, neither pets nor bicycles are allowed.

Getting There
From Mt. Rainier National Park's Nisqually (southwest) entrance, drive 4.4 miles east of the fee collection booth. A pullout on the left (north) side of the road provides room for half a dozen cars. A roadside marker explains the ecosystem of a low-elevation forest.

The Walk
Step into a sweet-smelling, shaded forest to be greeted by a massive horizontal log, a fallen giant. A carpet of needles forms the trail, with banks of moss and natural decay on either side. Observe nature's cycle of plant death, decomposition, and rebirth all around, as new trees and shrubs sprout from the carcasses of the old, and from the layer of humus atop the soil. Stay on the main, maintained trail; if you step over a log, you're going the wrong way.

Blue jays and other birds of the forest can be seen and heard. Watch for trailside flowers in the spring. Foamy fungi nestle in damp areas, and bracket mushrooms cling to the sides of tree trunks.

The trail climbs a bit, crossing creeks on sturdy little bridges, then descends gently to drop you off back in the parking area from which you started.

Nearest Lodgings: Any Ashford lodging.

GROVE OF THE PATRIARCHS
Old-growth magnificence, easily attained.

Map:	Mt. Rainier National Park Official Map & Guide; Green Trails #270, "Mt. Rainier East"
Distance:	1.4 mile round trip
Elevation Loss:	Negligible
Estimated Time:	45 minutes

One of the "must-see" attractions along the Mt. Rainier National Park scenic drive, this trail takes casual dayhikers of all ages onto an island in the

Ohanapecosh River to visit a stately grove of old giants. Interpretive signs along the way discuss the complexity and diversity of the old growth forest.

Getting There

The roadside trailhead for Grove of the Patriarchs is inside Mt. Rainier National Park, 3.5 miles from the park's southeast entrance. Take Highway 123 north past Ohanapecosh Campground, then turn left (toward Paradise and Stevens Canyon) at 3.0 miles. Watch for the large parking area, with picnic tables and restrooms, on your right, shortly after the turn.

Grove of the Patriarchs can also be reached by hiking north from Ohanapecosh on the Silver Falls Trail (see *Silver Falls Loop,* below). The combination of these two trails results in about a 4.5-mile loop.

Hikers of all ages will love Grove of the Patriarchs

.ıke

ın the north end of the parking lot, descend gently on a wide path of hard-packed dirt and conifer needles. Almost immediately, the cool, emerald waters of the Ohanapecosh River can be seen and heard immediately to your right. Its distinctive green color and clarity can be attributed to its origins in snowfields and inactive glaciers; other, cloudier streams in the park are sullied by their active glacial sources.

At 0.3 mile, just before the trail turns to the right (east) to cross the river, it intersects the East Side Trail. Persons taking the East Side Trail up and to the left would reach Deer Creek in 6.2 miles and Cayuse Pass in 9.3 miles. Continue right on the main trail. A split-rail fence leads down a switchbacking staircase to the bridge over the Ohanapecosh.

Once on the island, you enter a world of ancient Douglas-fir and Western red cedar, some trees over 1000 years old. This is the Grove of the Patriarchs. Red alder and Pacific silver fir tower above as well. Massive trees, standing and fallen, lend an air of reverence to this special place.

At about 0.5 mile, the path forks, creating a keyhole loop path; proceed in either direction. Interpretive signs point out such notable trees as the Twin Douglas-firs (two mighty, 1000-year-old trunks that continue to live despite the loss of much heartwood and most of their tops) and Big Cedar (whose gnarled base measures perhaps 15 feet in diameter).

Complete the loop and return the way you came.

Nearest Lodgings: Any Packwood or White Pass lodging.

CARTER FALLS
Easily-attained waterfall drama.

Map:	Mt. Rainier National Park Official Map & Guide; Green Trails #269, "Mt. Rainier West"
Distance:	2.2 miles round trip
Elevation Gain:	460′
Estimated Time:	I hour

An excellent leg-stretcher for almost anyone passing through Mt. Rainier National Park, the Carter Falls segment of the Wonderland Trail is a gentle rise through old forest to a plunging falls on the Paradise River. The trail is wide and well-graded, but the deep-woods experience is genuine. At just over a mile each way, you'll want to bring the family for this one. The only exception to its overall family appeal is an initial crossing of the Nisqually River. While the 3 log bridges with cable handrails are perfectly safe (in fact, older children will enjoy the bridges' bounce and sway), the second one is narrow enough to make parents of toddlers nervous, especially in wet weather, when surfaces are slick. If everyone in your party is comfortable with the Nisqually crossing, the rest of the walk is a piece of cake.

No pets or bicycles on this trail; stock is permitted.

Getting There

One-tenth of a mile west of Cougar Rock Campground (2.1 miles east of Longmire, 9.3 west of the Paradise visitor center), a pullout on the south side of the road provides room for 8 or 10 cars parallel to the road, and access to the Wonderland Trail. Via this trail, Longmire is 1.6 miles to the right (southwest), Paradise is 4.1 to the left, and Carter Falls is 1.1 to the left.

The Hike

Descend immediately from the parking area to a crossing of the Nisqually River and its rock-strewn basin. Flow varies with the season and snowmelt, but bridges and boulders make the crossing fairly easy. Contrast the milky-gray Nisqually, which originates from an active glacier, with the clear, emerald Ohanapecosh River (see Grove of the Patriarchs, above, or Silver Falls, below), which originates from a still, inactive glacier.

Once across the basin, ascend briefly through a stand of alder before entering coniferous forest on the wide, well-graded path.

The first 0.4 mile of the hike ascends at the gentlest of inclines, following the route of the Paradise River. At about 0.4 mile, you will cross a rubble field (the path remains clear and well-delineated), after which the ascent steepens to a moderate pitch for the remaining 0.7 mile. Stay alert for deer; the sound of the river mutes your footfalls and makes sighting them more likely.

The exposed pipe that can be seen alongside the trail in several places is a remnant of a now-defunct power generation plant.

After about half an hour, you'll reach two viewpoints, the second of which is signed CARTER FALLS, ELEV. 3660. The falls are below you, an impressive (although not terribly photogenic due to the angle and the intervening trees) cascade. Continuing beyond the signed viewpoint yields no further views of Carter Falls. Return the way you came.

Nearest Lodgings: Any Ashford lodging.

Doe and fawn on Carter Falls Trail

,ONE LAKE

swimming lake.

Map:	Green Trails #302, "Packwood"
Distance:	1.25 miles round trip
Elevation Gain:	300´
Estimated Time:	45 minutes

This steep but short trail takes you to a fine little lake, warm enough for a swim, making it a great add-on hike at the end of an active day. Pack a picnic and take your sweetheart, but leave the kiddies behind—the water is deep, the climb is steep, and local custom does not preclude bathing in the buff. And, please, leave this pristine place the way you found it—it's a jewel.

Getting There

About 4.5 miles east of Packwood on Highway 12, turn northwest on Road 1270, a paved, one-lane road. Cross the signed CLEAR FORK COWLITZ RIVER; stay left. The road goes to gravel after 1.0 mile. Just before the road ends at 2.5 miles (with room to park a dozen cars), you'll see the Backbone Lake trailhead on the left. Park at road's end and walk back about 50 feet to the trailhead.

The Hike

Begin at the signed BACKBONE LAKE, TR. 164 trailhead you passed about 50 feet before the parking area. The trail is steep, dusty, and exposed for the first 0.1 mile, after which the grade moderates a bit and offers some shade. The surface is rocky and rooty. Watch for the antics of the plump, busy grouse that frequent the shrubbery alongside the trail.

Backbone Lake is a great swimming hole

At 0.3, the trail is almost flat, briefly, and well-shaded by Western hemlock, Douglas-fir, and Western red cedar.

At 0.4, you reach a fork, which may be unsigned. Backbone Lake is to the right. (If you went left, you would climb north along Backbone Ridge, reaching the Mt. Rainier National Park Boundary in just over 3.0 miles.)

From the junction, head downhill to your right. The lake is in sight within 75 feet; you reach its banks at 0.5 mile. A 0.25-mile trail encircles the lake; the best swimming access is to your left, about 1/4 of the way around. After a swim and a picnic, complete the loop around the lake and return the way you came.

Nearest Lodgings: Any Packwood or White Pass lodging.

SILVER FALLS LOOP
Stunning, deep-forest trail to a magnificent waterfall.

Map:	Mt. Rainier National Park Official Map & Guide; Green Trails #302 & #270, "Packwood" & "Mt. Rainier East"
Distance:	2.4 miles round-trip
Elevation Gain:	260´
Estimated Time:	1 hour, 30 minutes

A short, popular, yet surpassingly beautiful trail, Silver Falls Loop takes you from Mt. Rainier National Park's Ohanapecosh Campground to an impressive waterfall, passing the historic Ohanapecosh Hot Springs en route. A great hike for families.

To avoid the crowds, hike this one in the shoulder season if you can. Check with the park service rangers; it's often open when other trails are not. It's also a good rainy-day choice, since sweeping views are not the attraction. The attraction is the dense, fragrant forest, the deep, emerald-green Ohanapecosh River, and the powerful cascade of Silver Falls, all of which are made more beautiful by a bit of gauzy fog or glossy rain.

Restrooms are available within the campground and at the visitor center.

Getting There
Access the Silver Falls trail from the Ohanapecosh Campground, 1.25 miles inside the southeast (Highway 123) entrance to the park.

Upon entering the campground from Highway 123, follow the signs toward the VISITOR INFORMATION CENTER (a helpful stop as well as a place to leave non-hikers), then proceed to the DAY USE AREA. Following the signs, drive a short loop through camping section B; en route, you will see the signed SILVER FALLS trailhead. At the end of the loop is a day use parking area for 10-11 cars. Check at the visitor center for additional parking if this is full.

The Hike
Find the silver trailhead sign at the far end of the camping section B loop, a short stroll from your vehicle. The sign says LOOP TRAIL, HOT SPRINGS 0.1, LAUGHINGWATER TRAIL 1.0, SILVER FALLS 1.1.

Begin on a wide, needle-carpeted trail surrounded by moss and ferns and canopied with magnificent old-growth forest. The emerald Ohanapecosh River rushes to your left.

Just a few hundred feet from the trailhead, you enter a marshy clearing that is part of the Ohanapecosh Hot Springs. A one-time resort site, the area is now closed to bathing and preserved in a natural state. As you tread across a board-walk, warm water beneath you is heated as it moves between pressured rock layers. Just beyond this first marsh, a trail to your right leads up to the rest of the hot springs site. This side trail is also part of the Life Systems Interpretive Loop, which begins behind the information center (see Life Systems Interpretive Loop under *Other Hike Notes,* below). If you won't be walking that loop, take a moment to wander off to your right and look at the sulfurous, steaming pools, surrounded by turquoise-green algae.

Continue on the main trail, which ascends gently, surrounded by giant trees, deep-green foliage, and the burbling sounds of water. A sturdy little bridge

Silver Falls

crosses a tributary to the river at 0.25 mile; another at 0.4. Bridges and trail surfaces are well maintained along this popular trail.

At 1.0 mile, cross Laughingwater Creek, the largest tributary to the Ohanapecosh on the route. Climb the final, steeper 0.1 mile to the falls. Just before the falls, the Laughingwater Creek Trail intersects on your right; stay left, descending to the falls viewing platform.

Silver Falls is a mighty, foaming, multi-tiered waterfall, stunning and powerful. Observe it from the platform, then again from the bridge below, crossing the Ohanapecosh at the base of the falls. On the other side, ascend to a final lookout point, an eye-level, up-close perspective of the top of the falls. Children will enjoy getting soaked by the spray, and you'll find yourself saying the Parent's Prayer ("Be careful!"), despite the railing separating you from the plunging water.

Continue uphill on the trail to the next junction, less than 0.1 mile. This is the loop's halfway point, 1.2 miles. Continuing straight would take you via the Eastside Trail to the Grove of the Patriarchs (see above; while these trails can be done together as a longer hike, I have listed them separately, as both are particularly well-suited for hiking with children). Turn left to complete the loop and return to the campground.

Pass another junction—with the Ollalie Creek trail—at 1.3 miles.

This side of the loop is quieter and farther from the river. The first 0.3 mile ascends gently; the rest descends, until it drops into the campground, where several social trails connect on your right. Stay left until you exit the trail onto a campground road just west of the Ohanapecosh River bridge. Turn left, walk across the bridge, and turn left again into the day use parking area.

Nearest Lodgings: Any Packwood or White Pass lodging.

BENCH AND SNOW LAKES
Colorful meadow, icy lake, and late-season snowfield.

Map:	Mt. Rainier National Park Official Map & Guide; Green Trails #270 or #270S, "Mt. Rainier East" or "Paradise"
Distance:	2.6 miles round-trip
Elevation Gain:	250′
Estimated Time:	1 hour, 30 minutes

This largely open, subalpine hike features lush meadows, two lakes, and a short but modestly challenging, well-maintained trail. At the end, Snow Lake gleams black, icy, and mysterious at the base of the late-melting snowfield that gives it its name. A quick dip in its inky waters will take your breath away. Great trail for families with older kids.

Getting There
From the Stevens Canyon entrance off Highway 123 at the east side of the park, go 16 miles west (5.7 miles west of Box Canyon) to a pullout for 10–12 cars on the south side of the road. Coming from the other direction, you'll find the

pullout 4.6 miles east of Paradise, or 2.6 miles east of where the one-way road down from Paradise intersects the main road.

You'll find the trailhead at the east end of the parking pullout. It's marked SNOW LAKE TRAIL: BENCH LAKE .7 MI., SNOW LAKE 1.3 MI.

The Hike

This hiker-only (no bikes, no pets) trail starts off uphill. Lupine and other flowering foliage crowd close around the trail as you ascend. It is a well-maintained path, with log-inset steps on steeper sections, and boardwalks across damp meadowed areas.

Snow Lake

Reach "The Bench," for which Bench Lake is named, after about 0.25 mile. This broad, flat meadow is packed with color from snowmelt through August: violet-blue lupine, lavender-and-yellow mountain daisy, magenta paintbrush, creamy white beargrass, rose-hued spirea.

After a quarter-mile of meadow, begin descending toward Bench Lake. At 0.7 miles, you may take a spur trail to the lake shore, just a few dozen feet to your left and down.

Leaving Bench Lake, you'll cross a stream at 0.9, then tuck into a fairly steep 0.2-mile ascent. At 1.1 mile, descend slightly into the Snow Lake basin. By 1.2, the lake is in sight, and you have a choice of turning left, toward Snow Lake Camp, or right, toward the snowfield, to access the banks of the lake. Either direction offers good access to the lakeshore after 1.3 total trail miles.

Nearest Lodgings: Any lodging in this section.

NACHES PEAK/TIPSOO LAKE LOOP
World-class wildflower meadows and outstanding views of Rainier.

Map:	Mt. Rainier National Park Official Map & Guide; Green Trails #270 & #271, "Mt. Rainier East" & "Bumping Lake"
Distance:	3.6 mile loop
Elevation Gain:	600´
Estimated Time:	2 hours, 30 minutes (with lunch stop)

Flower-decked meadows, several lakes, and breathtaking views of Mt. Rainier—what more could you want in a hike? The only drawback to this trail is that it often remains snowy until late in the season. Be sure to check with the Park Service at (360) 569-2211 before heading out. (Your best bet for a first-hand report is Mt. Rainier National Park's White River Ranger Station, extension 2356, but the Hiker Information Center at Longmire, extension 3314, should also be able to help.) Also, the trail is largely open to the elements, with very little shade, so take extra water if the day is warm.

The picnic area at Tipsoo Lake, from which the loop begins, is an excellent spot for non-hikers as well, offering views of the meadows and lake, as well as short paths for easy exploration.

Getting There
From the Highway 123/Highway 410 junction on the east side of Mt. Rainier National Park, proceed east on 410 toward Yakima (away from the mountain). After a series of switchback turns, watch for the signed Tipsoo Lake picnic area on your left. This large, asphalt parking area offers restrooms, picnic tables, and a fine scenic view of little Tipsoo Lake. A boardwalk path along the side of the lake gives non-hikers the opportunity to explore a bit while the hikers take off on the loop trail.

The Hike

You may begin this hike from several points: the Tipsoo Lake picnic area, one of the Tipsoo Lake pullouts east of the picnic area, or the Chinook Pass parking area just outside the National Park boundary. These directions begin at the picnic area and proceed clockwise, maximizing views to the west on the return. Dog owners can hike part of the trail by starting at the Chinook Pass area and proceeding east across the footbridge to the Dewey Lake junction. This segment is part of the Pacific Crest Trail and is open to equestrians and leashed pets.

Find the information sign and plaque commemorating Stephen Mather at the end of the parking lot. Read the memos posted and make sure everyone in your party understands the importance of staying ON the path and OFF the fragile meadows.

Follow the path as it drops down from the parking lot toward the lake. After about 80 feet, take the path that intersects to your left and leads uphill. Ascend moderately steeply across a meadow bright with magenta paintbrushes, violet-blue lupines, lavender aster-daisies, and starry-white avalanche lilies. Throughout the hike, watch for mountain pasqueflowers in their various stages: first white flowers with yellow centers on ferny, chamomile-like leaves; then homely brown heads as the petals fall; finally, shaggy little pelts as they reach their "old man of the mountains" stage.

Switchback through a bit of forest cover, one of the few shady spots on the hike, then top out in another meadow at about 0.3 mile. Here, a network of paths joins the trail from the alternate starting point at Chinook Pass, outside the national park boundaries; the next 1.7-mile section of the loop is open to horses and dogs. Stay to your right, avoiding the delta of access paths dropping down to the Chinook Pass parking area. You will cross a footbridge over the highway that is also an archway entrance to the park.

Naches Peak Loop overlooking Dewey Lake

Contour along the east side of Naches Peak, ascending moderately for the next 0.4 mile along a ridge flanked with Western hemlock and noble fir. The ascent gentles along the backside of the peak. Here, as elsewhere in the hike, the trail is primarily dirt with jutting rocks; ankle support is important.

Pass a couple of small mountain lakes over the next mile. As views open up to the southeast, the tip of Mt. Adams is visible over the ridge in front of you. The best stop-and-sit point comes just before 2.0 miles: follow a spur path to your left and slightly downhill a few hundred feet to a cluster of large rocks overlooking gemlike Dewey Lake deep in the valley below.

Shortly after 2.0 miles, a signed junction informs you that the Pacific Crest Trail continues downhill to your left to Dewey Lake. To continue on our loop, turn right and proceed uphill, following the sign toward Tipsoo Lake. (This ends the segment of the loop where dogs are allowed.) Just before 2.1 miles, you pass from the William O. Douglas Wilderness into Mt. Rainier National Park. The path bends around to the left shortly thereafter, offering a breathtaking vista of Mt. Rainier's east flank, a view that continues for the remainder of the hike.

Dip down into a meadow and pass a small lake. Wildflowers abound and photo opportunities are at their peak between miles 2.0 and 3.0, as the trail contours along the south side of Naches Peak.

At 3.1 miles, the trail curves north, along the west side of the peak, beginning its final descent to Tipsoo Lake. Huckleberries abound along this section of trail.

Nearest Lodgings: Any Packwood or White Pass lodging; Whistling Jack's (see *Additional Lodgings,* above).

GLACIER LAKE
Shady, green hike to a secluded lake.

Map:	Green Trails #302, "Packwood;" US Forest Service "Gifford Pinchot National Forest" or "Goat Rocks Wilderness"
Distance:	4.4 miles round-trip
Elevation Gain:	800´
Estimated Time:	2 hours, 30 minutes

This mossy, green trail in Goat Rocks Wilderness takes you to a pretty forest lake. Attractive in the early season because of its low elevation, it's also a good family hike for sturdy school-aged children throughout the season. The trail is deeply wooded and undulating. It is a contemplative hike of abiding beauty, rather than a "gee-whiz!" trail with lookout towers, interpretive plaques, waterfalls, or mountain views.

Getting There
From Packwood, go west about 2.0 miles on Highway 12. Turn south on Forest Service Road 21/Johnson Creek Road, which is signed WALUPT LAKE. Follow this one-lane gravel road 5.0 miles. Turn left on Road 2110, clearly signed GLACIER LAKE TRAIL 89. Take this narrow, steep road uphill 0.5 mile. At the elbow of a

switchback on Road 2110, an old road stub in front of you serves as the parking area for the Glacier Lake Trail.

The Hike

From the trailhead marker, where you fill out your self-issuing wilderness permit, the trail goes to the right. The narrow, dirt path is closely flanked by a mix of conifers. Early season hikers will find the trail moist, with creeklets to ford—little rivulets that run down the grade from Hall Ridge to the north to Glacier Creek to the south.

Gain some altitude on a steep stretch between 0.1 and 0.3 miles. Plants along the path include Oregon grape, vanilla leaf, salal, swordfern, and wild raspberries. Thick carpets of moss add to the rich tone-on-tone tapestry of green.

At 0.4 mile, you can see Glacier Creek below on your right. At 0.6, the trail descends to its banks briefly before climbing again. Notice the massive tree trunks as you climb.

Just past a mile, officially enter Goat Rocks Wilderness. Gain much of your altitude in the next 0.7 mile, whereupon you enter a moss-covered boulder field, through which you climb more gently the final 0.5 mile to the lake.

The canopy of evergreens thins, giving way to a profusion of vine maple as you near the lake. The sky opens up and, straight ahead (to the east), you can see the pyramid of Johnson Peak, from which the headwaters of Glacier Creek flow to create the lake now in front of you. Follow the path around to the left to a primitive campsite/picnic area and the best lake access.

Nearest Lodgings: Any Packwood lodging.

The lush, green route to Glacier Lake

HIGH ROCK
Stunning view of all four major peaks, with Mt. Rainier up close.

Map:	Green Trails #301, "Randle"
Distance:	3.6 miles round-trip
Elevation Gain:	1400′
Estimated Time:	2 hours

This is one of the most dramatic lookout tower dayhikes in the Cascades. For the mere investment of 1.8 miles (each way), you can rise to the dizzying height of 5700 feet. There, you stare Mt. Rainier in the face and, if you're lucky, look *down* on mountain goats. On a late July evening, with The Mountain bathed in the pink of twilight, High Rock is a near-mystical experience.

On a serious note, acrophobics and hikers with small children may want to think twice about this one. The top of High Rock is a sheer cliff—you wouldn't even bounce on the way down. Exercise caution.

Getting There
It takes a bit of driving to get to this trail, but it's worth it.

From Ashford, find Kernahan Road, which is also Forest Service Road 52, 3.2 miles west of the Nisqually archway entrance to the National Park; take this road south. Stay on Road 52, passing turnoffs to Osborn Road/Road 85 and Big Creek Campground. After 4.6 miles, turn right on Road 84, a one-lane gravel road with turnouts. Pass right turnoffs for roads 8410 and 8420, but stay left, following signs for HIGH ROCK LOOKOUT. After 6.8 miles on Road 84, turn right on Road 8440. Proceed 2.6 miles to the trailhead, which is on the right-hand, uphill side of the road inside the elbow of a 10-mph-hairpin turn.

A trailhead sign identifies this as HIGH ROCK LOOKOUT 266. There is parking for half a dozen cars.

Great view of Rainier from the High Rock Trail

The Hike

From the trailhead sign, you can see the lookout tower perched high above and to the north. Begin by climbing a narrow goat-path across a brief stretch of clearcut, now a recovering meadow full of lupine, tiger lilies, and beargrass. After the first couple of switchbacks, Mt. Rainier is visible over the ridges ahead of you to the northeast.

After 0.2 mile, you enter forest. From here, you are climbing a ridge; the hillside drops away from you on either side, affording fabulous views both east and west. Your ascent steepens just before 0.6 mile. At 0.75, a bench provides welcome respite for those unaccustomed to climbing. Views of Mt. Rainier are partially obscured by a stand of Pacific silver fir.

From here, the trail swings over to the east side of the ridge, sacrificing views to the west for better views of Rainier. Huckleberries surround the path; pick a few to munch at the second bench, just past 1.0 mile.

You'll come to a good view of Mt. Rainier at 1.4 miles. Step cautiously to the edge of the precipice for a nearly unimpeded view of Rainier; Mt. Adams is also visible to the southeast.

At 1.7 miles, don't miss the Johnnie T. Peters memorial viewpoint to your left. A plaque commemorates Peters' efforts in building the lookout tower. This point of rock, perched above a sheer drop-off, offers a jaw-dropping look at Mt. Rainier and, to your left, the aptly named Sawtooth Ridge.

Ascend the final 0.1 mile, passing an emergency shelter just before you step out onto the exposed rock on which the manned lookout tower is perched. Step carefully on the final hundred feet up the bare rock, avoiding a crevice, and staying back from the edges. The edges can be crumbly, and sudden gusts of wind are not uncommon up here.

The view of Rainier is predictably smashing from the top. You can also see Cora Lake just below and to the east, the vast expanse of Alder Lake to the west, and the snow-tipped crags of the Goat Rocks to the east, south of Mt. Rainier. Mt. Adams sits to the southeast, the symmetrical snow cone of Mt. Hood is directly south, and Mount St. Helens is to the southwest. Few points offer such a view of all four major peaks. If you're fortunate, lookout Bud Panco may be on duty at the tower. A wealth of information, Panco has worked at High Rock since the mid-1980s.

Nearest Lodgings: Any Ashford or Packwood lodging.

COMET FALLS

Magnificent 320-foot, sunlit waterfall.

Map:	Mt. Rainier National Park Official Map & Guide; Green Trails #269, "Mt. Rainier West"
Distance:	3.8 miles round-trip
Elevation Gain:	1200′
Estimated Time:	2 hours, 15 minutes

Climb a steep, wooded path to one of Mt. Rainier's most popular hiking destinations, a dramatic 320-foot cascade set amidst meadows. On a sunny summer day, this trail is chockablock with "hikers," including the ill-prepared sandal and tennis shoe variety. (Even though it's only 1.9 miles each way, any path this steep and rooty suggests hiking boots, if you want your feet to survive to hike another day.) Try catching this trail early or late in the day, or in overcast or drizzle, to avoid the worst of the throngs. And bring the camera—this waterfall is a can't-miss Kodak moment.

Getting There

The Comet Falls/Van Trump Park trailhead is 4.0 miles east of Longmire in Mt. Rainier National Park. Parking is limited; go early or late in the day to avoid disappointment.

Comet Falls

The Hike

Begin on a steep, rooty, dirt path lined with salal, coral root, pipsissewa, and Canadian dogwood, and shaded by mixed conifers including Pacific silver fir, Douglas-fir and Western red cedar. The path is heavily used but well-maintained.

Cross Van Trump Creek at 0.3 mile; Christine Falls (which can be seen from below, just off the highway) is to your right. Continue ascending, past huckleberries and deer ferns, with the music of Van Trump Creek to your left.

Tuck into some serious switchbacks at 0.6 mile. After 1.0 mile, you'll get some relief; a few short, exposed segments are nearly flat. At 1.4 miles, ascend a series of switchbacks through an open boulder field.

Just before 1.7 miles, arrive at a bridge over Falls Creek, a tributary of Van Trump Creek. Ascend the opposite bank and, about 50 feet up, BOOM! Comet Falls! Your first view is dramatic, but, as you ascend the final 0.2 mile, any residual stinging in your quadriceps evaporates, because the views keep getting better and better up to the 1.9-mile point, where the trail narrows and many hikers turn around. (When conditions permit, you can continue an additional mile past Comet Falls to the splendid meadows of Van Trump Park.)

Nearest Lodgings: Any lodging in this section.

RAMPARTS RIDGE LOOP
Great early season climb with views of Rainier.

Map:	Mt. Rainier National Park Official Map & Guide; Green Trails #269, "Mt. Rainier West"
Distance:	4.8 mile loop
Elevation Gain:	1300'
Estimated Time:	2 hours, 45 minutes

One of the earliest trails to melt out in the park is Ramparts Ridge Loop. Because it begins in Longmire, at about 2700 feet in elevation, and tops out just over 4000 feet, it is snow-free earlier than the trails at Paradise and those en route.

Because it is a good shoulder-season hike, Ramparts gets hit hard as soon as the snow melts, resulting in mucky springtime tread. Your reward for trudging through the early-season mire is a profusion of trillium and beargrass in bloom.

There are no really good picnic spots on this loop, so take water and a light snack for energy, but plan to treat yourself to lunch at the National Park Inn Restaurant (see *Dining*, above) in Longmire when you finish your hike.

Getting There

Begin in the historic community of Longmire, 7 miles east of the park's Nisqually entrance. The trailhead is on the west side of the road, across the street from the National Park Inn.

The Hike

Begin across the road from the National Park Inn at Longmire, where you'll find the Trail of the Shadows historical stroll (see *Other Hike Notes*, below). Head left on this trail, as though you were going to do the Trail of the Shadows clockwise.

Walk through the skunk cabbage, snake grass, rushes, and cattails of Longmire Meadow, then pass into a forest environment of devil's club, ferns, vanilla leaf, and shady conifers.

Just after 0.1 mile, you come to a signed junction with RAMPARTS RIDGE TRAIL. Turn left.

Begin the fairly steep, steady, switchbacking ascent that will take you up to the ridge, attaining most of your 1300 feet over the next 1.3 miles. As you gain altitude, you can look back down at the Longmire complex and the Nisqually River.

Just after 1.4 miles, the relentless grade becomes gentler, and you sense you are reaching the ridgetop. Just before 1.7 miles, a sign points you toward a viewpoint trail off to your right. Here, you gain your first good view of Mt. Rainier, and it's worth the struggle up the hill.

Return to the main trail, where you continue to glimpse the mountain through the trees, then, finally, score an unimpeded view as you crest the ridge summit at about 1.9 miles. Enjoy this wide-open view, because you descend rather quickly into deep forest and lose the mountain for the remainder of the hike.

Ramparts Ridge loop offers an up-close look at Mt. Rainier

At 2.8 miles, you intersect the Wonderland Trail; turn right. The descent becomes steeper as you head downhill toward Longmire.

At 3.0 miles, the Van Trump Trail intersects on your left; continue straight ahead on the Wonderland Trail, following the sign for LONGMIRE. Descend on a trail lined with Canadian dogwood, beargrass, Indian pipe, and mushrooms.

At 4.4 miles, you can begin to see and hear the road. A creek flows alongside you. Intersect with the road at 4.5. Cross the road and follow the trail straight ahead, signed LONGMIRE. (You are still on the Wonderland Trail.)

At 4.6 miles, the Wonderland Trail doubles back and to your left toward Cougar Rock and Paradise. You can see the roofs of Longmire buildings straight ahead; continue forward on the unmarked path into Longmire.

Nearest Lodgings: Any Ashford lodging.

MT. FREMONT LOOKOUT
Lookout tower and good chance for mountain goat sighting.

Map:	Mt. Rainier National Park Official Map & Guide; Green Trails #270, "Mt. Rainier East"
Distance:	5.6 miles round-trip
Elevation Gain:	800´
Estimated Time:	3 hours, 15 minutes

This trail is a prime choice when visiting the Sunrise visitor center in the northeast part of Mt. Rainier National Park. It offers a good look at Emmons Glacier, the largest of Mt. Rainier's many glaciers, and a relatively easy climb to a lookout tower. The tower is open most weekend afternoons during peak season, when it is staffed by park personnel who provide interpretive talks. When it's closed, you can still enjoy views from its deck.

En route to the tower, you'll pass the aptly-named Frozen Lake with its ever-present snow overhang. If you keep a sharp eye between the lake and the tower, chances are good you will see mountain goats.

Getting There
The Mt. Fremont trail is accessed from Sunrise, Mt. Rainier National Park's "other" visitor center. It is less flashy than Paradise, has no lodgings, and opens later due to its higher elevation (6400 feet to Paradise's 5400 feet).

The road to Sunrise goes west off Highway 410, 3.5 miles north of Cayuse Pass (the Highway 410/Highway 123 junction), in the northeast part of the park. Follow this scenic, switchbacking road 15.3 miles to its end.

Trailhead access is at the east end of the parking lot, by the restrooms.

The Hike
From the trailhead, head north on NATURE TRAIL. At a signed junction, go left toward WONDERLAND TRAIL and BURROUGHS MOUNTAIN. The path is wide, graveled, and inclines gently to moderately to a viewpoint at 0.3 mile. Continue following signs for WONDERLAND TRAIL and BURROUGHS MOUNTAIN; the trail narrows to a rocky dirt surface and climbs steeply from this viewpoint.

The Sunrise area trails are distinctly "east Cascade" in character—drier and dustier than those found at Paradise or on the south and west sides of the park. Lupine is the dominant flower; hellebore, bistort, mountain daisies, and phlox are also common. As you head west, looking south-southwest at the mountain, Emmons Glacier—the mountain's largest—stretches northeast toward you, and Fryingpan Glacier is the one to its left, running east-west, forming the horizon of your vista. The distinct pointed peak rising high on the mountain's shoulder west of Fryingpan Glacier is Little Tahoma Peak.

A signed junction at 0.7 mile tells you that HUCKLEBERRY CREEK TRAIL and FOREST LAKE are to the right. Stay to the left at this fork. While the Huckleberry Creek Trail climbs steeply from the junction, your trail begins to level out, then decline slightly at 0.8. Continue gently downhill along the exposed south-facing slope; soon Frozen Lake comes into view, straight ahead.

Frozen Lake is a stunning, turquoise-blue lake with a late-season snowfield that hangs over it much or all of the season. When the trail is snow-free and the temperatures warm to downright hot, you can watch ice floes shift around on the surface of this lake. The lake serves as a water supply, and bathing is not permitted.

At 1.6 miles, you arrive at a 5-way junction. Mt. Fremont Trail is to the right. Wonderland Trail is straight ahead. Burroughs Mountain is a soft left. When open, the hard left is also a part of the Wonderland Trail, a segment that provides an alternate route back to Sunrise; this trail may be closed due to construction taking place in the valley below. A former camping site is being reclaimed as a natural area.

Turning right, you contour around the west side of Frozen Lake, then begin ascending to the northwest. Mountain goats are frequently visible on the slopes and ridgetop ahead of you and to your right as you ascend.

At 2.3, the trail rounds a bend to head north. From here, you can see the lookout tower. The remaining half-mile is an easy, though rocky, incline. The wrap-around deck of the sometimes-manned tower is open for your viewing pleasure.

Nearest Lodgings: Any Packwood or White Pass lodging; Whistling Jack's (see *Additional Lodgings,* above).

Mt. Fremont Lookout

PARADISE LOOP
Best-of-the-best Mt. Rainier trail from Paradise.

Map:	Mt. Rainier National Park Official Map & Guide;
	Green Trails #270S "Paradise," or #270 "Mt. Rainier East"
Distance:	5.3 mile loop, including spur to Pebble Creek
Elevation Gain:	1900′
Estimated Time:	3 hours, 30 minutes

The créme de la créme of Mt. Rainier dayhikes, the 5.0-mile Skyline Trail at Paradise can't fail to impress. Beginning at 5400′, it climbs through resplendent meadows to unsurpassed glacier vistas, following the route taken by bona fide mountain climbers as they ascend to Camp Muir, where they catch a few hours sleep before beginning their assault on the summit in the wee dark hours of the morning. The variation presented here includes a brief out-and-back spur trail to Pebble Creek, a segment of High Skyline Trail, and the Golden Gate Trail cut-off (an alternative that cuts a mile off the standard Skyline loop by dropping through the best of all wildflower meadows: Edith Creek Basin). Pick up a "Paradise Trail Information" handout at any ranger station for more options. If 4-and 5-mile trails are more than you had in mind, check out the Nisqually Vista Loop, a 1.2-mile trail (see *Other Hike Notes* at the end of this section), also at Paradise.

Before embarking on any of the Paradise trails, check with park rangers for current conditions; snow patches remain on parts of the trails much of the season. Be prepared for all surfaces: asphalt, gravel, rocky-dusty dirt, and snow. The measurements given below may vary from your actual experience, as a significant amount of the upper trail was under snow when this route was measured.

Getting There
It seems that "all roads lead to Paradise" in Mt. Rainier National Park. On the southern side of the park, right at the base of the mountain, Paradise is by far the most popular tourist stop. It's 11.0 miles east of Longmire, and 21.0 miles west of the Stevens Canyon entrance gate.

The two main structures at Paradise are the Henry M. Jackson Memorial Visitor Center, an incongruous, spaceship-looking thing that bears only a cursory investigation, and Paradise Inn, the historic lodge and climbing headquarters. A network of trails connects the two, so you can start at either place. I prefer to drive past the visitor center to the large parking lot below the Inn. A small, historic A-frame ranger station sits on the north side of this parking lot. To the west (left) of this are restrooms, and some 50 feet west of these is a large trailhead map, from which I began this clockwise loop.

The Hike
From the trailhead map, ascend north toward the mountain on a wide, moderately steep asphalt path (the first 0.6-mile is paved). At the first junction, just before 0.1 mile, continue straight ahead and slightly to the left, following signs

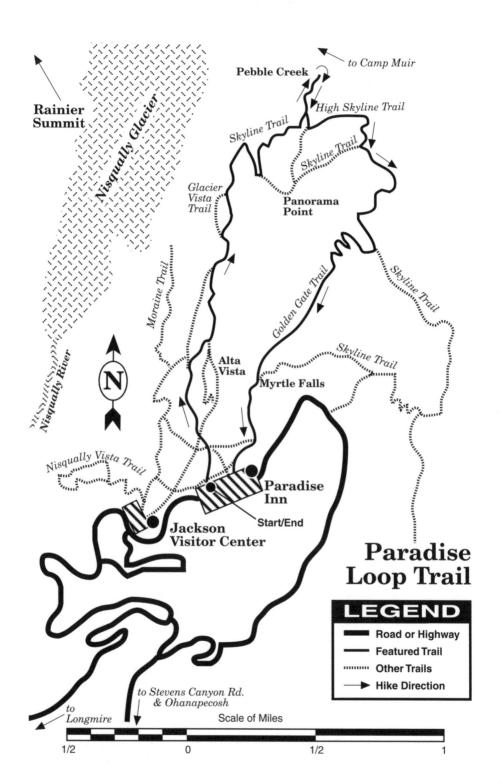

Rainier
Summit

Nisqually Glacier

Nisqually River

to Camp Muir

Pebble Creek

High Skyline Trail

Skyline Trail

Skyline Trail

*Glacier
Vista
Trail*

**Panorama
Point**

Moraine Trail

Golden Gate Trail

Skyline Trail

N

**Alta
Vista**

Skyline Trail

Myrtle Falls

Nisqually Vista Trail

**Paradise
Inn**

**Jackson
Visitor Center**

Start/End

Paradise
Loop Trail

LEGEND

▬▬	Road or Highway
—	Featured Trail
·········	Other Trails
→	Hike Direction

to Stevens Canyon Rd.
& Ohanapecosh

to
Longmire

Scale of Miles

1/2   0   1/2   1

for SKYLINE TRAIL. Another junction, signed for the ALTA VISTA TRAIL, follows almost immediately; stay the course on SKYLINE, toward CAMP MUIR.

The unrelenting incline continues to 0.4 mile, when a bench offers respite for those who thought that paved trails were always easy. Folks not accustomed to hiking will want to take their time, enjoying the displays of lupine, pasque-flower, and paintbrush along the way.

Just before 0.5 mile, reach a junction with MORAINE TRAIL; stay right.

At 0.6 is a flat, paved area for photo-taking and enjoying views to the south of the Tatoosh Range and Pinnacle Peak, and of Mt. Adams and Mount St. Helens. The knoll in front of you as you look back toward Paradise is Alta Vista. Those wishing to turn around at this point can hike up this knoll for unob-structed views south, and return to Paradise down the other side of the knoll, on the Alta Vista Trail (a 1.5-mile total hike).

Continuing on, the Skyline Trail leaves the north side of the paved viewpoint, becoming a gravel trail from this point. Park crews do a fine job of marking and maintaining the trail; please do your part by staying on it. Stay inside the stone borders or, on snow patches, between the areas marked with sticks. Meadows and fellfield areas are very fragile.

At 1.1, Glacier Vista Trail forks off to the left. By this time, you can turn to enjoy unobstructed views of Adams and St. Helens to the southeast and south-west, respectively; on a clear day, you may catch a glimpse of Hood between them. As you look up the trail, the icy expanse of the Nisqually Glacier is imme-diately on your left; you are no longer "at the base" of the mountain; you are "on" the mountain! Take time to savor this view at a resting plateau at 1.3 miles, where Glacier Vista Trail (a loop) rejoins Skyline Trail.

For the first 1.5 miles, you are traveling basically due north; a little past 1.5, the trail turns to head southeast. At 1.7 miles, the trail to Camp Muir and Pebble Creek intersects on the left; our route takes this hard left turn up the hill and back to the north. (This route bypasses a toilet conveniently located at about 2.0 miles on the main trail near Panorama Point. If your party would prefer, you can continue straight ahead. When High Skyline Trail intersects Skyline Trail, turn left and proceed a few dozen feet to the facility. Continue east on Skyline or north, then east, on High Skyline; both trails end up in the same place.)

A junction at 2.0 miles tells you that High Skyline Trail is to the right (you will return to this junction). Continue straight ahead toward Pebble Creek and Camp Muir. Reach Pebble Creek at 2.3 miles. At 7300´, this is our high point, our turn-around point, and the ideal lunch or rest spot. Camp Muir is a mere 2.2 miles far-ther, but it's a steep climb over a snowfield, topping out at about 10,000 feet. Leave Camp Muir to the climbers and enjoy Pebble Creek; it doesn't get any bet-ter than this.

Retrace your steps 0.3 mile back down to the last junction; go left for High Skyline Trail. This is your last uphill before descending for the remainder of the hike. After just a few dozen feet, the trail leading to Panorama Point, the main Skyline Trail, and the toilet goes to the right; go left to continue on High Skyline. Chances for seeing late-season snow bridges and caves off the trail are good over the next mile; remember to stay on the trail and enjoy them from a distance. You may also find groups participating in climbing exercises, using these snowfields to practice mountaineering maneuvers in preparation for a later climb.

Arrive at the Golden Gate Trail cutoff at 3.6 miles; turn right. The Skyline Trail continues straight ahead. Note that the ice caves mentioned on the junction sign no longer exist.

The remainder of the hike, utilizing the Golden Gate Trail, is a visual feast and downhill all the way. Every wildflower on the mountain seems to be represented here: paintbrush, lupine, daisy, phlox, bistort, pasqueflower, avalanche lily, groundsel, meadow parsley…acres of color.

At 4.6 miles, you come to a bridged crossing over Edith Creek—an outstanding photo opportunity looking up the creek through the meadow at the mountain. Just past the bridge, a very short, paved trail leads to your left down to Myrtle Falls viewpoint. Complete the loop on pavement, arriving at Paradise Inn at 5.1 miles and the trailhead at 5.3.

Nearest Lodgings: Any lodging in this section.

DRY CREEK
Good early season workout with Mt. Rainier and Cowlitz River Valley views.

Map:	Green Trails #302, "Packwood;" US Forest Service "Gifford Pinchot National Forest"
Distance:	8.0 miles round trip
Elevation Gain:	2700´
Estimated Time:	4 hours

When the early season hiking bug bites, take on Dry Creek for a good workout and splendid views. While this trail climbs a healthy 2700+ feet from trailhead to summit, it tops out at just over 3800 feet—much lower than most of the Mt. Rainier National Park trails to the north—making it a good choice when the mountain trails are still snow-covered.

Another reason to hike this trail early is that, while it is open to stock, bicycles, and motorcycles, they are less likely to access it early in the season when the Dry Creek crossing is difficult or impossible for anyone but pedestrians. The mosquitoes, however, love the spring; you'll want to slather on the industrial-strength bug juice for this climb. The only other fault of this trail is limited trailhead parking. On the balance, for views and solitude, it's a super trail.

Getting There
From Packwood, proceed west on Highway 12 toward Randle. You will pass a road marked WALUPT LAKE and CHAMBERS LAKE (Road 21). Turn left at the next opportunity, on the gravel road marked FOREST ROAD 20, 2.5 miles from the west end of Packwood. The first signs you will see state KLICKITAT TRAIL 7–12 MI. and ONE LANE ROAD WITH TURNOUTS 20 MPH. Pass a couple of residences before coming to an unmarked trailhead on the right, 0.2 miles from Highway 12, and just before Road 20 inclines up a small hill. If you are unable to park at or opposite

the trailhead, proceed up the hill, where a few pullout spaces are available on the left side of the road.

The Hike

The unmarked, but clearly visible singletrack is moss-lined, needle-carpeted, and begins fairly flat. The route is flanked by ferns and vanilla leaf and canopied with young timber.

A few hundred feet into the walk, you come to a crossing of Dry Creek, which can be anything but dry early in the season. Choose a left-forking trail and head upstream a bit, where you'll find an easy crossing on a sturdy log.

The trail veers right and through a clearing after the creek crossing, then begins to climb as it returns to forest. The moderately steep ascent is steady and unrelenting for the next mile, during which the sound, if not the sight, of Dry Creek continues to your left. Watch for little spur paths on your left. One of these, at about 0.5 mile, affords a view of a significant waterfall unseen from the main path.

The pitch of the climb and frequency of the switchbacks decrease after the first mile.

At about 2.0 miles, watch for a narrow bootpath to the north (on your right) at the crook of a switchback. Wending your way carefully some 30 or 40 yards down this path and over an embankment, you will emerge on a rocky outcropping overlooking the Cowlitz River Valley far below and majestic Mt. Rainier dead ahead. Beverages and trail mix are in order.

A mile farther, the path forks. Take the right, uphill fork. In the final mile ahead, other prospective forks present themselves; in each case, take the uphill choice.

The smells of deep-woods humus soil surround you as you ascend. In another half mile, as you contour around the northwest side of the knob, the path begins to flatten. Moss-covered stumps remind you that giants once dwelled here.

Resting at the top of Dry Creek Trail

At 3.75 miles, the canopy above opens up, and you tuck in for the final ascent. The soil is sandy here, with a heather groundcover dotted with lupine.

The summit is the site of the former Smith Point Lookout. Four cement piers are still in place. Your rewards are views of the Cowlitz Valley and Mt. Rainier to your north, and Goat Dike to the southwest.

Nearest Lodgings: Any Packwood lodging.

LAKE GEORGE
Pretty cirque lake away from the crowds.

Map:	Mt. Rainier National Park Official Map & Guide;
	Green Trails #269, "Mt. Rainier West"
Distance:	9.0 miles round-trip
Elevation Gain:	1400´
Estimated Time:	5 hours

Lake George would be a wildly popular 1.8-mile hike if Westside Road were kept open for vehicle traffic. Unfortunately, the frequency of flooding and slides on Westside make it impractical for the park to continue maintaining it. The result is that hikers need to walk an additional 7.2 (round-trip) miles to reach the trail. The good news is that Lake George is still a beautiful hike, it's just longer than it used to be. Those with mountain bikes can pedal the first (and last) 3.6 miles.

Getting There
From the Nisqually (southwest) entrance to Mt. Rainier National Park, proceed 0.9 miles to Westside Road. Turn left (north). Proceed 3.1 miles to the road closure, which is the trailhead. Portable toilets are usually provided. Room for about 20 cars.

The Hike
Begin by walking along the old roadway. Admittedly, this is not the most inviting of trail surfaces, but it's worth it in the end. Mountain bikers and pet owners can appreciate this part of the hike, as it is open to bikes and leashed pets. As you pick your way gradually uphill, along the route of Tahoma Creek and the wreckage of previous floods, be aware that the area is still susceptible to flash floods, especially on rainy or extremely hot days.

After 1.25 miles, the road swings west, away from the creek. The knoll in front of you in the distance is Gobbler's Knob, the summit of which is a potential extension to this trail.

Just before 2.2 miles, you will come around a bend and see a rock retaining wall on your left. This wall runs alongside a switchback, as the road doubles back here. Straight ahead of you, at the elbow of the switchback is a circular, overgrown former parking area—this is the once-popular Tahoma Vista parking area. Before continuing up the road, walk to the right, across the circular drive and toward some low rock walls (sort of contemporary "ruins"). There you will find an old sign, TAHOMA VISTA, partially obscured by overgrown alders. Push your way 50 feet or so through the overgrowth, following a boot-beaten path to a little circular meadow with a couple of large sitting stones and a postcard-perfect view of the mountain natives called "Tahoma." This is not a bad picnic spot, or a turnaround destination for families, hikers with dogs, or others who want only a 4.4-mile, 2-hour outing.

Continuing up the road toward Lake George, you will reach the summit of Round Pass, elevation 4000 feet, at 3.6 miles. On your left is a former parking lot, and the Lake George trailhead. Cyclists can park their bikes at a rack provided here and walk in to the lake. Dogs and bikes are not allowed on the trail from here to the lake.

At last, after the open, exposed roadway, you are embraced in the green shade of the forest. Climb the final 300 feet to the lake on this moderately ascending trail surrounded by Canadian dogwood, vanilla leaf, huckleberries, devil's club, and other woodland shrubs.

As you near 4.0 miles, you can see the mountain behind you and to the left. At 4.3 miles, the grade flattens out. At 4.4, the path begins to descend toward the lake, which you reach at 4.5 miles.

From the shores of this deep green cirque lake, you can gaze up at Gobbler's Knob and Mt. Wow, listen to jays squabble with one another, enjoy a picnic, and, perhaps, catch a measure of solitude unattainable on most of the park's dayhike

Lake George

trails. Lake George is a popular stopover for backpackers. A sturdy emergency shelter is available for their use, and pit toilets are provided.

Dayhikers up for a bigger adventure can take this trail an additional 1.5 (steep!) miles up to Gobbler's Knob.

Nearest Lodgings: Any Ashford lodging.

OTHER HIKE NOTES

Life Systems Interpretive Loop
This trail is a 0.6-mile self-guiding nature loop behind the visitor information center at Ohanapecosh Campground. Purchase a 50¢ trail guide and learn to recognize Western hemlock, Western red cedar, and Douglas-fir, as well as maidenhair, colt's foot, vine maple, huckleberry, and bunchberry (Canadian) dogwood. Also takes you past the site of the historic Ohanapecosh Hot Springs, open for viewing only, not bathing.

Trail of the Shadows
Across the road from the National Park Inn at Longmire, this 0.5-mile interpretive loop takes you to sites of historic interest such as an early homestead cabin. The current plant and animal life is also explained.

Nisqually Vista Loop
This 1.2-mile loop leaves the Henry M. Jackson Memorial Visitor Center at Paradise and meanders through the colorful meadows for which the Paradise area was named. A self-guiding trail booklet, available at the trailhead, enhances this easy walk by explaining the sights along the way.

Lake Christine
For a short hike near Ashford and outside the national park boundary, turn north off Highway 706 onto Road 59 (also signed MOUNT TAHOMA SKI TRAILS), 2.7 miles west of the Nisqually park entrance. After almost 4 miles, turn right onto Road 5920. Drive about a mile to the road's end, and the trailhead for Lake Christine Trail 249. The lake is about 0.8 miles in, and the trail continues about another mile to intersect with Puyallup Trail 248 at Beljica Meadows. Turning right on Trail 248 takes you to Goat Lake after a little over a mile, then into the national park in another third of a mile. Lake Christine and Goat Lake are in the Glacier View Wilderness area of the Gifford Pinchot National Forest; wilderness regulations apply.

Wonderland Trail
Not a dayhike, this 93-mile backpacking trail encircles Mt. Rainier, passing through both remote and popular areas of the park. A backcountry permit is required, and most hikers allow 9 to 12 days for the journey. Dayhikers can enjoy sections of this magnificent trail (see Carter Falls and Ramparts Ridge Loop above), which crosses the park's main roads at several points.

Table 1.
Lodgings in the Mt. Rainier-Ashford vicinity

	ALEXANDER'S INN	GROWLY BEAR	JASMER'S	MOUNTAIN MEADOWS	MOUNTHAVEN	NISQUALLY LODGE	WELLSPRING	WHITTAKER'S BUNKHOUSE
PRICE (1997 SUMMER RATES, PRE-TAX, 2 PERSON)	$89–$135	$80–$105	$45–$95 B&B; $75–$145 cabins	$75–$110 B&B; guest house suite $125–$165	$56–$149	$67–$77	$85–$300	$20/ person (bunkhouse); $60–$80 for 2 (motel)
EXTRA PERSON	$15	$30	$10	$15	included	$10	$10	$5
PAYMENT METHODS	VISA, MC, Checks, Cash	VISA, MC, AmEx, Checks, Cash	VISA, MC, Checks, Cash	VISA, MC, Checks, Cash	VISA, MC, Disc, Cash	VISA, MC, AmEx, Cash	VISA, MC, Checks, Cash	VISA, MC, Checks, Cash
# OF UNITS	12 rooms, 2 houses	4	2 B&B rooms; 7 cabins	3 B&B rooms; 2 guest house units	12	24	8	18 motel, 1-10 person bunkhouse
PRIVATE BATH	Yes	Yes, 2 rooms; No, 2 rooms	Yes	Yes	Yes	Yes	Yes	Yes, 18 rooms; No, bunkhouse
BREAKFAST INCLUDED	Yes	Yes	Cont. at B&B Not in cabins	Yes	No	Continental	Yes, most (Continental)	No
COOKING FACILITIES	No in rooms; Yes in houses	No	Yes in cabins; some in B&B	Yes, in guest house	Yes, 10 units	No	Yes, 2 units	No
POOL	No	No	No	No	No	No	No	No
HOT TUB	Yes	No	Yes at B&B, some cabins	No	No	Yes	Yes	Yes
CHILDREN	OK	OK	OK over 10	By arrange.	OK	OK	OK in 1 unit	OK
PETS	No	No	No	By arrange.	OK, $10 fee	No	No	No
HANDICAPPED ACCESSIBLE	No	No	Call	No	Yes, 1 unit	Yes	Yes, main lodge	Yes, 1 unit

	COWLITZ RIVER LODGE	HOTEL PACKWOOD	MOUNTAIN VIEW LODGE	TATOOSH MEADOWS	VILLAGE INN CONDOS
PRICE (1997 SUMMER RATES, PRE-TAX, 2 PERSON)	$50–$60	$25–$38	$34–$73	$110–$220	$48–$98
EXTRA PERSON	$5	$5	$3	included	included
PAYMENT METHODS	VISA, MC, AmEx, Cash	VISA, MC, Disc, Checks, Cash	VISA, MC, AmEx, Disc, Checks, Cash	VISA, MC, AmEx, Disc, Checks	VISA, MC, Check, Cash
# OF UNITS	32	9	22	10	56
PRIVATE BATH	Yes	Yes, 2 rooms No, 7 rooms	Yes	Yes	Yes
BREAKFAST INCLUDED	Continental	No	No	No	No
COOKING FACILITIES	No	No	Yes, some	Yes	Yes
POOL	No	No	Yes	No	Yes
HOT TUB	Yes	Yes	Yes	Yes	No
CHILDREN	OK	OK	OK	OK	OK
PETS	No	OK, credit card deposit	OK, $3 fee	OK in some units, $25 fee	No
HANDICAPPED ACCESSIBLE	Yes	No	No	Yes	No

Table 2. Lodgings in the Mt. Rainier-Packwood/White Pass vicinity

Section 2—Mount St. Helens

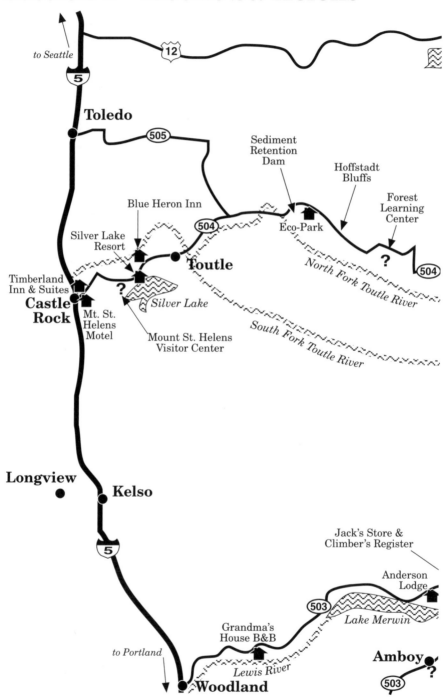

to Seattle

12

5

Toledo

505

Sediment
Retention
Dam

Hoffstadt
Bluffs

Forest
Learning
Center

Blue Heron Inn

504

Eco-Park

?

504

Silver Lake
Resort

Toutle

North Fork Toutle River

Timberland
Inn & Suites

?

Castle
Rock

Mt. St.
Helens
Motel

Silver Lake

South Fork Toutle River

Mount St. Helens
Visitor Center

Longview

Kelso

5

Jack's Store &
Climber's Register

Anderson
Lodge

503

Lake Merwin

Grandma's
House B&B

to Portland

Amboy

503

Lewis River

Woodland

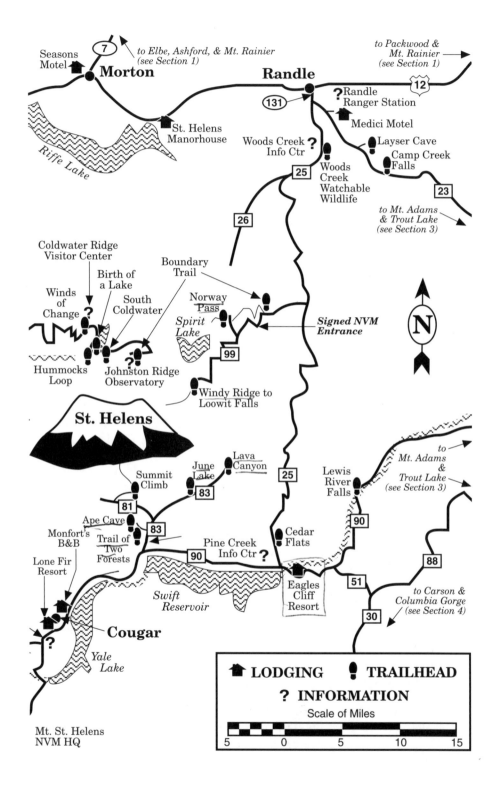

Seasons Motel

7

to Elbe, Ashford, & Mt. Rainier
(see Section 1)

Morton

Randle

to Packwood &
Mt. Rainier
(see Section 1)

12

131

? Randle
Ranger Station

St. Helens
Manorhouse

Medici Motel

Rifle Lake

Woods Creek
Info Ctr ?

Layser Cave
Camp Creek
Falls

25

Woods
Creek
Watchable
Wildlife

23

to Mt. Adams
& Trout Lake
(see Section 3)

26

Coldwater Ridge
Visitor Center

Birth of
a Lake

Boundary
Trail

Winds
of
Change ?

South
Coldwater

Norway
Pass

Spirit
Lake

Signed NVM
Entrance

N

Hummocks
Loop

Johnston Ridge
Observatory

99

Windy Ridge to
Loowit Falls

St. Helens

Lava
Canyon

Summit
Climb

June
Lake

25

Lewis
River
Falls

to
Mt. Adams
&
Trout Lake
(see Section 3)

83

81

90

Ape Cave

83

Monfort's
B&B

Trail of
Two
Forests

Pine Creek
Info Ctr ?

Cedar
Flats

88

Lone Fir
Resort

90

51

Eagles
Cliff
Resort

to Carson &
Columbia Gorge
(see Section 4)

Cougar

Swift
Reservoir

30

?

Yale
Lake

Mt. St. Helens
NVM HQ

🏠 LODGING   👣 TRAILHEAD

? INFORMATION

Scale of Miles

5   0   5   10   15

Mount St. Helens

OVERVIEW

"Mount St. Helens." Two decades after its cataclysmic blast on May 18, 1980, its name still evokes images of disaster: the 12-mile high steam plume, the raging mudslide up the Toutle River valley, the blanket of ash that covered eastern Washington, the weather-disturbing cloud that circled the globe in the two weeks following the eruption.

It takes a bit of study to get your bearings before visiting Mount St. Helens today. First, it pays to understand the basics of the 1980 blast, so you'll have a sense of the geology affecting the landscape. Second, you'll need to understand the logistics of visiting the mountain: three distinct roads lead to the mountain, each with its own set of lodgings and trails. You can easily visit and hike all three, but not in the same day.

When Mount St. Helens erupted, the north side of the mountain blew out. The result is that the south side remains in many ways the way it was before 1980: timberland with forested hiking trails and lava tube caves and canyons— remnants of other, long-ago volcanic events. The south side of the mountain still looks more or less like a mountain, albeit a flat-topped one. This is the side that climbers climb, and, upon reaching the top, find themselves at the upper edge of a volcanic rim, looking down into a crater that cannot otherwise be seen from the south side. (See South Side Summit Climb under *Walks and Hikes*, below.) I refer to Highway 503 and Forest Service Road 90 and its access roads as the mountain's "south approach."

The north side of the mountain is a different story. Here, the side of the mountain blew away, leaving a denuded mountainside with a huge crater dominating its top and side. Inside the crater, a lava dome has risen (and continues to rise), forming a bump in the middle. Here, two decades after the eruption, visitors can still see the three distinct devastation zones: the blast zone, 0–6 miles from the crater, where virtually no life remained (and precious little is present today); the blowdown zone, 6–14 miles from the crater, where trees were killed and blown down, and still lay like so many tossed toothpicks; and the heat-kill zone, 14–18 miles from the crater, where trees were killed but remained, and still remain today, as upright snags. Visitors can approach the north side of the mountain from Highway 504 (I refer to this as the "west approach") and Forest Service Road 99 on the mountain's northeast side (I refer to this as the "east approach").

The effects of the blast upon the immediate area were numerous and complex. The prevailing winds were from the west, resulting in most of the ash and pumice blowing east. Visitors to the east approach will see much of the ash and pumice from the blast when they visit the Windy Ridge viewpoint or hike trails such as Hummocks Loop and Windy Ridge to Loowit Falls. The tremendous heat generated by the blast also caused thousands of tons of snow to melt, resulting in floods and mudslides which re-contoured the land. Spirit Lake was literally moved and redefined. Coldwater Lake was formed. The Toutle River valley became a raging river of mud and an instrument of mass destruction. Visitors along the popular west approach will follow the route of the Toutle River and can learn about the mudslide, the blast, and the "stone-filled wind" that changed the landscape to the north and west.

Much of the area around the mountain has been designated Mount St. Helens National Volcanic Monument (NVM). This area has been preserved in its natural state: no reforestation efforts have been undertaken. Instead, scientists from around the world have used this post-volcanic landscape as an in-situ laboratory to study the natural recovery process following a cataclysmic eruption. Beyond the boundaries of the monument, parts of the Gifford Pinchot National Forest were affected, as were some privately owned parcels of land—most notably, 68,000 acres of Weyerhaeuser Company timber. These areas were harvested and have been replanted.

To find the west approach, the mountain's most popular visitor route, take Interstate 5 to Exit 49 at Castle Rock, then take Highway 504, also known as Spirit Lake Highway, east toward the mountain. This popular highway was finished in 1992, built along the hillside north of the Toutle River valley to avoid the unstable valley floor which was the route of the pre-eruption highway now deeply buried. Lodging and dining is available, though not exactly abundant, along this route. Nonetheless, this corridor is "tourist central," with five visitor centers.

The first, and largest, visitor center is called simply Mount St. Helens Visitor Center. It's 5 miles east of Castle Rock. Helpful personnel can answer all your questions about the 1980 eruption and other facets of the mountain's history, geology, and biology. It's a good visitor center, especially for those who don't have time to venture far off Interstate 5, but it's too far west for a really good look at the mountain.

The next "visitor center"—using the term loosely—is Hoffstadt Bluffs, 27 miles east of Castle Rock. The facility, which was built by Cowlitz County, not the forest service, includes a restaurant, helicopter tours, and souvenir shops.

Next is the Weyerhaeuser-sponsored Forest Learning Center, 33.5 miles east of Castle Rock. This free center includes fabulously replicated dioramas of the wreckage and reforestation efforts. A short, 4-minute film is also worth viewing. Other displays explain conservation and forest management. The indoor "helicopter tour" should be a hit with kids.

At mile 43 is Coldwater Ridge Visitor Center, a dramatic building with a green, peaked roof which rises above the barren, windswept ridge. Opened in 1993, this impressive facility includes a 16-screen video presentation, interactive exhibits, gift shop, book store, cafeteria, and lots of glass, so you can view the surrounding landscape even on the windiest of days, including Mount St. Helens, the Toutle River valley, and Coldwater Lake.

At the absolute end of Highway 504, 53.8 miles east of Castle Rock, is the crown jewel: Johnston Ridge Observatory. Named for volcanologist David Johnston, who lost his life in the blast, this newest of visitor centers opened in 1997. Built low and set unobtrusively into the hillside, the center is part memorial, part laboratory, and part visitor center. It includes interpretive displays, interactive exhibits, and a magnificent film. The film begins with Johnston's now-eerie recorded last words announcing—in a panic—the eruption, and ends with the raising of the screen and wall to show the crater outside. It is moving and disturbing—perhaps too much for small children.

To approach the mountain from the east, take Highway 131/Forest Road 25 south out of Randle from Highway 12; after 20 miles, turn right onto Road 99. (You can also wind your way over from Mt. Adams or up from the Columbia Gorge. One way to get there from Mt. Adams is to take Road 88 north out of Trout Lake to Road 90, then head west until 90 junctions with Road 25. Take 25 right [north] to Road 99. From the Columbia Gorge, take Road 30 north out of Carson, then Road 51 west to connect with 90. Go left [west] on 90 to its junction with Road 25, then right [north] to Road 99.) Once you're on Road 99, continue west, following signs for the mountain and the volcanic monument. This is the most dramatic approach to the mountain, because you experience the effects of the blast they way they happened: all at once. One minute, you are driving through lush timberland of the Gifford Pinchot National Forest; the next, just before milepost 7, you come around a sharp elbow in the road, pass the sign ENTERING MOUNT ST. HELENS NATIONAL VOLCANIC MONUMENT, and BOOM! there it is: death and devastation as far as the eye can see. Trees downed like toothpicks or standing, gray and ghostly, a naked testimony to the heat and force of the eruption. There are no formal indoor visitor centers on this route, but there are several impressive viewpoints with interpretive plaques, and rangers are often on hand to give formal and informal talks, especially at Windy Ridge viewpoint at the end of the road. Windy Ridge, while not nearly as popular as Coldwater Ridge and the Johnston Observatory, is the closest viewpoint to the crater. There is no lodging along Road 99; the nearest opportunities are north in Randle and Morton, or those listed along the south side.

To approach the mountain's forested south side, take Interstate 5 to Woodland, then turn east at Highway 503, which becomes Forest Service Road 90 a few miles east of the tiny town of Cougar. (You can also reach Road 90 from Mt. Adams; one way is to take Road 88 out of Trout Lake to Road 90, then head west. From the Columbia Gorge, take Road 30 north out of Carson, then Road 51 west to connect with 90.) Beautiful, forested trails are found on the south side, including Lewis River Falls and Cedar Flats, as well as sites of geological curiosity such as Ape Cave and Lava Canyon. The south side is where the climbers go. Climbing permits are obtained in Cougar (see details under South Side Climb, below), and the Climbers Bivouac is reached from the south. Lodgings are available in Cougar, Woodland, and points in between on Highway 503.

Many viewpoints and most visitor facilities within the National Volcanic Monument require the purchase and display of a Monument Pass. In 1997, these sites were:

- Mount St. Helens Visitor Center
- Coldwater Ridge Visitor Center Complex
- Coldwater Lake Recreation Area
- Loowit Viewpoint
- Johnston Ridge Observatory Complex
- Ape Cave Interpretive Site
- Lava Canyon Interpretive Site
- Lahar Viewpoint
- Road 99 Viewpoints including: Windy Ridge, Smith Creek, Donney Brook, Cedar Creek, Harmony Falls, Meta Lake, Miner's Car, Blast Entry Viewpoint, Bear Meadows

As of 1997, this pass was $8 for general admission (16 and over; children 15 and under free); $4 for senior citizens and disabled individuals holding Golden Age/Golden Access cards. This pass is valid for 3 days, and must be displayed on your person. Surprisingly, you may park at many trailheads (including those at the visitor centers) and use the trails without a pass. If you plan an extended stay near Mount St. Helens, purchase an annual pass for $24 ($12 Golden Age/Golden Access). Otherwise, group your visitor center visits and fee trail hikes into three consecutive days. All this is, of course, subject to change. As visitor facilities are still being added and trails are in a constant state of construction and improvement, the Mount St. Helens area, even more than the other areas in this book, is subject to change in terms of both trails and policies. To be on the safe side, request a current list of sites and trails where the Monument Pass is required.

LODGINGS

Listed according to "west approach," "east approach," and "south approach," as explained in OVERVIEW, above.

Highway 504 (West Approach):

BLUE HERON INN
2846 Spirit Lake Hwy. • Castle Rock, WA 98611
(800) 959-4049 or (360) 274-9595
www.blueheroninn.com • e-mail jeanne@blueheroninn.com

If you want to stay in style on the mountain's popular west approach, choose the Blue Heron Inn. The 7700-square-foot contemporary mountain lodge, its stone-and-log-columned façade reminiscent of a grand winery chateau, was built by John and Jeanne Robards to fulfill a deeply held dream. They wanted to be self-employed, and they wanted to do it by starting the classiest

> **BLUE HERON INN**
>
> Spacious new B&B;
> rates include dinner

bed and breakfast they could imagine. After scouting a number of locations, they chose John's grandfather's 5-acre property at the edge of Silver Lake, with its sweeping view of Mount St. Helens. Conceiving and supervising every detail of the con-

Upscale Blue Heron Inn

struction and decorating themselves, the energetic couple opened for business in 1996.

The interior of the Blue Heron Inn is flowing and open, with casually elegant decor in the common spaces, including three graciously appointed conversation areas and the dining room. Tea, coffee, water, and wine are always available in the kitchen, and a selection of books and games is available for guests' use inside or on the attractive outdoor deck. Your hosts' quarters are separate but adjacent, offering proximity with a measure of privacy.

Each of the Blue Heron Inn's six guest rooms has a queen bed, private bath, cable TV, and balcony, and each is decorated in a unique fashion—one with a sleigh bed, another with a country-quilt motif, another with a lacquered art nouveau look. Each room is $135 for two persons; $110 for a single.

Your room rate includes not only a full breakfast, served in the dining room at 9 A.M., but also a full dinner, complete with salad, wine, and dessert, at 7 P.M. Given the limited selection of restaurants in the area, this is a particularly important feature. Rather than spending your evening trying to ferret out a palatable meal along the Highway 504 corridor, perhaps driving an hour or so to do it, relax with your fellow travelers at the Blue Heron, then spend the balance of the evening sipping a glass of wine and watching the sunset tint the mountain pink in the distance.

Getting There

From I-5, take Highway 504 east at Castle Rock. In about 5 miles, you'll see the Blue Heron Inn on the hill to your left.

Hikes and Walks Nearby: Anything in the West Approach subsection.

ECO-PARK AND TENT & BREAKFAST
Mount St. Helens Adventure Tours • P.O. Box 149 • Toutle, WA 98649
(360) 274-6542

What would you do if your family lost everything in a catastrophic act of God? That's exactly what happened to the Smith family in 1980, when their Spirit Lake Lodge was buried under several hundred feet of ash, mud, and debris in the wake of St. Helens losing her top. Some folks would pack their bags and move as far away as they could, but not Mark Smith. Eleven years after the blast, the young entrepreneur whose family had lost everything started over, offering van tours into the blast zone. By 1992, with permission from Weyerhaeuser Company, the State of Washington, and the US government, he had begun to offer a special tent camping service. Today, operating under a Special Use Permit from the US Forest Service, Mark Smith's Mount St. Helens

> **ECO-PARK AND TENT & BREAKFAST**
>
> Environmentally sensitive tent and cabin camping as close as you can get to the crater

Adventure Tours offers both a deluxe Tent & Breakfast service and Eco-Park, an environmentally sensitive camping and cabin experience.

Both of Mark Smith's lodgings are as close to the mountain as you can get. Both offer hot showers and soft beds, but neither are standard lodgings in any respect.

Eco-Park—simple, clean cabins near the crater

Having evolved from its 1992 inception, today's Tent & Breakfast experience is what Mark calls "Cadillac camping." In other words, this ain't your grandpappy's tent camping. For $125 per person, per night, you get to commune with "the world's youngest landscape"—the recovering Mount St. Helens blast zone—in a very personal way, but you won't sacrifice comfort to do it. Your tent features a wooden floor to support your futon couch, top-of-the-line cots (high-quality sleeping bags provided), and pellet stove. The cook tent serves up a delicious dinner (complete with dessert) and breakfast daily, on real dishes, at a real table with chairs. And what about hot showers? They've taken care of that, too, with propane-heated water, along with a unique propane toilet system. All power is via propane or 12-volt battery; no noisy, polluting generators. (Price for two is $220/night; groups of 10, $1000/night.)

The Tent & Breakfast experience runs Thursday, Friday, Saturday, and Sunday nights from mid-May to October and reservations are required, as a maximum of 10 guests is allowed at a time. Winter programs are evolving. Children are welcome; no pets.

In 1995, Smith started offering special camping cabins on his 90-acre Eco-Park. These roomy cabins are rudimentary, clean, and, of course, environmentally low-impact. Furnishings consist of a double bed and two bunk beds, a table and chairs. Bottled drinking water, waterless biodegradable hand soap, and propane light and heat are provided. Shared toilet and shower facilities (both propane-fueled) are nearby, as is an open-air cooking area, available to cabin guests as well as to the RV and tent campers at Eco-Park. If you plan to cook, you must bring all cooking and eating utensils.

The five Eco-Park cabins each rent for $55/night for up to 4 people. More cabins are planned for the future. Wall tents may also be available. Bring your own bedding or sleeping bag. Limited self-serve linens may be available from the office for a fee. Children are OK at Eco-Park, and leashed pets are allowed on the grounds, but not inside the cabins.

The grounds at the Eco-Park are beautiful, and include miles of trails available only to Eco-Park guests. Even though you are right next to the highway, the whole place feels almost Jurassic in its isolation and simplicity.

Everything at both the Eco-Park and the Tent & Breakfast is designed for your comfort and minimal environmental impact. There are no telephones, no TV, no electrical power, so it's not for everyone, but, for those seeking the unusual, you can't beat these unique facilities for getting close to the mountain.

Getting There
From I-5, take Highway 504 east at Castle Rock. Pass through Silver Lake, Toutle, and Kid Valley (gas station and "19 Mile House" café). About 2 miles after Kid Valley, pass a road leading to the Sediment Dam. To find Eco-Park, watch for the chain-saw sculpture totem pole with thunderbird indicating "next right turn" just east of the Sediment Dam turnoff.

Hikes and Walks Nearby: On-site trails, plus anything in the West Approach subsection.

MT. ST. HELENS MOTEL
1340 Mt. St. Helens Way NE • Castle Rock, WA 98611
(360) 274-7721

This clean, comfortable motel was built by Mal and Ellen Rose in 1981. It's just off Interstate 5 in Castle Rock, the gateway to Highway 504 and the west approach to Mount St. Helens.

The Roses, nice folks and conscientious hard-workers, still own and operate the motel. Its 32 rooms are spacious, if standard, with newer carpets and bedspreads. Each has one or two queen beds, a private bathroom, in-room telephone, and cable TV with remote. Two rooms are handicapped-accessible, and equipped with oversized shower only; all other rooms have tub and shower. Most units have a small refrigerator.

> **MT. ST. HELENS MOTEL**
>
> Clean, affordable, family-run motel

Room rates are $40 for 2 persons in a room with one bed; $48 for 2 in a room with two beds. Extra persons sharing the room are $5 each. Three rooms are designated OK for pets; a $6 fee is charged.

A café is adjacent, and all the Castle Rock services are just across the highway, in town.

Getting There
From Interstate 5, take Exit 49 at Castle Rock. As you begin to head east, toward the mountain, Mt. St. Helens Motel is on your right.

Hikes and Walks Nearby: Anything in the West Approach subsection.

SILVER LAKE MOTEL & RESORT
3201 Spirit Lake Highway • Silver Lake, WA 98645
(360) 274-6141

A semi-rustic retreat geared toward the fisherman, Silver Lake Resort offers motel rooms, cabins, and RV and tent camping on the shores of Silver Lake. The location is beautiful: right on the lake, with a postcard-perfect view of Mount St. Helens to the east.

The six motel rooms take excellent advantage of the lake—not only does each have a lake view, but each has a deck built over the water that enables you to fish from your room. Single units have a queen bed and sleep two, for $70. Suites have a separate bedroom and a living room with table and chairs, dresser, and hideabed or double bed; they sleep up to four for $85. All motel rooms have complete kitchens, and bathrooms with tub and shower unit. They are well-decorated and furnished, and include cable TV.

> **SILVER LAKE MOTEL & RESORT**
>
> On-the-water motel and cute cabins

The five cabins are funky and aging—but in a good way! They offer an authentic, established-fishing-resort ambience. They are clean, well cared for, and have been updated a bit, with newer carpet, vinyls, mini-blinds, valances, and quality bedding. Each has its own bathroom with shower, and full kitchen with stove, oven, refrigerator, toaster, and coffee maker. While cozy, they are well laid out. Bedrooms are separated from the living area, and a dining table is provided. All units have electric

Fish from your room at Silver Lake Resort

baseboard heat. Each unit rents for $75/night for 2–4 people (extra persons $5), with varying bed configurations.

In addition to being a good place to stay when you're visiting the popular west approach to Mount St. Helens, Silver Lake Resort offers many on-site diversions for the fishing and water enthusiast. Rental boats (motorboat, rowboat, pontoon boat, canoe, or pedal boat) are available, and the resort store/office stocks all you need to take up fishing or re-rig your tackle box. Silver Lake is renowned for its trophy-size largemouth bass, bluegill, crappie, perch, catfish, and trout.

Children are welcome at Silver Lake Motel & Resort, and they'll love it. Besides the lake, there is a play area, a bonfire pit, barbecue area, and convenience store, making the property especially well-suited for families and longer stays. Pets are allowed in the cabins, but not in the motel. On the grounds, they must be leashed at all times.

Getting There

From Interstate 5, take Exit 49 at Castle Rock. Go east 6 miles on Highway 504/Spirit Lake Highway. Watch for the signed turnoff on your right.

Hikes and Walks Nearby: Anything in the West Approach subsection.

TIMBERLAND INN & SUITES
1271 Mt. St. Helens Way • Castle Rock, WA 98611
(360) 274-6002

Timberland Inn & Suites is a well-built, quiet, modern motel just off Interstate 5 in Castle Rock, the gateway to Highway 504 and the west approach to Mount St. Helens.

Rooms range from $65 for 2 people in a single queen room to $119.50 for 4 people in a Family Suite. Every room has air conditioning, a refrigerator, cable TV, telephone, and a private bath with tub and shower unit. Most of the rooms have 2 queen beds, but some have a king, and some have just one queen. Five rooms are set up as Family Suites, with 2 queen beds in a bedroom and a queen hideabed plus table and chairs in an adjoining sitting room. Two Jacuzzi Suites are also available. All suites have a microwave oven and wet bar. Children are accepted, and rollaway beds are available. Extra persons in a room are $5 each. Some rooms are designated OK for pets; a $5 fee is charged.

> **TIMBERLAND INN & SUITES**
>
> Comfortable, modern motel

Timberland Inn & Suites is run by a congenial staff and is conveniently located near the services of Castle Rock.

Getting There

From Interstate 5, take Exit 49 at Castle Rock. As you begin to head east, toward the mountain, Timberland is on your left.

Hikes and Walks Nearby: Anything in the West Approach subsection.

Highway 12 (East Approach):

The following are the closest lodgings to Mount St. Helens' east approach. See also lodgings in Packwood (Section 1, Mt. Rainier) and Trout Lake (Section 3, Mt. Adams).

MEDICI MOTEL
471 Cispus Road • Randle, WA 98377
(800) 697-7750 • (360) 497-7700

Medici Motel & Campground advertises itself as "off the beaten path," and that it is. The simple, older cinderblock building sits on 40 acres in a secluded, private glen apart from the world.

Arriving at the Medici grounds, you're likely to be greeted by a welcoming committee of geese as you approach the owners' home and the humble little motel itself. If not geese, perhaps the resident peacocks or another critter will greet you. Deer frequent the pastureland as well. On my visit, an orphaned fawn was being nursed back to health by the proprietors in one of the large animal corrals on the premises.

> **MEDICI MOTEL**
>
> Quiet, secluded location; inexpensive

The motel consists of five simple rooms, four with kitchenettes and four with satellite TV. Each has a private bath with shower and rents for $45. Children and pets are OK; rooms 1 and 2 rent together as a family unit for $80. If you appreciate the charms of rural living, and don't mind the simplicity of an older motel, this is a good pick.

Getting There

Take Highway 12 to Randle. From there, go south on Highway 131/Road 25. After 1.0 mile, take the left fork onto Cispus Road, which is also Forest Service Road 23. After 1.8 miles from the fork, turn left onto Judd Road. From here, wind your way through a maze of partially paved roads, using Medici Motel's "Burma Shave"-style signs to guide you ("YOU'RE NOT LOST," "KEEP GOING,"

"ALMOST THERE," etc.). After 0.7 mile, you arrive at a gate. Continue straight ahead, passing a former cattle pasture.

Hikes and Walks Nearby: Anything in the East Approach subsection.

ST. HELENS MANORHOUSE
7476 Highway 12 • Morton, WA 98356
(800) 551-3290 • (360) 498-5243

There is no contest: Susyn Dragness makes the best breakfasts in the Pacific Northwest.

At $65 for a room with a shared bath, or $75 for a room with a private bath, St. Helens Manorhouse is also an excellent B&B value. The charming 1910 country home is appointed with original glasswork, local mill-

ST. HELENS MANORHOUSE
Charming English country B&B with fabulous breakfasts

work, and vintage decor, lending an atmosphere of abundance and ease. The grounds are reminiscent of the English countryside, with sprawling herb gardens, flowering fruit trees, and an assemblage of wicker and white wrought iron furniture from which to enjoy it all. The lawn is bordered by one of the nation's last stands of American chestnut trees, a remnant of the 1000-acre farm that once occupied the property.

Susyn has run the Manorhouse as a B&B since 1992. She offers four spacious rooms, two with private baths. Sophie's Choice, a bright, airy, pink and lavender room with a queen bed, shares a clawfoot tub bathroom with The Twins, a roomy unit with two twin beds. The Limoges and Winterthur rooms each have queen beds and private baths; the former features floral decor, the latter, a burgundy-and-forest color scheme.

From your designer bedroom to the inviting lawn to the casual French country parlor, you'll be at ease here. Try to arrive early enough to enjoy the ambience and perhaps an evening treat prepared by your hostess.

And now—about that breakfast. Some people just have a way with food and hospitality, and Susyn is one of those. Her cooking is fresh, inventive, and seasonally inspired; it must be experienced to be appreciated. A sample menu: cream-cheese-and-honey-stuffed French toast with blueberry compote; spicy sausage; mushroom-and-green-pepper omelette with parmesan and feta cheeses, fresh herbs, and a Dijon sauce; homemade hash browns; fresh fruit, juice, tea, and coffee. If a Denny's Grand Slam is your idea of breakfast, you're in for an eye-opener. Served family-style at 9 A.M.

St. Helens Manorhouse's central location enables daytrips to Mount St. Helens, Mt. Rainier, and even Mt. Adams, and the inn is also adjacent to fishing, swimming, and boating at Riffe Lake, and to a wildlife preserve with 400+ varieties of birds.

Getting There
To reach St. Helens Manorhouse, take Highway 12 east from Morton or west from Randle. Turn south at the purple mailbox, on Fisher, between mileposts 103 and 104.

St. Helens Manorhouse

Hikes and Walks Nearby: Anything in the East Approach subsection; also close to *Section 1,* "Mt. Rainier," and *Section 3,* "Mt. Adams" hikes.

SEASONS MOTEL
P.O. Box 567 • 200 Westlake Ave. • Morton, WA 98356
(360) 496-6835

This 50-room motel offers clean, comfortable lodgings at the edge of the town of Morton, right on Highway 12. Conveniently located, you can access either Mt. Rainier or Mount St. Helens from here. By staying in Morton, you are also near restaurants and services.

Rooms at Seasons are standard, modern motel units, with newer carpets, fixtures, vinyls, bedspreads, and draperies. Amenities include satellite TV, clock radio, shampoo, and in-room telephones with free local calls. All beds at Seasons Motel are queen beds; 19 rooms have two queens, and 31 have one. Several rooms are designed to connect, making them especially

SEASONS MOTEL
50-room, modern motel

appropriate for families. Of the 50 rooms, all but one include tub units in the bathroom. The one room without a tub (it's a bit smaller than the others) rents for $42. Other one-bed rooms are $55 for two; rooms with two queens are $65 for two. Extra persons in the rooms are $5. Children 12 and under stay free, and small pets are allowed ($5 fee charged).

The staff at Seasons Motel are cheerful and service-oriented. Complimentary coffee and hot beverages are available in the lobby from 6 A.M. to 10 P.M. Adventures Restaurant (see *Dining,* below) is located immediately adjacent.

Getting There
Take Highway 12 to Morton, which is also the junction of Highway 7. Seasons Motel is at the northwest corner of the junction.

Hikes and Walks Nearby: Anything in the East Approach subsection; also *Section 1,* "Mt. Rainier" hikes near Ashford.

Highway 503/Road 90 (South Approach):

ANDERSON LODGE
Home Office • 18410 NE 399th St. • Amboy, WA 98601
(360) 247-6660

Perfect for large groups, Anderson Lodge is a family-run, Scandinavian-themed retreat center five miles west of Cougar and 23 miles east of Woodland on Highway 503. Facilities include a main lodge and bunkhouse that sleeps 20–60 people, a cabin suitable for 2–6, and a house that accommodates 15–30.

Situated on 90 forested acres, Anderson Lodge is more of a self-contained retreat center than mere lodging for dayhikers. In addition to the lodgings, detailed below, the grounds include softball and soccer fields, volleyball/badminton nets, tennis courts, basketball courts, tetherball, horseshoe pits, children's playground equipment, and an amphitheater with campfire pit.

The Main Lodge/Malung Bunkhouse has a warm, hand-hewn ambience with its open-beam ceilings, hardwood floors, and Scandinavian heirloom decor. In addition to providing flexible sleeping accommodations for 60+ people, the premises include a glassed-in sunroom, a log-framed conference room, large commercial kitchen (use fee is charged), spacious dining room, outdoor barbecue, hot tub, sauna, and bathroom facilities appropriate to large groups. In July and August, the Main Lodge and Malung Bunkhouse rents for $1450 on weekends for up to 50 persons (extra persons $14.50); weeknights are $625 for 50, $12.50 each extra person.

> **ANDERSON LODGE**
> Scandinavian lodge & grounds perfect for groups

Groups can arrange to use the kitchen for $30 per day, or have their meals catered; contact the lodge for foodservice information.

The Dalarna Cabin, situated near the main lodge, offers a private space for a small party. Also Scandinavian-styled, its sleeping quarters, kitchenette, and private bathroom accommodate up to 8 people. For up to 6 guests, the rate is $87 on a weekend (extra persons $14.50); $75 on weeknights (extra persons $12.50).

Another unit, the Hilltop House, is situated across the road and up the hill from the rest of the Anderson Lodge property. From its hilltop perch overlooking the Yale Valley, this cozy home has a kitchen (use fee $15, or catering available), 3 bathrooms, hot tub, TV/VCR, ping-pong and pool tables, board games, and more. It sleeps up to 30, renting for $580 per night on weekends and $250 on weeknights. This rate covers up to 20 people; extra persons $14.50 on weekend nights, $12.50 on weeknights.

All rates quoted above are for the peak months of July and August. September through June, rates are lower.

Anderson Lodge is a unique property, with many options and policies different than standard motel, cabin, lodge, or B&B accommodations, particularly with respect to groups. Be sure to contact them for information including policies regarding cleaning, linen rental, foodservice options, and reservation deposits.

Getting There

To reach the main Anderson Lodge property, site of the Main Lodge/Malung Bunkhouse and Dalarna Cabin, turn south off Highway 503 just west of the Amboy turnoff (watch for the small sign and tennis courts). The turnoff for Hilltop House is a bit farther west; turn north on a gravel road and continue 0.75 mile uphill.

Hikes and Walks Nearby: Anything in the South Approach subsection.

EAGLES CLIFF RESORT
Box 250 • Cougar, WA 98616
(360) 238-5335 • (360) 607-6408

Its mailing address is Cougar, but Eagles Cliff is "miles from anywhere." This rustic cabin and camping resort is about 18 miles east of Cougar, about a mile east of the Pine Creek information center and the Road 90/Road 25 junction. In other words, it's a perfect location for hiking: far from the crowds and right in the middle of some of the most beautiful, wooded hikes on St. Helens' south side, including those along the

EAGLES CLIFF RESORT
Rustic cabins and bunkhouse, excellent location

Lewis River. It's also an easy and scenic drive from Eagles Cliff to north Windy Ridge (the "east approach" to Mount St. Helens). Indian Heaven Wilderness, described in *Section 3, Mt. Adams,* is just to the east.

Eagles Cliff is definitely the most rustic recommended lodging in this book. Lodgings consist of 4 rudimentary camping cabins, a 25-person bunkhouse, and

Eagles Cliff offers rustic, budget cabins

a bathhouse with coin-operated showers. The cabins are one-room affairs with sleeping lofts. The lofts are very low-ceilinged and cozy; each has a single and a double bed, and is accessed by ladder. The main room has a double bed or hide-abed couch, a dining table, and a very basic kitchen. Heat, lights, and stove are propane-fueled; there is no electricity in the cabins. Each cabin has a half bath (toilet and sink), but no hot water. Showers are in the bathhouse. Outside your cabin is a picnic table and a fire pit. The cost for up to three people in a cabin is $28; $38 for 4–5 people.

The bunkhouse rents for $100/night (ask about weekly rates). It has four bed-rooms, and can sleep up to 25 (friendly!) souls, with 8 double beds, 4 single beds, and 1 hideabed. It has 2 bathrooms (only one shower), a kitchen with 2 stoves, and a woodstove with wood. Unlike the small cabins, the bunkhouse has a refrigerator and hot water, both propane-fueled. A fire pit and picnic table are provided outside.

Children are welcome at Eagles Cliff, as are pets; the latter must be leashed. Bedding is not supplied; bring your own bed linens or sleeping bags. The cab-ins have no refrigerator, so bring a cooler for your perishables.

While the cabins have no electricity, the property does have a generator. When it is running, laundry facilities are available. The Eagles Cliff General Store sells basic groceries, firewood, and fishing supplies.

Owner Kevin Landacre is usually on hand to help with anything you might need. He and his staff are friendly, hardworking, and always busy doing some-thing to make Eagles Cliff a going concern. They know the roads, the trails, and the "ins and outs" of the mountain and the forest, including where to hunt, fish, hike, and find everything from mushrooms and huckleberries to picnic sites and swimming holes. Eagles Cliff is great for families wanting a rugged "outdoor experience" without sleeping on the ground; you can't beat the price.

Getting There
From I-5, take Highway 503 (Lewis River Road) east at Woodland. Pass through Cougar (after which Highway 503 becomes Forest Road 90), then continue another 17-18 miles to the Pine Creek information center and the junction of Road 90/Road 25. Continue straight on Road 90 about a mile; watch for Eagles Cliff on your left.

From Randle and points northeast, take Road 25 south to the Road 90 junc-tion, then turn left (east) on Road 90. Proceed one mile.

Hikes and Walks Nearby: Lewis River Falls, Cedar Flats, and anything in the South Approach and East Approach subsections; also good access to trails in *Section 3*, "Mt. Adams," and *Section 4*, "Columbia Gorge."

GRANDMA'S HOUSE B&B
4551 Old Lewis River Road • Woodland, WA 98674
(360) 225-7002
email gmasbb@pacifier.com
You really do feel like you've gone to visit Grandma when you stay at Louise and Warren Moir's adorable old farmhouse bed and breakfast. Flowered

wallpaper and "real" antiques—the genuine artifacts of Louise's growing-up years—make the premises warm and homey. Wicker fur-nishings brighten the sunny shared living room, and updated carpets and paint make the house fresh and com-fortable for modern tastes despite its age. ("...now, of course, we have running water," jokes the brochure.)

> **GRANDMA'S HOUSE B&B**
>
> Cozy old farmhouse B&B

Grooviest of all is the kitchen, where retro-cool fixtures like an old Hotpoint refrigerator and original wooden cabinets mingle companionably with a mod-ern dishwasher, microwave, and a double stainless-steel sink.

Grandma's House is a traditional, or "European-style," B&B—all three rooms share one large bathroom on the main level. The main-level bedroom is cozy and cute; it's adjacent to the bathroom and kitchen. The two upstairs rooms are slightly larger and sunnier, and each has a sink. The house has no air-condition-ing, but fans are provided. All three rooms have queen beds, and each rents for $55 for two persons ($39 for a single person), including a full breakfast. Shared areas include the large, pink bathroom with clawfoot tub/shower and dressing area, the kitchen, a living/dining room with TV and VCR, and a pleasant out-door deck.

The 35-acre property overlooks the lazy, green North Fork Lewis River, affording anglers a good opportunity for salmon and steelhead, and the rest of us a sense of peace and relaxation. The grounds are lovely—flowers, flowers everywhere: in containers, in the garden, cultivated, and wild. And the black-berry bush! You're in for a treat if the berries are ripe, and you've never seen a more prolific stand.

Grandma's House B&B lives up to its name

Your hosts live next door in a separate home, giving you a bit more privacy. They'll be happy to provide information and insight on the area. Maps and flyers on trails and other recreational pursuits can be found in the living/dining area.

A filling, no-frills country breakfast is prepared fresh and served family-style in the dining room at the time of your choice.

Situated west of St. Helens on the south corridor, near Woodland, this charming house is a bit farther from the mountain, but its peaceful location and reasonable prices make up for driving a few extra miles. It's a great place for families, small groups, travelers on a budget, or anyone who appreciates peace and quiet and the old-fashioned comforts of home.

Getting There

From I-5, take Highway 503 (Lewis River Road) east at Woodland. Proceed 8.0 miles; turn right on Fredrickson, then right again on Old Lewis River Road and follow the signs (about a mile).

Hikes and Walks Nearby: Anything in the South Approach subsection.

LONE FIR RESORT
16806 Lewis River Road • Cougar, WA 98616
(360) 238-5210

When passing through the town of Cougar, you can't miss its only motel: Lone Fir Resort. The "resort" refers to the fact that, in addition to a 16-unit motel, the property includes an RV park, swimming pool, and laundry facilities ($5 fee). Coming east from Woodland on Highway 503, you will find Lone Fir on the left side of the highway, which is also known as Lewis River Road as it passes through town.

> **LONE FIR RESORT**
>
> Conveniently located in Cougar

The smallest motel room at Lone Fir is a simple unit with a queen bed, priced at $38 for two people. The largest is a 2-level unit with 4 bedrooms, full kitchen, and 2 baths; it sleeps up to 10, and is priced at $85 for up to 4 people, $12 for each extra person. In between, the humble but tidy and reasonably-priced units run from $40 to $65 for two. Each sleeps from 2 to 6 people; extra persons $7 each in most units. Eight of the units have kitchens, including microwave, full stove and oven, full-size refrigerator, toaster, and percolator coffee pots. Two units—one with kitchen at $60, and one without at $50—are designated non-smoking. Children are welcome; cribs are available for $7. No pets or sleeping bags are allowed in the motel.

Getting There

From I-5, take Highway 503 (Lewis River Road) east at Woodland to Cougar. Lone Fir is the only motel in town, located right in the center of things on the north side of the road.

Hikes and Walks Nearby: Anything in the South Approach subsection.

MONFORT'S B&B
132 Cougar Loop Rd. • Cougar, WA 98616
(360) 238-5229

Conveniently located in Cougar, Monfort's Bed & Breakfast is the perfect place to call home when you're hiking the south side of Mount St. Helens. Start your day with Marilyn Monfort's stick-to-your-ribs break-fast, hike the day away, then return to your queen bed, private bath, and shared sitting room with kitchenette.

> **MONFORT'S B&B**
>
> Closest B&B to the south side trails

True to the spirit of the *Hot Showers, Soft Beds, & Dayhikes* experience, Monfort's is not a luxurious lodging, but a practical one. It has just the right balance of comfort, amenities, location, and affordability. Gary and Marilyn Monfort built the B&B adjacent to their home in 1992, and have operated it with care and good cheer ever since. The property is up for sale, but won't change hands until they find just the right buyer, and chances are good it will remain a B&B.

Each of Monfort's two rooms has a queen bed and a private bath. The larger, at $75, has a shower and a two-person jetted bathtub; the smaller is $65. They share a common room with a sitting area, TV/VCR, dining room table, and kitchenette. The kitchenette includes a microwave, refrigerator, and a supply of popcorn and hot beverages. A trundle bed is also located in this room. It can be moved into either room, or, if one party is taking both rooms, can be used in the common room. Fifteen dollars extra is charged for each person over two per room.

The two guest rooms are located in a building separated from the main house by a walkway. In the morning, Marilyn Monfort brings breakfast across on a serving cart, and serves it at the common room dining table. Typical fare might consist of orange juice and coffee, a ham and cheese omelette, hash browns, toast, and rhubarb-strawberry pudding. If you're lucky, you'll arrive on caramel-pecan-sticky-buns day—these are a delight, serving as both fuel and incentive for a hard day of hiking. The bottom line is, if you go away hungry, it's your own fault.

Children are welcome at Monfort's, but pets are not.

Getting There
From I-5, take Highway 503 (Lewis River Road) east at Woodland to Cougar. Turn left (north) at the sculpture of the Cougar on the corner next to the gas station. Take the first right, and watch for the sign on your right.

Hikes and Walks Nearby: Anything in the South Approach subsection.

DINING

Listed according to "west approach," "east approach," and "south approach," as explained in OVERVIEW, above.

Let's just say that the Mount St. Helens area, while definitely "loaded for bear" when it comes to tourism, lags behind in providing dining options for those tourists. For the most part, you have to be willing to drive west toward I-5 if you want a decent meal: Woodland if you're in the south corridor, Castle Rock if you're in the north corridor, and Morton if you're in the east corridor. I recommend the following as reasonable picks.

Highway 504 (West Approach):

TOUTLE DINER
5037 Spirit Lake Highway • Toutle, WA 98649
(360) 274-6208
Ten miles east of Castle Rock, Toutle is the last town you pass through as you head east up the highway to the mountain. On the south side of the road, across from the big, red-brick high school, is the Toutle Diner. Scott and Gabriela Hill took over the café in 1995, and they serve breakfast, lunch, and dinner.

Breakfast at the Toutle Diner includes the standard egg, meat, and griddle fare, reasonably priced. To fuel up for a busy day of hiking and visitor center touring, add a blueberry pancake on the side for $1.50, or a half order of biscuits and gravy for $2.50. Or try the hearty Mount St. Helens Hash—eggs, hashbrowns, onions, green peppers, cheese, and your choice of meat for $4.95.

Lunchtime is a bargain, with sandwiches starting at $2.75 (grilled cheese) and topping out at $5.50 for a good-sized clubhouse; each includes chips. Burgers, in a basket with fries, run $4–$5.50, including such festive features as the Ash Burger with chili and the Super Big Blast with Swiss, each $5.25.

Dinner choices include an assortment of chicken, fish, steaks, and chops, priced from $7.99 to $12.95 complete with all the trimmings. Future menu plans call for lighter and more creative fare including big salads, stuffed potatoes, and an appetizer menu.

Highway 12 (East Approach):

ADVENTURES RESTAURANT
Morton, WA 98356
(360) 496-6660
A trendy, fun-loving place with a head-spinning menu, Adventures Restaurant bills itself as "the ultimate trip for your tastebuds." That might be a bit strong, but what you *can* count on is something for every taste. A hang-glider, airplane propeller, ski paraphernalia, and photos of foreign and domestic adventures decorate the walls and ceiling, but the emphasis is on good food, and plenty of it, served with a smile in a clean, lighthearted, family atmosphere. The airy, high-ceilinged contemporary café has both indoor and outdoor patio seating.

Adventures serves breakfast, lunch, and dinner at the junction of Highway 7 and Highway 12 in Morton. Gourmet burgers are a specialty, at around $5 each with fries or potato salad. The meal-sized salads and sandwiches are economical lunch or dinner choices, or try a full dinner of steak, chicken, or seafood, served complete with bread, vegetable, potato or rice, and soup or salad. The many dinner choices include fried oysters ($10.95), artichoke-and-shrimp stuffed chicken dijonnaise ($8.95), and a "climber's cut" 12 ounce prime rib ($14.95)

A "Seniors & Kids" menu features four small-size standards (fish & chips, chicken strips, burger, spaghetti) for under $6. If you're in a snacking mood, Adventures is famous for their Macho Nachos, a prodigious pile of chips with all the fixings that you *won't* be able to finish. For more south-of-the-border fare, come on Thursday—Mexican Night—when a range of Mexican entrées are offered in the $7 price range.

Beer, wine, and cocktails are available, as well as espresso drinks. The "bottomless soda" (unlimited refills) for $1.50 can be a welcome beverage option at the end of a long, hot day of hiking.

PIZZA DELI & COMPANY
210 W. Main St. • Morton, WA 98356
(360) 496-EATS (3287)

I stopped in for a latté, but was seduced by the menu: pizza with not only a wide choice of toppings (including shrimp, BBQ chicken, 3 types of sausage, sun-dried tomatoes, and spinach), but 9 sauce choices! Granted, not everyone would want a pizza topped with burger sauce or ranch dressing, but you have to admire them for trying. Steve and Star Kenfield offer an ambitious menu of sandwiches, salads, burgers, pasta, gyros, calzone, and more at their two restaurants (the other one is about 30 miles north in Eatonville), but the pizza is what brought me in, and it's what brings the locals back. Start with a large cheese pie at $9.95 and build from there, or try one of their 15 specialty combos. Jim's Logger Special, The Mountain, and Husky Combo are typical meat-heavy bruisers at $14.95 to $16.95. More unusual fare includes the Oriental (with teriyaki chicken and veggies), the Quarto (4 pizzas in one), and the South Pacific (shrimp and veggies on garlic white sauce), each $14.95 for a large.

This is the kind of hometown enterprise that deserves applause and a big tip—they do a great job. From Highway 12, head north on Highway 7 into Morton, then left on Main.

Highway 503/Road 90 (South Approach):

ARIEL STORE
288 Merwin Village Road • Ariel, WA 98603
(360) 225-7126

Sometimes you stumble across something so interesting you want to share it. The Ariel Store falls under the category of "local color" more than the category of "restaurant," but this was the closest fit.

You might at first assume that this quirky little establishment was a tavern, but you'd be wrong. Despite the pool table, the bar (complete with bar stools and bartender-like individual behind it), and the vintage Rainier Beer posters plastered on the rustic, wooden walls, this is a STORE, not a tavern. As such, children are welcome. It's also a restaurant. Sort of. There is always something to eat here. Chances are, you can get a burger (with or without chili or cheese) or a deli sandwich, and there's usually some other specialty-of-the-moment. Bottled beer, wine coolers, and soft drinks are also available—in the coolers, help yourself. This is a *store*, after all. It's also home of D.B. Cooper Days, a celebration of the now-legendary bank-robber-turned-parachutist who was said to have bailed out directly over Ariel.

To find the Ariel Store, take Highway 503 east from Woodland 9 miles, then turn south on Merwin Village Road. Go 0.4 mile; the store is on your right.

CASA MARIA'S
P.O. Box 1600 • 1175 Lewis River Road • Woodland, WA 98674
(360) 225-3104

Fresh mex is the fare at Casa Maria's, a truly exceptional Mexican restaurant worth the drive to Woodland. Located right on the main drag, it's easy to find, and you'll be glad you did.

Casa Maria's prides itself on using fresh ingredients, and rightfully so. In addition to standard mexi-platter combos (which are also done well), specialties that take advantage of their culinary prowess include a sautéed-red-snapper ceviche salad, and the veggie enchiladas, a decadent duo of corn tortillas stuffed with fresh seasonal veggies, topped with a cream sauce and served with black beans and rice. Three other Mexican vegetarian entrées are also offered, and are equally delicious; none is over $6.95. Casa Maria's fajitas—steak, chicken, or shrimp—are melt-in-your-mouth excellent, at $9.95. American-style steak and seafood are also served with pride, and beer, wine, and cocktails are available.

PARK PLACE PIZZA & SUBS
545 Park Street • Woodland, WA 98674
(360) 225-8851

Another good reason to drive to Woodland! The evening after my assault on the south summit of Mount St. Helens, I was not looking for a feature restaurant, I was looking for sustenance. Food, vittles, nourishment, chow. I was looking for pizza, which, even at its worst, is pretty good post-hiking fodder.

Ariel Store & Cafe (don't call it a tavern!)

Park Place turned out to be a pleasant surprise. After polishing off half of a family-size artichoke-heart-and-sundried-tomatoes-over-pesto pie, I realized this place deserved mention. They start with a tender, flavorful crust, then top it with your choice of sauce: red, alfredo, cheddar, or pesto. Fresh garlic may be added upon request. A selection of toppings includes seasoned steak and marinated chicken (featured on the specialty Fajita Pizza), Italian sausage, zucchini, pepperoncini, and (when in season) sweet red peppers. A family-size pie will set you back $10.75 to $22.95; my two-item selection was $14.25. Salads, sub sandwiches, calzone, pasta, and chicken dishes are also available.

WALKS AND HIKES

Listed according to "west approach," "east approach," and "south approach," as explained in OVERVIEW, above. Within each subsection, listed in approximate order of difficulty.

The trails in this section are either in the Mount St. Helen's National Volcanic Monument, or are in the Gifford Pinchot National Forest. The national monument has a fee system that is explained in *Overview,* above. I have indicated in the individual trail descriptions which ones require purchase and display of a Monument Pass. Gifford Pinchot National Forest participates in the Trail Park Pass system; hikes from any trailhead in the forest require purchase and display of a pass. See *Trail Park Pass System,* in the Introduction.

Highway 504 (West Approach):

WINDS OF CHANGE
Short, interesting interpretive stroll.

Map:	US Forest Service "Mount St. Helens National Volcanic Monument"
Distance:	0.25 mile loop
Elevation Gain:	negligible
Estimated Time:	30 minutes with guided tour

This 6-foot wide, paved, barrier-free trail winds through the recovering post-volcanic landscape next to the Coldwater Ridge Visitor Center. Narrated interpretive walks are provided at frequent intervals; check inside the visitor center for times. The name "Winds of Change" refers both figuratively to the process of change over time and literally to the hot, stone-filled wind that scoured Coldwater Ridge at hundreds of miles per hour during the 1980 blast.

Getting There
From I-5, take the Castle Rock exit (Exit 49). Travel 43 miles east on Highway 504, Spirit Lake Highway, to the Coldwater Ridge Visitor Center. The trailhead for this short interpretive loop is just to the right of the visitor center as you face the visitor center.

Winds of Change Interpretive Trail

The Walk

This easy stroll is suitable for everyone. (Wheelchair hikers may find one 15% grade challenging; it lasts for only about 50 feet.) Try to catch one of the naturalist-led guided walks for additional insight and an opportunity to ask questions.

Along the way, you will see examples of the scouring effects of the hot, rocky winds that blasted this ridge during the 1980 eruption. Ghostly tree snags (including two concrete "fakes" put in place of original snags for safety's sake) dot the landscape, remnants of the devastation. But many species of plants have returned to the once-nitrogen deprived soil: lupine (a special plant that makes more nitrogen than it uses, thereby helping other species to get started), ferns, dandelions, foxglove, daisies, pearly everlasting, fireweed, and more. Even alders have returned, defying scientists' predictions that it would take 30 years for these trees to come back.

The walk offers sweeping views over the Toutle River valley and the hummocks below (for more information on the volcanic phenomenon known as "hummocks," see Hummocks Loop hike, below).

Nearest Lodgings: Anything in the West Approach subsection.

BIRTH OF A LAKE
Barrier-free walk onto Coldwater Lake pier.

Map:	US Forest Service "Mount St. Helens National Volcanic Monument"
Distance:	0.5 mile round-trip or loop
Elevation Gain:	none
Estimated Time:	30 minutes

This pleasant stroll is appropriate for anyone, even those with significant mobility impairment. A 6- to 8-foot wide aggregate/concrete path, gently graded for wheelchair access, leads to an extra-wide boardwalk pier. Interpretive plaques explain Coldwater Lake's "birth" in the post-blast mudslide, and the subsequent cycle of pollution and self-clean-up. The lake is 5 miles long and up to 200 feet deep.

Getting There
Take Highway 504, the west approach to the mountain. Go 45 miles east from Castle Rock (two miles past Coldwater Ridge Visitor Center), and turn left at the sign COLDWATER LAKE. Where the road forks, go right to reach the trailhead. (To the left is a boat launch. No gas-powered motors are allowed on the lake; electric or human-propelled craft only.) Restrooms are available here.

The Walk
From the parking lot, walk along a paved path to the boardwalk pier, then out onto Coldwater Lake. Several interpretive plaques explain the history of the lake and speculate on its future.

On the way back, you can either make a loop, which involves a paved, but steeper (up to 12.6%) grade, or—preferable for some wheelchair users—retrace your route back. It's about 0.5 mile round-trip either way.

Mount St. Helens and its blast crater are visible during the course of the stroll.

Nearest Lodgings: Anything in the West Approach subsection.

HUMMOCKS LOOP
Loop through post-volcanic landscape.

Map:	US Forest Service "Mount St. Helens National Volcanic Monument"
Distance:	2.3 mile loop
Elevation Gain:	200′
Estimated Time:	1 hour, 45 minutes

"Hummocks" are mounds or hills created by boulders thrown from volcanoes then covered with the ensuing dirt and mud from the blast. Most hummocks are just the "tip of the iceberg," with the bulk of the rock buried beneath the surface of the ground by the force of its landing and the mud that flowed around it. An excellent example of a visible, isolated hummock is the big rock in Coldwater Lake. The hummocks through which you will walk on this hike range in size from molehills to mountains—up to 500′ tall.

Getting There
Take Highway 504, the west approach to the mountain. Pass Coldwater Ridge Visitor Center, 43 miles east of Castle Rock. Just past a sign reading VOLCANO OBSERVATORY 7 and just after crossing Coldwater Creek, you will see a parking area on your right for the Hummocks Trail. This parking area is right across the road from the entrance to Coldwater Lake boat launch and Birth of a Lake trail

Hummocks Loop

(see above). Parking is provided for a few dozen cars at the Hummocks Loop trailhead. Restrooms are available across the road at the Coldwater Lake parking area.

The Hike
To do the loop counterclockwise, begin at the trailhead marked HUMMOCKS TRAIL 229, and proceed straight ahead, up and over a small rise. The little hummocks surrounding you make this look like Land of the Mole People.

Coming over the rise at 0.1 mile, you find yourself looking into the valley below. Larger, mountainous hummocks sit on the other side of the basin. Follow the trail down through a glen shaded by red alder toward the valley floor.

After descending for about half a mile, you reach a small pond and the valley floor, then begin crossing a flat, meadowed area. A great deal of vegetation has reestablished itself along this trail: lupine (one of the first plants to return after the blast, due to its "nitrogen fixing" properties—it makes more nitrogen than it consumes), clover, groundsel, alder, daisies, monkeyflower, mosses, lichens.

After 0.25-mile of flat, descend to the North Fork Toutle River. Here, the trail leads along a lush oasis of greenery and startling, bright yellow monkeyflowers.

Just after 1.0 mile, you ascend back up, away from the river. Reach the most desolate part of the hike at 1.4 miles. Here, a gravely surface is home to only a few struggling conifers. Rocks of varying colors—red, black, gray—surround you.

At 1.6 miles, pass through a stand of trees between two lakelets. At 1.8 miles, reach a junction with Boundary Trail; stay left to return to the parking lot.

Nearest Lodgings: Anything in the West Approach subsection.

BOUNDARY TRAIL EAST FROM JOHNSTON RIDGE
A close look at Mount St. Helens' crater.

Map:	Green Trails #332, "Spirit Lake;" US Forest Service "Mount St. Helens National Volcanic Monument"
Distance:	3.0 miles round-trip
Elevation Gain:	200′
Estimated Time:	1 hour, 45 minutes

Escape the madding crowds at Johnston Ridge Observatory and take a walk out on the Boundary Trail along the top of Johnston Ridge. Some of the most stunning, straight-on views of the crater can be seen along this 2.0-mile stretch of trail. While the trail is not long or steep, and therefore not physically challenging, it may not be for everyone. It can be windy, it's very exposed, and there are significant drop-offs and loose surfaces. This is not a trail for children unless they are trail-wise.

Getting There
The Johnston Ridge Observatory, opened in 1997, is at the absolute end of Highway 504. It is the be-all and end-all of tourist stops, home of the not-to-be-missed film that tells the story of the eruption with such noise and intensity it may frighten small children. The parking lot resembles that of a concert arena or sports stadium—it's that big.

Steep drop-off along the Boundary Trail east from Johnston Ridge

The trail system around Johnston Ridge is still undergoing refinement. At the time of this writing, access to Boundary Trail was at the north end of the parking lot—the end farthest from the observatory.

The Hike
From the trailhead, go right. Wind around the back of the hill just east of the observatory (the hill which is home to the short Eruption Trail stroll, still under construction at this writing; see *Other Hike Notes,* below). In less than 0.1 mile, you'll see the reason for taking this hike: dead-on views directly south into the breach and crater of Mount St. Helens.

This trail is all about views. Mostly, you'll be looking south: the crater, the lava dome within the crater, the pumice plain, the channeled scablands between you and the mountain. As you are walking along a ridgetop, however, you also have views to the north, where the downed trees of the blowdown zone stretch for miles. To the east, just a couple of miles, is Spirit Lake.

The trail gently undulates, dropping down overall for the first 0.75 mile, then rising after the first mile. You may notice that, unlike the ground at the Windy Ridge Visitor Center area, which is covered with pale tan, lightweight chunks of pumice, the ground here is largely void of ash and pumice. That debris blasted and blew northeast. Here, a sort of gray lateral-blast-deposit and rocks dominate.

At 1.5 miles, the trail narrows and the drop-offs to your right become steeper. A sign may be in place warning you that the upcoming section of trail is dangerous. In fact, the views of the crater don't get any better than this, so 1.5 miles makes a good turnaround point.

Those foolhardy souls like me wishing to continue will find a steep, narrow trail that hugs a cliff, first heading south, then doubling back in a hairpin turn around the end of a ridge known as "The Spillover," just above "Harry's Ridge," where northwest legend Harry Truman (not the president) met his demise in 1980. On the east side of the ridge, Truman Trail 207, a 7.5-mile trail to Windy Ridge viewpoint, intersects, and Boundary Trail continues north and west to Mt. Margaret and, eventually, Norway Pass. As these destinations are too far for most dayhikers, I suggest turning at 1.5 miles, for a 3.0-mile outing along the Boundary Trail.

Nearest Lodgings: Anything in the West Approach subsection.

SOUTH COLDWATER
Preserved logging equipment shows 1980 blast devastation.

Map:	Green Trails #332, "Spirit Lake" (partial); US Forest Service "Mount St. Helens National Volcanic Monument"
Distance:	7.5 miles round-trip
Elevation Gain:	1500'
Estimated Time:	4 hours, 30 minutes

This trail climbs a ridge south of Coldwater Lake to sweeping views across the lake basin. It's also an in-situ exhibit of logging equipment mangled and partially buried in the 1980 blast, preserved as a reminder of the devastating force of the "stone-filled wind" that buffeted Coldwater Ridge. The route is exposed and climbs steadily for over 3.0 miles, so bring sunscreen and plenty of water.

South Coldwater Trail does not access Coldwater Lake, but travels a ridge 400 to 1500 feet above the lake. For lake access, see Birth of a Lake, above, the short, barrier-free trail at the west end of the lake. Lakes Trail 211, which begins from the same west-end parking area as Birth of a Lake, also accesses the lake, traveling along its north side at or near water level. When each is open all the way, Trail 211, Trail 230, and Trail 230A (South Coldwater) can be combined to form a long (11+ miles) loop. This loop is dry, exposed, and difficult at best, with one

Mangled logging wreckage along South Coldwater Trail

extremely steep section. Washouts frequently render the loop closed; be sure to check with the National Monument staff at Coldwater Ridge Visitor Center before attempting it.

Getting There

Take Highway 504 east. Pass Coldwater Ridge Visitor Center at 43 miles, and the Hummocks Loop trailhead and Coldwater Lake recreation area at 45 miles.

At 45.3 miles, turn in at the parking area marked S. COLDWATER TRAILHEAD. You'll find no toilets or services at this parking area, just a paved lot with room for 14–15 cars and the trailhead, SOUTH COLDWATER TRAIL 230A.

The Hike

Climb through a mostly open area busily re-vegetating itself from the blast of two decades ago. Thistles, horsetail ferns, pearly everlasting, butterweeds, and lupine line the trail. The sensitive ecosystem of the recovering blast zone is still of major interest to scientists worldwide. Here, perhaps more than anywhere in the Cascades, it is important to stay on designated trails.

After switchbacking up a moderate incline from the parking lot, you can first see Coldwater Lake after about 0.2 mile. The Coldwater Ridge Visitor Center is visible on the hill above, and the Birth of a Lake boardwalk trail is visible at the west end of the lake below.

Continue ascending, passing through an alder grove, then winding around the south side of the ridge, out of sight of the lake, then back to the north side. Twisted carnage of scorched deadfall surrounds the trail, interspersed with new growth. From about 1.3 miles, you can see a large piece of rusted metal up ahead; this is the first of the preserved blast wreckage. As you approach it, you can also see a rusted, wrecked truck down below, to your left, at the bottom of the ridge. At 1.6 miles, you arrive at a tangle of pulleys, cables, pipes and half-buried logs. Just beyond it, a huge piece of machinery sits, its arms and cables and panels sheared, twisted, and fused, its cab filled with sand, ash, rock, and chunks of trees. Standing in front of this vehicle, and those that follow over the next quarter-mile, you can't help but think of the men and women who worked here, and how fortuitous it was that the eruption occurred on a Sunday, when most loggers were not on the job—a coincidence that may have saved thousands of lives.

The ascent gentles after the logging equipment, but continues uphill until shortly past 3.0 miles, after which it's a steady downhill to aptly named Tractor Junction. Here, an upturned tractor stands on end, partially buried in sand and ash, its tank-like treads jutting obscenely skyward. Chunks of tree are wedged in improbable places throughout what is left of its mangled frame.

Just beyond the tractor, at 3.75 miles, is the junction with Coldwater Trail 230. A left turn on Trail 230 would, if open, take you to Lakes Trail 211 in 2.5 miles (this is the often-closed loop route mentioned above). A right turn would take you uphill toward Boundary Trail, St. Helens Lake, and Coldwater Peak.

Tractor Junction is the turnaround point for this 7.5-mile hike.

Nearest Lodgings: Anything in the West Approach subsection.

Highway 12/Road 25/Road 99 (East Approach):

LAYSER CAVE

Honest-to-goodness former cave dwelling.

Map:	Green Trails #333, "McCoy Peak" (access only); US Forest Service "Mount St. Helens National Volcanic Monument"
Distance:	0.4 miles round-trip
Elevation Loss:	200´
Estimated Time:	20 minutes

One of the most important and recent archeological finds in the Northwest, Layser Cave was discovered by Tim Layser in 1982. Actually, according to the artifacts found in the cave, it was discovered—and inhabited—some 7000 years ago, and inhabited until about 4000 years ago. The 1982 finding of the cave was a "re-discovery." Today, the animal bones and stone tools have been removed from the cave, and it is open for exploration. Hidden from the road and trailhead, the cave is a short downhill walk.

Getting There
From Randle, go south on Highway 131/Road 25. After 1.0 mile, take the left fork onto Cispus Road, which is also Forest Service Road 23. From this fork, go 6.1 miles on a well-paved two-lane road to the signed LAYSER CAVE turnoff, Road 083. This is a one-lane, rather steep gravel road with turnouts. After 1.5 miles, you'll find pull-out parking for 6–8 cars.

The Walk
From the parking area, descend a wooden staircase with a sapling handrail to a dirt path below. Pass interpretive plaques which explain this area's geology and Native American inhabitants. The shady, green trail is sort of a loop—a lower

Layser Cave

trail leads to a lookout point across the adjacent valley en route to the cave, while an upper trail goes straight to the cave. Either way, it's only about 0.2 mile to the cave. On a clear day, you get a nice view of Mt. Adams to the east from the lookout point.

The cave itself is interesting and not the least intimidating. It's only 32 feet deep, so you'll want to duck down and go inside, where the "ceiling" is high enough to stand up. A plaque at the cave's entrance gives more information about the inhabitants who left this cave some 4000 years ago.

Nearest Lodgings: Anything in the East Approach subsection.

CAMP CREEK FALLS
Pretty walk to a small waterfall.

Map:	Green Trails #333, "McCoy Peak;" US Forest Service "Mount St. Helens National Volcanic Monument"
Distance:	0.5 miles round-trip
Elevation Gain:	300´
Estimated Time:	30 minutes

This short walk in the woods is rewarded by a view of a pretty 40´ waterfall. A nice addition to the end of a day or when you don't have time for a longer hike. Also fun for kids; the short but moderately steep climb will make them feel like they've done something worthwhile. At low elevation (1300–1600 feet), it's open when others are snowed under.

Getting There
From Randle, go south on Highway 131/Road 25. After 1.0 mile, take the left fork onto Cispus Road, which is also Forest Service Road 23. From this fork, go 8.5 miles on a paved two-lane road. (If you are leaving Layser Cave—see above—you will continue 2.4 miles past the Road 23/Road 083 junction.) Just past the turnoff signed CISPUS LEARNING CENTER, you'll see a pullout for a few cars on the right side of the road. On the left side of the road is a sign, CAMP CR. FALLS, TRAIL 260.

The Hike
From the trailhead, stroll a fluffy duff trail lined with ivy, Oregon grape, and ferns under a canopy of cedar, maple, and a few giant Douglas-fir. The route is flat for the first 0.1 mile, then climbs moderately-to-steeply to a pleasant, up-close waterfall viewpoint. The narrow, pretty trail makes a good first-time waterfall hike.

Nearest Lodgings: Anything in the East Approach subsection.

WOODS CREEK WATCHABLE WILDLIFE
Easy, pretty walk through five habitat areas.

Map:	Woods Creek Watchable Wildlife Interpretive Trail brochure (available at trailhead); Green Trails #333, "McCoy Peak;" US Forest Service "Mount St. Helens National Volcanic Monument"
Distance:	2.5-mile double loop
Elevation Gain:	none
Estimated Time:	1 hour, 30 minutes

Two loop trails, Woods Creek Loop 247 and Old-Growth Loop 247A form a sort of figure-8 double loop trail for a total hike of 2.5 easy miles. Wheelchair users and those wishing a shorter hike can opt for the first loop only, a 1.5-mile trail built to barrier-free standards, 4 feet wide with compacted gravel surface.

The "watchable wildlife" moniker refers to the evidence of wildlife seen along the trail: beaver dams, emptied seed-cones, game trails. The interpretive brochure provided at the trailhead helps illuminate these signs of animal presence.

Hikers on the Woods Creek trail view five habitat areas as they pass through a mixed hardwood-conifer forest, an open meadow, the edge of a stream and beaver pond, a deciduous forest, and an old-growth conifer forest. With benches at intervals, bridged stream crossings, and 3-dimensional animal print identification signs (a Boy Scout project) along the way, this is an interesting and pleasant trail for everyone.

Getting There
From Randle, go south on Highway 131/Road 25. After 1.0 mile, stay right when the road forks (staying on Road 25). You'll see the left turn into the trailhead parking area 5.7 miles south of Randle. The Woods Creek Watchable Wildlife trail is directly opposite the Woods Creek Information Center.

The Hike
You'll find the signed trailhead for WOODS CREEK LOOP TRAIL 247 on the east side of the spacious parking area, which includes picnic tables and a toilet. Pick up a well-done and informative interpretive brochure at the trailhead. The trail is open to hikers and leashed pets.

Walk about 0.2 mile through a mixed hardwood-conifer forest, to a fork. A bridged crossing of Woods Creek is to your right; you'll return that way. For now, go left, following Woods Creek for another 0.2 mile; watch for beaver dams. Cross a bridge over the creek and come to a marshy, cattail-filled beaver pond. The trail winds along the edge of the beaver pond for about 0.3 mile, then comes to a junction after a total of about 0.8 mile. Go left to do the full 2.5-mile loop, which narrows to a 3-foot native surface path and includes grades up to 12%; go right if you want to stay on the 4-foot, compacted gravel path and limit your walk to 1.5 miles.

Stay right as you begin the second loop, OLD-GROWTH LOOP TRAIL 247A. (You will come to another fork almost immediately, with the return trail to your left.)

Proceed counterclockwise up modest inclines along a duff surface. Towering Douglas-fir and Western red cedar form a high canopy over an understory of vine maple, devil's club, Oregon grape, salal, and ferns. This loop is a mile long; turn right at its end, then left when you re-join the Woods Creek Loop.

Nearest Lodgings: Anything in the East Approach subsection.

NORWAY PASS
Dramatic vista of Spirit Lake and the crater.

Map:	Green Trails #332, "Spirit Lake;" US Forest Service "Mount St. Helens National Volcanic Monument"
Distance:	4.6 miles round-trip
Elevation Gain:	850′
Estimated Time:	2 hours, 30 minutes

This hike takes you up a segment of the Boundary Trail to an overlook southwest across Spirit Lake into the crater of Mount St. Helens. Views along the way include Meta Lake, Mt. Adams, Mt. Rainier, and, all around you, the effects of the 1980 eruption. The vista of Spirit Lake and the crater remain hidden until the trail's end, a dramatic reward for your efforts.

Getting There
From Highway 12 at Randle, take Forest Road 25 south. Pass the right-forking junction for Forest Road 26 (toward Ryan Lake) after 8.5 miles; stay left on Road 25. About 20 miles south of Randle, reach the junction with Forest Road 99 and turn right.

Take Road 99 toward Mount St. Helens. Watch for the ENTERING MOUNT ST. HELENS NATIONAL VOLCANIC MONUMENT sign. Two and one-third miles past the sign—just before the Miner's Car roadside exhibit and the parking area for Meta Lake—you will turn right (north) on Road 26.

Road 26 is a one-lane, paved road with pullouts. Proceed 0.9 mile up this road to a large, paved parking lot on the left. (Note that Road 26 is probably not a through road, although many maps show it to be. Massive slides north of this trailhead and south of Ryan Lake have kept it closed in recent years, and opening is unlikely.)

The parking area has room for a few dozen cars and provides a double pit toilet facility. Note that this parking lot is the one at which the Boundary Trail West from Bear Meadows (see below) ends.

The Hike
Find the trailhead, marked BOUNDARY TRAIL 1, at the north end of the parking lot. Follow this dry, dusty, hiker-only trail through a bone yard of scorched and fallen logs interspersed with new growth. (As this area lies within the National Volcanic Monument, nothing has been planted here since the 1980 blast. All new growth has occurred naturally.) The trail curves in an arc, heading north first, then swinging west, then south.

The pumice and ash upon which you walk was deposited during the eruption, carried by prevailing winds on that day. These loose, friable surfaces are prone to washouts.

After 0.75 mile, as you head south, you can see Meta Lake below on your left; Mt. Adams is in the distance due east. Across the valley, you can see the contrast between the blowdown zone, with its blast-felled trees and, farther up the hill, the heat-kill zone, where trees were scorched bare but remain standing.

Switchback up the hillside to 1.3 miles, where a signed intersection tells you that Independence Ridge Trail 227A goes off to the left. Turn right to continue on Boundary Trail toward Norway Pass. As you ascend, heading north, you can see Mt. Rainier to the northeast, appearing as a double-domed mountain from this angle. At 1.75 miles, drop down into a valley, then climb again to reach the Norway Pass trail junction at 2.3 miles.

If you continued on Boundary Trail to the right, you would reach Mt. Margaret in 3.0 miles and Coldwater Peak in 7.75. Instead, turn left on Trail 227, toward Independence Pass, and walk out 200–300 feet for the best views of Spirit Lake and the mountain. When Trail 227 is open all the way through to the south, it connects with Trail 227A to form a 7.0-mile loop. However, frequent slides make its maintenance difficult; don't count on the loop being open. Your best bet is to return the way you came.

Nearest Lodgings: Anything in the East Approach subsection, or Eagles Cliff Resort.

Views from Norway Pass include 20-year-old flotsam in Spirit Lake, and Mount St. Helens

BOUNDARY TRAIL WEST FROM BEAR MEADOWS
Dramatic tour of three distinct zones affected by the 1980 blast.

Map:	Green Trails #332, "Spirit Lake;" US Forest Service "Mount St. Helens National Volcanic Monument"
Distance:	5.5 miles one way or 6.3 miles one-way with Ghost Lake side trip; 7.8 miles round-trip from Bear Meadows to Ghost Lake and back
Elevation Gain:	+500', -700', +600' for one-way hike
Estimated Time:	3 to 4 hours

Another dayhikeable segment of the 64-mile Boundary Trail (see also Norway Pass, above; Boundary Trail East from Johnston Ridge, *West Approach* subsection; and Boundary Trail in *Other Hike Notes* at end of chapter), this is the only hike in the book for which I suggest using a shuttle car. In fact, it's the perfect hike for a mixed group of hikers and non-hikers. Those wishing to hike it can be dropped off at the trailhead, and the others can drive 4.5 miles down the road to the Miner's Car exhibit. While they wait, they can stroll the less-than-half-a-mile, paved Meta Lake trail, then drive 0.9 mile up Road 26 to the Norway Pass parking lot, the endpoint of this hike.

The one-way hike is a dramatic look at the effects of the volcano. When hiked from east-to-west, it takes you through three distinct zones left behind by the 1980 eruption: first, the untouched, pre-eruption forest gives you a look at what the entire area used to look like; next, the heat-kill zone shows you still-standing trees stripped bare by the heat of the blast; finally, in the blowdown zone at trail's end, you see how the force of the blast laid the mighty trees of the forest

Deadfall along the Boundary Trail west from Bear Meadows

down on their sides like so many toothpicks. (For an intimate look at the final zone—the blast zone—see Windy Ridge to Loowit Falls, below.)

Getting There

From Highway 12 at Randle, take Highway 131/Road 25 south. When the road forks at 1.0 mile, stay right. Pass the right-forking junction for Forest Road 26 (toward Ryan Lake) after 8.5 miles; stay left on Road 25. About 20 miles south of Randle, reach the junction with Forest Road 99 and turn right.

After 4.8 miles on Road 99, you will see a parking area signed GIFFORD PIN-CHOT NATIONAL FOREST INTERPRETIVE SITE BEAR MEADOW on your left; turn in. Parking for about 15 cars is provided, as are toilets.

Drivers of the shuttle car will have plenty of time to take in the short viewpoint trail off the Bear Meadow parking lot, then continue west about 4.5 miles on Road 99. Here, at the junction of Road 26, you will find the Miner's Car exhibit and Meta Lake parking area on the right side of the road. Explore this area, including the short Meta Lake stroll, then head north 0.9 mile on Road 26 to the Norway Pass parking lot, the end point for the one-way hike.

The Hike

From the parking lot, a short trail leads off to the south to a viewpoint, but the trail you want, Boundary Trail heading north and west, is on the opposite side of the road. Find the trailhead and begin ascending.

The trail begins outside of the National Volcanic Monument, in the Gifford Pinchot National Forest, in a landscape of deep forest, peppered with paintbrush, lupine, and beargrass, and phlox. If you didn't know better, you might not realize you were just one ridge away from the devastation of America's most infamous 20th-Century volcano.

After 0.6 mile of fairly brisk climbing, reach an intersection with Strawberry Mountain Trail 220, which goes to the right. Go left to continue on Boundary Trail.

After 0.8 mile, curve around the end of a hill and leave the wettest, greenest part of the forest behind. The trail flattens out here, gently undulating as it hugs the hillside for the next mile or so. Catch a good view of Mount St. Helens on an open ridge at about 1.0 mile. Ford a couple of waterfalls just after 1.1 mile.

At 2.3 miles, after the trail has begun ascending again, you may start to notice a change underfoot. Pale, blonde chunks of pumice, about the size of nickels, are on the path, and the soil has taken on a gray, ashy element. You know you're nearing the ridge summit. Spikes of dead trees stick up along the ridgetop.

At 2.5 miles, you arrive at the summit, the boundary of the devastation. A new understory is establishing itself beneath the tall, ghostly skeletons of trees killed in the blast, but the sense of destruction is still overpowering. Wind down the hillside, through the still-standing sentinels whose naked, gray trunks bear witness to the intense heat that scorched this ridge, some six miles from the mountain. You can see Road 99 below as you descend.

Reach the bottom of the ridge at 3.5 miles, and walk across a moist, creek-fed draw filled with a rich confusion of new growth and deadfall. Keep your eyes peeled for spur trail 1H to Ghost Lake; it should intersect on your right alongside the creek. An optional side trip to Ghost Lake would add about 0.8 mile to the length of your hike (0.4 mile each way). Those without a shuttle car could turn around at the lake and return to Bear Meadow.

From this draw, climb again, up another ridge. Note how knolls and ridges afforded partial protection from the volcano's blast. In areas open to the full force of the blast, trees were all blown down; in more sheltered areas, trees were sometimes scorched, but remained standing. In some cases, they even survived the blast.

To experience the full drama of this hike, you really must go all the way to the end. As you descend the final quarter-mile to Road 26 and the Norway Pass parking lot, you are surrounded by a total boneyard of downed trees—a full measure of destruction, the magnitude of which must be experienced to be appreciated.

Nearest Lodgings: Anything in the East Approach subsection, or Eagles Cliff Resort.

WINDY RIDGE TO LOOWIT FALLS
Hike through the blast zone to within 2 miles of the crater.

Map:	Green Trails #364S, "Mount St. Helens NW" (also shows on #364, "Mount St. Helens," but scale is better on #364S); US Forest Service "Mount St. Helens National Volcanic Monument"
Distance:	9.0 miles round-trip
Elevation Gain:	640'
Estimated Time:	5 hours

This unique hike is an open, exposed trail through the restricted area of the volcanic monument. Hike right into the blast zone, across a pyroclastic plain of puffed pumice that, even 20 years later, has recovered very little life except in small oasis-like creek draws.

Utilizing part of the round-the-mountain Loowit Trail, hike to a junction and take a short spur trail up to an overlook of Loowit Falls, formed by a stream coming down from the crater. As you stand at the falls, you are just 1.75 miles from the center of the crater, looking straight into the "breach," the massive hole in the side of the mountain from which thousands of tons of rock were thrown.

Getting There
From Highway 12 at Randle, take Highway 131/Road 25 south. After 1.0 mile, the road forks; take the right fork. Pass the right-forking junction for Forest Road 26 (toward Ryan Lake) after 8.5 miles; stay left on Road 25. About 20 miles south of Randle, reach the junction with Forest Road 99 and turn right.

The hike begins at Windy Ridge viewpoint, at the end of Road 99. At this large parking area you will find toilets, interpretive plaques, and ranger talks. A quarter-mile path zigzags up from the parking lot to an impressive high viewpoint. Non-hikers will enjoy the views from the parking area, but may not find enough to amuse themselves for the approximately 5 hours it will take you to hike to the falls and back.

The Hike

At the south side of the Windy Ridge parking lot is a road. Now closed to vehicular traffic, this road is Truman Trail 207, upon which you begin. As you follow this trail, ascending at a moderate incline for the first half mile, Windy Ridge rises to your right and Smith Creek valley lies below on your left. Usually, I don't favor trails that utilize roadbeds, but it's not so bad to have a 12-foot-wide path upon which to walk when you're busy craning your neck to look at the devastation of North America's most famous recent volcano eruption.

After 0.7 miles, the trail veers west and you can begin to see the mountain, which has been hidden by Windy Ridge since the parking lot.

At 1.7 miles, a thin singletrack trail forks off to the left and ascends along a ridge. This is Abraham Trail 216D, a trail which connects with Loowit Trail 16 some 2.3 miles to the south. Do not take this trail; continue straight ahead on the wide trail, descending into the vast, scoured, taupe moonscape below.

After another 0.3-mile, you reach the floor of the basin, a signed junction, and the end of the former road. To the left is Windy Trail 216E and Loowit Trail; straight ahead is Truman Trail 207, leading to Boundary Trail. Go left. From here, all paths are mere boot trails through the featureless landscape. As you are in a restricted area (the super-fragile blast zone), it is important to stay on the trails at all times. Cairns help you find your way.

Wind across the floor of the basin, through a field of pumice and igneous rock expelled by the blast. (The pale, beige, and airy chunks of pumice dominate the

Windy Ridge to Loowit Falls Trail goes through the boulder-strewn moonscape of the blast zone

first half of this hike, gradually giving way to weightier, darker igneous rock as you draw nearer the crater.)

After about a quarter of a mile, you begin ascending. As you work your way west past Windy Ridge, views of Spirit Lake open up to the north. At 2.5 miles, you are walking alongside the first of several stream-carved canyons you will climb into and out of en route to the falls.

At 2.8 miles, junction with Loowit Trail 216, which goes both left and right from this point. Turn right. Descend into the canyon, then climb up the other side, continuing west. The third stream crossing, at about 3.5 miles, is perhaps the most dramatic. This water comes off the Forsyth Glacier and creates an oasis of greenery and deep-pink flowers.

At 4.25 miles, you reach the junction of the Loowit Falls spur trail 216F. From this point, if you look north and slightly west across the pumice plain, you can see Johnston Ridge Observatory in the distance. Give a wave to the folks up there, smug in your knowledge that you are a full 4 miles closer to the crater than they are. When you visit the observatory and find Loowit Falls with your binoculars, you won't believe you were this close!

Climb the final quarter-mile to the falls viewpoint, where you can rest up and reflect on the wonder and magnitude of the blast that created the barren landscape spread in front of you. The crater hangs above you, too high to see into from this angle, but with a palpable presence.

Nearest Lodgings: Anything in the East Approach subsection, or Eagles Cliff Resort.

Highway 503/Road 90 (South Approach):

CEDAR FLATS NATURE TRAIL
Unmolested old-growth forest.

Map:	Green Trails #364, "Mount St. Helens;" US Forest Service "Mount St. Helens National Volcanic Monument"
Distance:	1.0 mile loop
Elevation Gain:	negligible
Estimated Time:	30 minutes

Cedar Flats is a "research natural area." Its 112 acres were set aside in 1946 as an area that would be left untouched for comparison to "managed" forests. What a surprise to find that Mother Nature has done just fine without our management. Old-growth Douglas-fir, Western red cedar, and Western hemlock giants survive and thrive here, in a rich, complex ecosystem of decay and regeneration.

The one-mile loop trail through a section of the preserve gives walkers and hikers of all ages and abilities an opportunity to enjoy the needle-carpeted calm of a majestic old-growth forest.

Getting There
From points south and west of Mount St. Helens, take Highway 503/Road 90 to Pine Creek information center, about 17 miles east of Cougar. Just after the information center is the junction of Road 90 and Road 25. Go north 3.6 miles on Road 25.

From Randle and points northeast, take Road 25 south. Continue past the Road 99 junction, watching for the pull-out on the left (east) side of the road 3.6 miles before you reach the junction with Road 90.

A signed pull-out on the east side of Road 25 provides parking for half a dozen cars.

The Walk

Enter a cathedral of unspoiled old-growth on a wide, gentle path. This is not an "interpretive trail" in the sense of having signs or brochures to accompany and illuminate your walk. One sign near the beginning explains the nature preserve. After that, you are on your own to enjoy the serenity.

Cross a little footbridge at 0.1 mile, then come to a fork, at which you can go either way. As you walk the loop, you are surrounded by trees 3, 4, and more feet in diameter. The mulchy understory is home to a variety of ferns, mosses, and mushrooms. You can see the Muddy River flowing to the east.

A pleasant leg-stretcher on your way between Windy Ridge and Ape Cave, or Randle and Cougar.

Nearest Lodgings: Eagles Cliff Resort, Monfort's B&B, and Lone Fir Resort.

Old-growth trees along Cedar Flats Nature Trail

TRAIL OF TWO FORESTS
Easy walk includes a crawl-through lava-cast tunnel.

Map:	Green Trails #364, "Mount St. Helens;" US Forest Service
	"Mount St. Helens National Volcanic Monument"
Distance:	0.25 mile loop
Elevation Gain:	none
Estimated Time:	30 minutes

A fun walk for the whole family, and adjacent to a pleasant picnic area, this stroll takes you through remnants of a 2000-year-old lava flow, now thoroughly refor-ested. "Two Forests" refers to today's forest and to the visible remains of the long-ago forest, preserved in lava. Kids will love the lava tree castings and tubes, especially one "crawl-through" tube that, while short and perfectly safe, is not for the claustrophobic.

Getting There
From Cougar and points west, take Highway 503/Forest Road 90 east; 6.6 miles east of Cougar, turn left on Road 83. From the east, take Road 90 west; 11.9 miles west of the Road 25/Road 90 junction, turn right on Road 83. In either case, you'll be turning north on Road 83, which is signed APE CAVE and LAVA CANYON. The road is paved but patchy.

After 1.6 miles on Road 83, turn left onto Road 8303, following the sign APE CAVE. Proceed 0.2 mile to a signed left turn into a large parking lot with a pleas-ant picnic area and toilets.

The Walk
Follow a nearly level boardwalk trail (5 feet wide and wheelchair-accessible) through a forested landscape with vertical and horizontal castings of trees from a lava flow of almost 2000 years ago. Interpretive signs help explain the geology.

If you plan to explore "The Crawl," two underground, horizontal tree cast-ings that form a tunnel, wear long pants. The imprint from the centuries-old tree bark is rough on the knees!

Nearest Lodgings: Anything in the South Approach subsection.

APE CAVE
Easy, eerie walk in a dark lava tube cave.

Map:	Green Trails #364, "Mount St. Helens;" US Forest Service
	"Mount St. Helens National Volcanic Monument"
Distance:	1.5 miles round-trip (lower cave only)
Elevation Gain:	negligible
Estimated Time:	1 hour, 30 minutes

Okay, I confess. Technically, walking through Ape Cave could be called "caving" rather than "hiking." And perhaps an all-underground hike isn't a hike at all.

But who can resist the lure of a 0.75-mile-long lava tube? It's OK if you don't h. the idea of "spelunking"—even a six-footer can walk upright through the entire lower cave, except for a small (and totally optional) crawl at the end. Walking through this wide, high-ceilinged cave is more like walking through a huge cathedral (albeit a pitch-dark one) than crawling in a cave.

Ape Cave is a geologic wonder that shouldn't be missed. The lower cave, featured here, requires no special "caving" skills or equipment. All it requires is a light source (bring two *good* flashlights, or rent a couple of lanterns from the booth off the parking lot), warm clothes (honestly—even in August, you'll want a warm jacket or sweater and long pants), and a sense of curiosity.

Those who wish to explore the upper cave (1.25 miles each way) will need sturdy clothing, a headlamp, and caving skills. The upper cave can be entered at its lower end through the same entrance as the lower cave, or at its upper end by walking one mile up Ape Cave Trail 239 from the lower cave entrance.

Please don't make yourself and your family miserable by failing to wear warm clothes. I did Ape Cave on a 90° day in August, and I was doggone chilly in long cotton hiking pants, a T-shirt, and a fleece jacket. Winter coats are not a bad idea. The cave's temperature is about 42°F year-round.

It's up to you whether you take a guided tour or not. And it's up to your tour guide whether this service enhances the tour—some are better than others.

Getting There

From Cougar and points west, take Highway 503/Road 90 east; 6.6 miles east of Cougar, turn left on Road 83. From the east, take Road 90 west; 11.9 miles west of the Road 25/Road 90 junction, turn right on Road 83. In either case, you'll be turning north on Road 83, which is signed APE CAVE and LAVA CANYON. The road is paved but patchy.

After 1.6 miles on Road 83, turn left onto Road 8303, following the sign APE CAVE. Drive 1.0 mile to the parking lot.

The Hike

Begin by dropping down a steep staircase to the cave floor. The more obvious route, to the south, is the lower cave. This route is easier because it is wide and open, with a high ceiling and sand-packed floor.

Enter a cold, dark underground world created some 1900 years ago when flowing lava ran down a streambed and began cooling on the outside. As the outside cooled, it formed a shell, and the still-liquid center continued to flow out, leaving behind a tube. The interior of the tube was further scraped out by subsequent mud and water flow.

Inside the cave today, patterns created by the initial cooling and refined by time are everywhere around you. In places, it looks like chocolate that was cooled in mid-melt; other places have the glazed look of pottery.

Shine your lights onto the walls as you go along, looking for interesting features like "The Meatball"— a lava sphere wedged into an overhead crevice about 3/4 of the way into the cave.

the cave, those wanting to try some minor spelunking can get rs and crawl a few dozen feet along a claustrophobia-inducing wo small "rooms" and the absolute end of the tube.

Ape Cave was named after a youth group who explored it in 1951. They called themselves the St. Helens Apes, a reference to Sasquatch, a purported denizen of this part of the forest.

Nearest Lodgings: Anything in the South Approach subsection.

JUNE LAKE
Short hike to lake and waterfall.

Map:	Green Trails #364 or #364S, "Mount St. Helens" or "Mount St. Helens NW" (close-up scale); US Forest Service "Mount St. Helens National Volcanic Monument"
Distance:	2.6 miles round-trip
Elevation Gain:	480´
Estimated Time:	1 hour, 30 minutes

A knowing Cougar resident informed me that June Lake is "where all the rangers take their parents when they visit." That sounded like a good recommendation. And why not? A 1.3-mile hike on Mount St. Helens' un-devastated south side, the June Lake trail rises through a young fir forest to a pretty mountain lake and a waterfall. That's a lot of scenic bang for the buck. But before you haul your parents up this trail, remember that some moderate uphill walking is involved.

Getting There
From Cougar and points west, take Highway 503/Road 90 east; 6.6 miles east of Cougar, turn left on Road 83. From the east, take Road 90 west; 11.9 miles west of the Road 25/Road 90 junction, turn right on Road 83. In either case, you'll be turning north on Road 83, which is signed APE CAVE and LAVA CANYON. The road is paved but patchy.

After 6.8 miles on Road 83, turn left on the road signed JUNE LAKE. The trailhead is just off the road. It provides room for about 8 cars and is signed JUNE LAKE TRAIL 216B.

The Hike
Nice views of the south side of Mount St. Helens await you along this hike. At the beginning, the trail is wide, open, and dusty, making it a less-than-perfect choice at midday (late afternoon might be the best time—the light on the mountain is exceptional). The path draws near a creek almost immediately. Lupine, paintbrush, and huckleberries surround you.

The first 0.75 mile rises at a gentle incline. After that, things get steeper for a quarter mile. Just after 1.0 mile, the grade flattens out again, and you emerge into a clearing. The mountain looms above you, its summit less than 4.0 miles away.

Cross the creek at about 1.2 miles, then walk onto a flat, sandy pl
with volcanic debris, the foot of the Worm Flows mud and lava lahar. June Lake,
appearing first as an unremarkable puddle on your right, is actually quite beautiful up close. Its sandy shore invites you to take your shoes off. The lake itself,
while small, is clear and emerald, fed by a waterfall over a basalt cliff on the
opposite side. Ducks and other waterfowl may be seen on the lake.

Nearest Lodgings: Anything in the South Approach subsection.

LAVA CANYON

Fascinating trail includes a ladder drop, rope-assisted creek crossing,
and a suspension bridge. (Also has short, barrier-free section.)

Map:	Green Trails #364 "Mount St. Helens;" US Forest Service "Mount St. Helens National Volcanic Monument"
Distance:	3.8 miles round-trip
Elevation Gain:	900´
Estimated Time:	3 hours

Part history lesson, part obstacle course—a more unusual hike than Lava
Canyon you'll be hard-pressed to find. As such, this popular trail requires a
Monument Pass (see *Overview,* above).

The suspension bridge on Lava Canyon Trail

The canyon was formed by lava from a Mount St. Helens eruption 3500 years ago, and exposed again by mud flows created during the May 18, 1980, eruption.

The trail is actually three trails in one: an easy, barrier-free beginning, a moderately difficult loop in the middle, and an optional difficult, steep trail that includes a rope-assisted hillside creek crossing and a ladder climb. The whole length of Lava Canyon Trail 184 is 2.5 miles each way, but all the interesting features occur within the first 1.7 miles. This version, which includes the more challenging features, eschews the final 0.8 mile, and ends with a side trip up spur trail 184B, giving you the most impact for your effort.

Getting There

From Cougar and points west, take Highway 503/Road 90 east; 6.6 miles east of Cougar, turn left on Road 83. From the east, take Road 90 west; 11.9 miles west of the Road 25/Road 90 junction, turn right on Road 83. In either case, you'll be turning north on Road 83, which is signed APE CAVE and LAVA CANYON. The road is paved but patchy.

Follow Road 83 all the way to its end (about 11 miles) at the Lava Canyon trailhead. A large parking lot provides pit toilets and room for a few dozen cars.

The Hike

Begin on a wide, paved, barrier-free path off the parking lot. From the trailhead sign, the picnic area is to the right and the trail is to the left, descending toward Muddy River and its canyon. Interpretive plaques within the first 0.4 mile explain the formation of the canyon and the regeneration of its ecosystem. Wheelchair users will find this part of the trail steep but otherwise very user friendly.

A final viewing platform at 0.4 mile signifies the end of the barrier-free trail. From here, the moderately difficult loop trail begins. To do the loop clockwise, go straight ahead (to the north, or to your left as you face the river) descending on a dirt path signed MORE DIFFICULT over loose, crumbly surfaces, toward the canyon and river below. About 50 feet down this exposed rock surface, watch for a trail disappearing into an alder grove on your left; turn onto it. At 0.5 mile, you are walking along the west side of the canyon. Water rushes through the bottom of the deep canyon, and you can see the rocky, vertical striations on the opposite side of the canyon laid bare by the 1980 mud flow.

Just before 0.7 miles, arrive at the suspension bridge. This is the north end of the moderately difficult loop. Those not wishing to continue to the difficult section of the trail can cross the bridge onto Trail 184A and return up the east side of the canyon. Those wishing to continue should stay left, following the MOST DIFFICULT sign and staying on Trail 184; you'll return this way and cross the suspension bridge on your way back.

Continue along the west side of the canyon, heading north. Slippery, loose talus surfaces alternate with slippery, wet rock surfaces to make footing dicey; a sturdy cable acts as a handrail to help you cross one particularly steep, wet grade. Meanwhile, the tumbling cataract of the Muddy River roils deep in the gorge below. This is not a trail for children.

In between the difficult areas are opportunities for rest, ı
vation of the awesome power of nature that created this ca
croppings offer places to sit and take photos or just bask in

At 1.5 miles, you come to *the ladder*. I have to admit, this
It's only about a 35-foot descent, though, and it beats jumpin
horsetail-fern grotto, then continue on the path.

At 1.7 miles, you junction with Ship Trail 184B; turn right. (Trail 184 continues another 0.8-mile north to its endpoint at a junction with Trail 225 at Smith
Creek, but all the major scenic points of interest are now behind you.)

Climb up a couple of dusty switchbacks, a short ladder, and a section of lava
rock, to find yourself atop the rock formation known as Ship Rock. Follow the
narrow path south along the top of Ship Rock to the end. From here, you can see
a four-tiered waterfall, the ladder you descended earlier, and the trail below.
Return to the junction with the main trail; you have hiked 2.1 miles. Turn left to
retrace your steps to the ladder, up the ladder, and back up the canyon. The
return trip is a steep climb, but in many ways it's easier than the sometimes-slip-
pery descent was. Plus, you have the bonus of seeing all the waterfalls in this
direction without turning around.

Reach the suspension bridge at 3.1 miles, and turn left to cross it, returning
via Trail 184A. This side of the river offers close-up looks at the river and the lava
formations around it. Cross two bridges. After the second, at 3.5 miles, you come
to a fork. Go left to junction with the initial, barrier-free trail and return to the
trailhead. The total hike is just over 3.8 miles.

Nearest Lodgings: Anything in the South Approach subsection.

LEWIS RIVER FALLS
Three exceptional waterfalls and old-growth forest.

Map:	Green Trails #365, "Lone Butte" (access only); US Forest Service "Mount St. Helens National Volcanic Monument"
Distance:	5.7 miles round-trip
Elevation Gain:	380′
Estimated Time:	3 hours, 30 minutes

Lewis River Trail 31 is a gorgeous, 14.5 mile (each way) trail southeast of Mount
St. Helens that follows the west bank of the Lewis River from Curly Creek at the
south end to Quartz Creek at the north end. The segment featured here offers the
most scenic impact per mile—three exceptional waterfalls artfully arranged along
a shady, green, old-growth-forested river draw. As the path also roughly parallels Road 90, each of the falls can be accessed via short spur trails from the road,
so not everyone on the trail will be hiking the full trek suggested here.

Getting There
From Cougar and points west, follow Highway 503/Road 90 east, past Swift
Reservoir, to the Pine Creek Information Station and the Road 90/Road 25

‿ection. Continue on Road 90, proceeding 14.0 miles (from the Road 25 junc‿
‿n) to the Lower Falls Campground.

From Randle and the Windy Ridge area, take Road 25 south to its junction with Road 90, then left (east) on Road 90 14.0 miles to the campground.

Turn right (east) into the campground. Follow signs to the day use area, where you'll find composting pit toilets and parking for about 15 cars. Trailhead is adjacent to the toilets.

The Hike

This hike begins on a short barrier-free trail which leads to a series of excellent viewpoints of Lower Falls within the first 300 feet. Follow the wide, compact gravel surface from the trailhead. When you reach the first fork, go left to the viewpoints, following a split rail fence to your right to see all three. Those continuing beyond the barrier-free trail to the other two falls will re-connect with the main trail at 0.1 mile; go left.

Almost immediately, arrive at a fork. Go right, following the sign MIDDLE FALLS 1.25 MI. The trail doubles back to head north through the campground, crossing the road on which you entered the campground at 0.25 mile. The surrounding forest is typical west-slope-central-Cascades: Douglas-fir, Western red cedar, vine maple, ferns, Oregon grape, vanilla leaf.

After leaving the campground area at about 0.4 miles, the trail follows close along the route of Lewis River.

Cross a little bridge just before 1.0 mile. Spur paths down from Road 90 join the trail on your left at 1.1 and 1.25 miles.

Just before Middle Falls, the trail opens up into a meadow ecosystem that includes thistles, wild berries, and pearly everlasting. Cross a bridge over

Lower Lewis River Falls

Copper Creek at 1.5 miles, then descend to Middle Falls at 1.6 miles. Like Lower Falls, this is a wide, shelf-like waterfall.

From this viewpoint, regain the altitude you lost in a series of switchbacks to an unsigned junction at 1.7 miles—another access path up to Road 90. Stay right.

Impressive rock outcroppings and cliffs covered with electric-green lichens rise on your left and the river continues to flow below on your right as you head toward Upper Falls. This segment of the hike—between Middle and Upper Falls—is the most notable for old-growth timber. You will see Douglas-fir 6 and 8 feet wide, plus huge Western red cedar and Pacific silver fir.

Just after 2.4 miles, you begin to see and hear the rush of Upper Falls, just ahead. Just before the falls, an access trail joins the main trail on the left. At 2.5, arrive at Upper Falls. Continue on across a bridged crossing of Alec Creek (a tributary of the Lewis River) to the falls viewpoint. Those wishing to avoid a hill could turn around here and make this a 5.0-mile round-trip hike.

For another look at Upper Falls, continue up the trail—and I do mean *up*. The 0.1-mile rise is the only really steep part of the hike. At 2.8 miles, arrive at a spur trail junction. Take this trail to your right, downhill 250 feet, to an exceptional eye-level look at Upper Falls.

Return to the main trail and retrace your steps for a 5.7-mile total round-trip. (If you continued on Lewis River Trail 31, you would come to Road 90 after another 0.7 mile, but the only sights along the way are a small waterfall—Taitnapum Falls—and the confluence of Quartz Creek and the Lewis River. A parking lot here provides an opportunity for a 3.6-mile point-to-point shuttle hike. Alternately, you could return via Road 90 for a 6.0-mile loop.)

This is truly a four-star hike. For scenic, deep-forest beauty, you won't find a prettier trail in the Mount St. Helens area. The path is well-maintained and gently undulating (except for the section just north of Upper Falls!), the waterfalls are exceptional, the old-growth timber is massive, and you are within sight of the river most of the time.

Nearest Lodgings: Eagles Cliff Resort, Monfort's B&B, and Lone Fir Resort.

SOUTH SIDE SUMMIT CLIMB
Stand on the rim of America's most famous 20th-Century volcano crater.

Map:	Green Trails #364 or #364S, "Mount St. Helens" or "Mount St. Helens NW" (close-up scale); US Forest Service "Mount St. Helens National Volcanic Monument"
Distance:	11.0 miles round-trip
Elevation Gain:	4481´
Estimated Time:	9 hours

This excursion really qualifies as a "climb" more than a "hike," but, as it requires no special climbing gear or mountaineering skills, and since it provides the unparalleled experience of gazing down into the crater of America's most famous volcano, I had to include it.

If the idea of hiking 11 miles, with a 4500-foot elevation gain, topping out at nearly 8300 feet elevation isn't enough to deter you, consider this: it's not the distance, climb, or altitude that makes this trek difficult. It's the surfaces. The first 2.3 miles are normal—your basic forest hike. After that, spend over two miles scrambling up rocks—at best, a thigh-burning proposition, at worst, steep enough to require clambering on all-fours. Finally, if the route is snow-free, the last mile is straight from Hell: a deep, steep, soft pumice-and-ash climb during which your feet sink ankle-deep with every step and you slide 6 inches back for every 12-inch step you take.

Still interested? Since this isn't a book for mountaineers, you'll want to do this climb when the trail is snow-free—which might be late July through early September. This, of course, is peak season, so plan ahead. You'll need a permit; the cost is $15 per person. Between May 15 and October 31, only 100 climbers per day are allowed on the mountain. Up to 60 of these permits may be reserved in advance, while at least 40 are held in unreserved status. To reserve a permit, obtain an application from:

Climbing Coordinator
Mount St. Helens NVM
42218 NE Yale Bridge Road
Amboy, WA 98601

Permit reservation applications are available after February 1 for the coming season. On this permit, you request several dates, in order of preference. The forest service will mail you a response within two weeks. This is not your *permit*, this is your *reservation*, guaranteeing your permit on a particular day. All climbers, with and without reservations, must pick up and pay for their permits

Mount St. Helens' Crater Rim

at Jack's Restaurant and Store on Highway 503 (23 miles east of Woodland and 5 miles west of Cougar) the day before their climb. Those with reservations must come before 5:30. At 5:30, all unreserved permits and unclaimed reserved permits are sold to those present at Jack's. If more climbers than permits are on hand, a lottery is held to distribute permits.

Finally, climbers must register by signing in and out before and after their climb at a 24-hour registry box outside of Jack's.

The morning of your climb, rise early, pack plenty of water (about 3 quarts per person) and snacks, and don't forget sufficient clothing to layer—it may be cool during the forested start, warm to hot on the exposed ascent, and windy and cold at the top. Other useful items (besides the usual "ten essentials") include a disposable camera (the blowing ash is liable to ruin your good one), eye protection (especially for contact lens wearers) and leather-palmed gloves (for hand-scrambling on abrasive surfaces). Tie your permit on your pack, lace up your best boots, and prepare for the "hike" of your life. For a dayhiker, it's a Spartacus experience.

Getting There

From Cougar and points west, take Highway 503/Road 90 east; 6.6 miles east of Cougar, turn left on Road 83. From the east, take Road 90 west; 11.9 miles west of the Road 25/Road 90 junction, turn right on Road 83. In either case, you'll be turning north on Road 83, which is signed APE CAVE and LAVA CANYON. The road is paved but patchy.

After 2.9 miles on Road 83, turn left on Road 81, signed CLIMBERS BIVOUAC. Proceed 4.2 miles on this sometimes-rough road, following signs, to the spacious bivouac parking loop. Toilets are adjacent to the trailhead, on the northwest side of the parking area.

The Hike

This most-popular of Mount St. Helens climbing routes begins on the Ptarmigan Trail 216A, a wide path that takes you through high-altitude forest to the tree-line. You gain nearly 1000 feet in the first two miles, so the grade is fairly steep, seeming especially so if you're fully loaded with everything you need for the climb. By 1.3 miles, the forest begins to thin. Pass through meadows between 1.6 and 1.7 miles; the tiger lilies, columbine, and beargrass bloom late at this altitude. As you rise and switchback, watch for Mt. Adams, due west.

Intersect with the round-the-mountain Loowit Trail at 2.1 miles. It goes both left and right; you want to continue straight ahead on the remaining 0.2 mile of the Ptarmigan Trail. As the trees peter out, so does the trail. At 2.3 miles, you reach 4800 feet, the point after which climbing permits are required. From here, the route is marked by tall poles. Lupine and other vegetation give way to a few scraggly subalpine fir and patches of pink heather as you walk northwest across what promises to be your last flat section of trail toward the beginning of the boulder-strewn climb up Monitor Ridge.

As you climb up through the boulders, winding your way from pole to pole along ashy paths, you can see Mt. Adams to the west and, looking behind you, Mt. Hood to the south. The higher you climb, the less obvious the path, until you are hand-and-foot-scrambling up rocks with nothing but distant poles and other hikers to guide you.

Around 4.5 miles, a flat area provides a good opportunity to rest and regroup. The snowfield on the west side of the ridge is a popular glissade descent route; to the east is Swift Glacier. A mile above you is the crater rim, your destination. You can see it well from here.

From here on up, it's a struggle. The deep, pumice-ash-sand surface sucks at your feet like a Sahara dune, and the steep pitch has you sliding one step back for every two you take forward. Here's another argument for starting *real* early—if you're among the first to reach this point, you won't have to deal with the humiliation of sprightly descenders—some of them sure to be teenage Boy Scouts—hip-hopping down the dune from the top.

And, speaking of the *top*…

OK, it's worth every step. After slogging up the Slope From Hell, the summit comes all at once. Chances are, you'll do what every other climber does at the top—you'll sit down immediately on the 6-foot crater rim. That's right, it's only about 6 feet wide, and it's 2000 feet straight down. You'll sit, not out of fatigue, but out of awe and the need to overcome vertigo. Then, sitting or standing, take it all in: Spirit Lake and Rainier to the north, Goat Rocks to the northeast, Adams to the east, Hood to the south. But what really commands your attention is the crater itself. Elephant-gray and featureless from the popular viewpoints to the north, the crater is actually a striated, multi-hued gorge as beautiful and as variegated as the walls of the Grand Canyon: pink, gold, charcoal, copper. And enormous! From a mile-and-a-half to two-and-a-half miles across, the span of the crater is more than the eye and the brain can deal with.

Just below the crater rim, a snow shelf stays in place most of the summer. This wide, flat cornice creates a false sense of security. Remember, while this shelf is dingy with ash and looks solid as earth, it's only *snow*, dangerously cantilevered and unstable. Do not hop down to stand on it, even for the sake of the ultimate photograph. If you reach the summit early enough that snow remains on the crater rim itself, remember to stay well away from the edge. While snow remains on the rim, what appears to be the inner edge of the rim may in fact be a dangerous, unstable snow-and-ice cornice jutting out over the crater.

You'll want to savor the views for a good hour up here. Walk off to the west, past Dryer Glacier (the mountain's highest point is about a third of a mile this direction). Take lots of photos. Eat lunch. Pound your chest. Then tighten your bootlaces and prepare to be one of the smug ones who barrel down the first mile past the struggling uphill climbers.

Nearest Lodgings: Anything in the South Approach subsection.

OTHER HIKE NOTES

These hikes not personally reviewed or not as highly recommended as the above hikes.

Eruption Trail

This newly constructed trail at Johnston Ridge Observatory was unfinished in 1997, but was planned to be a half-mile loop past a site commemorating the 57 individuals who died during the 1980 eruption. A Monument Pass will likely be required to walk on this trail.

Loowit Trail

Named for one of the Native American words for the mountain, Loowit Trail 216 is a round-the-mountain trail about 29 miles long. It is shown in its entirety on Green Trails Map #364S, "Mount St. Helens NW." This 1:40500-scale map shows the trail in good detail, with its side trails including Loowit Falls and June Lake. The full loop is not a dayhike, but many segments of it can be.

Boundary Trail

Boundary Trail 1 is a 64-mile point-to-point trail with many dayhikeable segments, including those I've called Norway Pass, Boundary Trail East from Johnston Ridge, and Boundary Trail West from Bear Meadows, featured above. The trail extends from the west side of Mount St. Helens National Volcanic Monument east through the NVM and into the Randle Ranger District of the Gifford Pinchot National Forest, terminating about 7.5 miles east of Council Lake. Outside the NVM, the trail is open to bicycles, horses, and motorcycles as well as hikers. Boundary Trail traces its history to the early 1900s, when Forest Service rangers used it for horseback patrols. Its name comes from its location on the boundary between what used to be the Columbia and Rainier national forests.

Sediment Retention Dam

On the west approach to the mountain, 21 miles east of Castle Rock, a signed spur road leads to the Sediment Retention Dam, an engineering marvel that was built swiftly and without precedent to stem the threat of additional mud flooding in the wake of the 1980 eruption. Down the spur road, you'll find a parking area on your right. Stroll 300 feet to a viewing platform overlooking the structure, or take the 2.0-mile round-trip walk down to the dam and back. Interpretive plaques just off the parking lot tell the story behind the nearly 20-story structure. Picnic tables are available near the viewing platform and around the parking lot. Bathrooms and a gift shop are also in the parking lot.

Table 3.
Lodgings in the Mt. St. Helens–West Approach vicinity

	BLUE HERON INN	ECO-CAMP (Mount St. Helens Adventure Tours)	MT. ST. HELENS MOTEL	SILVER LAKE MOTEL & RESORT	TENT & BREAKFAST (Mount St. Helens Adventure Tours)	TIMBERLAND INN & SUITES
PRICE (1997 SUMMER RATES, PRE-TAX, 2 PERSON)	$135	$55	$40–$48	$70–$85	$220	$65–$119.50
EXTRA PERSON	$20	up to 4 included	$5	some, up to 4; others, $5	$110	$5
PAYMENT METHODS	VISA, MC, Disc, Checks, Cash	VISA, MC, Checks, Cash	VISA, MC, AmEx, Disc, Cash	VISA, MC, Disc, Cash	VISA, MC, Checks, Cash	VISA, MC, AmEx, Disc, Cash
# OF UNITS	6	5	32	6 motel rooms, 5 cabins	10 persons allowed per night	40
PRIVATE BATH	Yes	No	Yes	Yes	No	Yes
BREAKFAST INCLUDED	Yes—also dinner	No	No	No	Yes—also dinner	No
COOKING FACILITIES	No	Yes	No	Yes	No	No
POOL	No	No	No	No	No	No
HOT TUB	No	No	No	No	No	No; Jacuzzis in 2 suites
CHILDREN	By arrange.	OK	OK	OK	OK	OK
PETS	No	OK on grounds, not in cabins	OK, $3 fee	OK in cabins, No in motel	No	OK, $5 fee
HANDICAPPED ACCESSIBLE	Yes	No	Yes	Call	No	Yes

	MEDICI MOTEL	SEASONS MOTEL	ST. HELENS MANORHOUSE
PRICE (1997 SUMMER RATES, PRE-TAX, 2 PERSON)	$45	$42–$65	$65–$75
EXTRA PERSON	N/A	$5 over 12	N/A
PAYMENT METHODS	VISA, MC, Checks, Cash	VISA, MC, AmEx, Disc, Cash	Checks, Cash
# OF UNITS	5	50	4
PRIVATE BATH	Yes	Yes	Yes, 2 rooms No, 2 rooms
BREAKFAST INCLUDED	No	No	Yes
COOKING FACILITIES	Yes	No	No
POOL	No	No	No
HOT TUB	No	No	Yes
CHILDREN	OK	OK	By arrange.
PETS	OK	Small OK, $5	By arrange.
HANDICAPPED ACCESSIBLE	Yes	Yes	Call

Table 4. Lodgings in the Mt. St. Helens-East Approach vicinity

	ANDERSON LODGE	EAGLES CLIFF RESORT	GRANDMA'S HOUSE B&B	LONE FIR RESORT	MONFORT'S B&B
PRICE (1997 SUMMER RATES, PRE-TAX, 2 PERSON)	$75 & up (see listing)	$28	$55	$38–$85	$65–$75
EXTRA PERSON	See listing	Up to 3, $28; 1–2 more, $10	N/A	$7–$12	$15
PAYMENT METHODS	Checks	Checks, Cash	VISA, MC, Checks	VISA, MC, Cash	VISA, MC, Cash
# OF UNITS	3 facilities; 65 + guests	4 cabins, 1 bunkhouse	3	16	2
PRIVATE BATH	Yes & No	Yes, toilet only in cabin units	No	Yes	Yes
BREAKFAST INCLUDED	No (Catering available)	No	Yes	No	Yes
COOKING FACILITIES	By arrange.	Yes	Yes	Yes	Kitchenette
POOL	No	No	No	Yes	No
HOT TUB	Yes	No	No	No	No
CHILDREN	OK	OK	OK	OK	OK
PETS	Not in bldgs.	OK	No	No	No
HANDICAPPED ACCESSIBLE	Yes	Call	No	No	Yes

Table 5. Lodgings in the Mt. St. Helens-South Approach vicinity

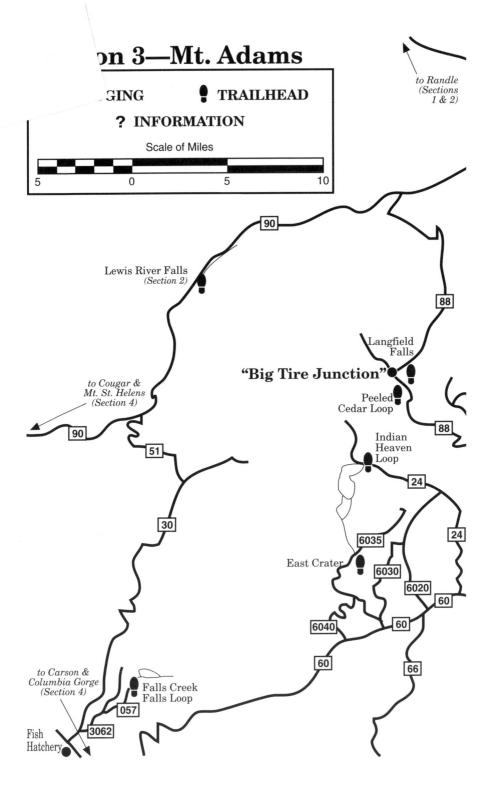

on 3—Mt. Adams

GING   ● **TRAILHEAD**

? **INFORMATION**

Scale of Miles

5   0   5   10

to Randle
*(Sections
1 & 2)*

`90`

Lewis River Falls
(Section 2)

`88`

Langfield
Falls

"Big Tire Junction"

to Cougar &
*Mt. St. Helens
(Section 4)*

Peeled
Cedar Loop

`88`

`90`

`51`

Indian
Heaven
Loop

`24`

`30`

`6035`

`24`

East Crater

`6030`

`6020`

`60`

`6040`

`60`

`60`

`66`

to Carson &
*Columbia Gorge
(Section 4)*

Falls Creek
Falls Loop

`057`

Fish
Hatchery

`3062`

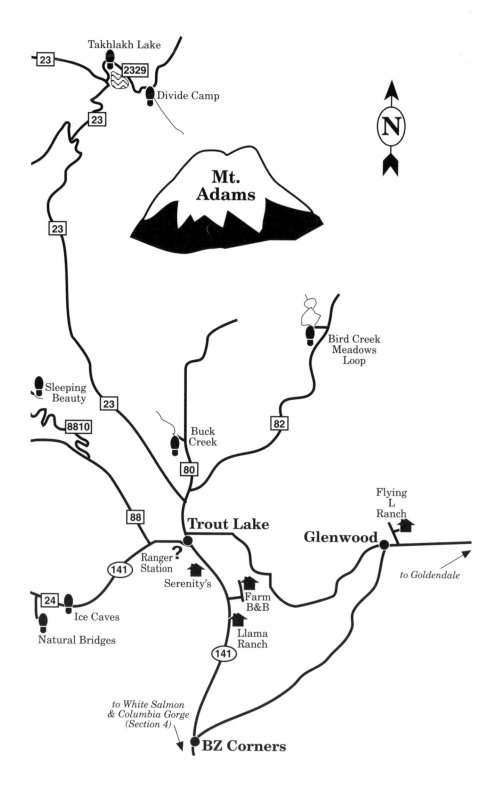

Takhlakh Lake

23

2329

Divide Camp

N

Mt.
Adams

23

Sleeping
Beauty

23

8810

Buck
Creek

Bird Creek
Meadows
Loop

82

80

88

Trout Lake

141

Ranger
Station

?

Serenity's

Glenwood

Flying
L
Ranch

to Goldendale

24

Ice Caves

Farm
B&B

Natural Bridges

Llama
Ranch

141

to White Salmon
& Columbia Gorge
(Section 4)

BZ Corners

Mt. Adams

OVERVIEW

Known to Native Americans as Klickitat, Mt. Adams tends to be Washington's "forgotten" Cascade peak. Situated south of Rainier and east of St. Helens, Adams is a massive, broad-shouldered mountain that ranks second only to Mt. Rainier in height, at 12,276 feet. Its recreation areas are less organized than the national park at Mt. Rainier and the national volcanic monument at Mount St. Helens, and nearby services are fewer than any other section in this book. Since travelers from the major metropolitan areas of Portland and Seattle must pass Rainier, St. Helens, and/or Hood to reach Adams, most find themselves at one of the other three peaks. But the Trout Lake valley and the dayhikes on and near Mt. Adams provide compelling reasons to make the journey.

The mountain has long held spiritual significance for Native Americans. Its ownership has been contested for over a century, beginning with a 1855 treaty between the Yakama Nation and the US Government. Subsequent surveys changed boundaries, resulting in fewer and fewer acres for the Yakama people over the years. Finally, in 1972, the US returned a 21,000-acre parcel, including much of the mountain's east face and its summit, to the Yakama Nation. Part of this parcel is accessible to the general public for hiking.

Hiking within the Yakama Indian Reservation requires a special permit. The Bird Creek Meadows Loop hike, featured below, and Bench Lake Loop and Heart Lake, listed in the *Other Hike Notes* at the end of this section, require this permit. The Yakama Nation permit system is rather loosely organized and not always strictly enforced; permits are available on site, but it is often difficult to find anyone to sell you one. The cost is $5.00 for one day's use. For current information, call the Bureau of Indian Affairs in Toppenish, Washington, at (509) 865-2255, and ask for the Department of Natural Resources. Or just head on up, and, if you can't find anyone to sell you one, they'll find you (unlike US Forest Service Wilderness Area permits, there seems to be no penalty for being found without a permit).

Most of the hikes featured in this section lie to the west of the mountain, outside the reservation and within the Gifford Pinchot National Forest and its Indian Heaven and Mt. Adams wilderness areas. Gifford Pinchot participates in the Trail Park Pass system (see *Trail Park Pass System* in the *Introduction*); vehicles parked at trailheads must display a pass decal in the window.

Mt. Adams is east of the Cascade crest, so the area is green and pretty, but not sodden like the west side. Where Mount St. Helens' view is obscured by weather some 200 days out of each year, Mt. Adams' is clear more often than not.

As you drive the roads outside of Trout Lake and Glenwood, you will encounter many open range areas; cattle may be present in the roadway. Plan extra time, and take it easy, especially on gravel roads and around corners.

For those seeking a hot shower and a soft bed at the end of their hiking day, lodgings immediately adjacent to Mt. Adams are few. The four featured here are delightful, each in its own way. Other lodging opportunities within striking distance can be found in the Mount St. Helens and Columbia Gorge sections of this book.

The Trout Lake valley is a beautiful and largely unexploited place. Much of the farming here is organic, and the water, tested on a regular basis, is drinking-pure (if a local offers you a glass of tap water, don't decline). The area has a long dairy heritage, with milk, cheese, and butter production and storage facilitated by the naturally occurring lava ice caves. (See Ice Caves under *Other Hike Notes* at the end of this section). It is also renowned for its huckleberries. Native Americans and early settlers converged on the hillsides to lay in their winter's supply each September. If you visit the area in the fall, be sure to find a café that serves homemade huckleberry pie or cobbler.

LODGINGS

In Alphabetical Order
See also lodgings in Section 4, Columbia Gorge

THE FARM B&B
490 Sunnyside Road • Trout Lake, WA 98650
(509) 395-2488

Tucked away from the highway in the quiet farming valley southeast of Trout Lake, a charming farmhouse nestles at the base of Mt. Adams. Inside, the comfortable home is a combination of antique charm and modern ease. Freshly cut flowers from the perennial garden decorate the parlor. Join your hosts for a complimentary afternoon beverage. Relax on the deck or in front of a cozy fire in the stove.

THE FARM B&B
Comfortable 1890s farmhouse; great breakfast

The farmhouse was built in 1890, and your hosts, Rosie and Dean Hostetter, have owned it since 1985. They can fill you in on information about the area, including ideas for daytrips in addition to the featured hikes in this section. If you want to pedal around and check out the valley, or into town for a bite to eat, Rosie and Dean provide mountain bikes at no charge.

Choose one of two guest rooms, the 1890 Room or the Quilt Room. The 1890 Room has a queen and a single bed, quilts, hardwood floors, and an antique vanity; its corner location provides lots of light. The Quilt Room has a double bed and attractive decor. The two rooms share a bathroom with a large, tile-and-glass-block shower big enough for two. Thick, terry robes are provided in your room. Rates are $80 for two in the 1890 Room ($10 for third person), and $70 in the Quilt Room. Ask about possible arrangements for additional guests.

The Farm B&B—charming, 1890s farmhouse

Call ahead to reserve your room. The Farm requests notice when you are traveling with children, and pets are not allowed. (Animal lovers will enjoy Levi, the farm dog.)

In the morning, a fresh, creative breakfast awaits you, served in the dining room at an elegant table set with antiques, or, weather permitting, on the deck. You'll start with fresh fruit (perhaps including the raspberries and strawberries raised in the Hostetter's garden), juice, and home-baked scones, followed by a carefully prepared entrée. Individual apple Dutch babies are a specialty, accompanied by sausage. A box lunch can be prepared by arrangement, to simplify your hiking day.

Getting There
To find The Farm, turn off Highway 141 east onto Warner Road (which is about 4 miles south of Trout Lake and just south of milepost 21). Go 1.0 mile to the end of Warner, then turn left. Go 0.2 mile; it's the first charming farmhouse on the right. A small sign on the mailbox identifies it.

Hikes and Walks Nearby: Any in this section.

FLYING L RANCH
25 Flying L Lane • Glenwood, WA 98619
(888) MT ADAMS (682-3267) • (509) 364-3488

What better way to start the hiking day than relaxing in a hot tub, watching the sunrise grace the snow-swathed slopes of Mt. Adams, with the distant sounds and smells of someone cooking a hearty, ranch-style breakfast for you? That's the kind of high-country ease you'll find at The Flying L Ranch.

The Ranch traces its heritage to 1945, when construction began on the building now known as The Lodge. Originally a private home, The Lodge now offers five guest rooms; a spacious living room complete with games, piano, stereo system, stone fireplace, and a Mt. Adams view; and a big old kitchen. Another five-unit building, The Guesthouse, was constructed later. It has its own small kitchen, and each of its rooms has a separate entrance. Three cabins are also available on the property.

FLYING L RANCH

Sprawling ranch; rooms & cabins with private baths

The sprawling campus of Flying L Ranch can house over 35 people in its 10 rooms and 3 cabins. It is especially well-suited to groups, but is also appropriate for families, couples, and individuals.

Rooms in The Lodge and The Guesthouse all have private bathrooms, and range in price from $80–$110 for two; extra persons $10–$15. Most rooms have a sleeping capacity of two or three people; the Mt. Adams Suite, with queen bed, two twins, fireplace, sofa, desk, and mini-refrigerator, sleeps up to four.

Flying L cabins are a short stroll away from the main buildings. Each has a complete kitchen and bathroom, and both electric and woodstove heat. Woods Cabin, at $110 for two, has a bedroom with a queen bed, and two twin beds in the living room. Wild Rose Cabin, at $120 for two, has a bedroom with a queen bed, and a full bed and twin bed in the living room. The Log Cabin, at $140 for two, sleeps up to six, with a bedroom, a sleeping loft, and a futon couch.

Breakfast, included in the price of your room, is served family-style in The Cookhouse dining room, a building adjacent to The Guesthouse and The Lodge. Dinners and other meals can be catered, or sack lunches prepared by arrangement. The complete kitchens in all lodging facilities make meal preparation easy,

Flying L Ranch has a great view of Mt. Adams

and Glenwood, with a grocery store and a couple of eateries, is just a mile away. (Trout Lake restaurants are 18 miles, and The Logs at BZ Corners is 20 miles.)

Other Flying L amenities include the 24-hour community hot tub, a 20-foot yurt (ideal for meetings), outdoor games, bikes, a small horse corral, barbecues, picnic tables, a pond, and strolling/cross-country skiing trails through its acres of woods and meadows. Firewood is provided for the fireplaces and wood-stoves.

The Flying L was owned for many years by Darrel Lloyd, a renowned local photographer, and his family. The Lloyds still live nearby. In 1997, the property was purchased by Jacquie Perry and Jeff Berend, who bring their new energy to the ranch, while respecting the tradition of its considerable heritage in the valley.

Getting There

Take Highway 141 north from the Columbia Gorge 12 miles to BZ Corners. Turn right and continue 19 miles to Glenwood. Go east through town, following signs for Goldendale. Watch for the Flying L sign 0.5 mile past town; turn left. Proceed another 0.5 mile to a signed driveway; turn right.

Hikes and Walks Nearby: Any in this section.

LLAMA RANCH B&B
1980 Highway 141 • Trout Lake, WA 98650
(509) 395-2786

Ever been kissed by a llama? Ever hugged or walked a llama? Ever hiked or picnicked with a llama? The Llama Ranch B&B poses these questions in their brochure. If your answer is "no," and you wish it were otherwise, this is the place for you!

Even if locking lips with a llama is not on your to-do list, chances are you'll enjoy the laid-back atmosphere and simple hospitality of Jerry Stone and Dee Kern at the Llama Ranch. The ranch is not your "shi-shi" Victorian B&B

Get friendly with a llama at Llama Ranch

Llama Ranch B&B sits at the base of "Klickitat"

dripping with lace and antiques—it's more like staying with relatives. A former Montessori school, the bed and breakfast is separate from the hosts' living quarters, and includes a kitchen, dining, living, and laundry area for guests' use. The result is a comfortable place for friendly couples and families.

LLAMA RANCH B&B

Working llama ranch

Five of the seven guest rooms share two full bathrooms; these each have a queen bed and rent for $79. A room with two queens and a private bath rents for $89, and a one-bedroom apartment with king bed, queen hideabed, private bath, and separate kitchen rents for $99 (when available). These prices are based on double occupancy; extra persons sharing any room are $10 apiece.

The Llama Ranch is a working ranch, with some 60 of the curious, vocal, woolly creatures in residence. Prices include full breakfast and a walk with the llamas. Pets are welcome at the llama ranch, and llama boarding is free for guests traveling with their own llama.

Your hosts, former educators, are fascinating people. Plan to spend time with them learning about the llamas and about the Trout Lake valley. They are a wealth of first-hand information about the local trails, most of which they have hiked—with and without the llamas.

Getting There
Take Highway 141 north 19 miles from White Salmon; watch for the sign on the east side of the road just before you get to Trout Lake.

Hikes and Walks Nearby: Any in this section.

SERENITY'S
2291 Highway 141 • P.O. Box 217 • Trout Lake, WA 98650
(800) 276-7993 • (509) 395-2500

SERENITY'S
Classy, romantic cabins with Mt. Adams views

"Serenity's" is a good name for these four splendid, romantic cabins. Nestled in the woods just south of Trout Lake, each has a view of Mt. Adams that inspires tranquility, and an atmosphere of classic calm. The chalet-style studio units were opened in late 1995. They are small but light and airy, with high, peaked ceilings, lots of glass, and warm, blued-pine paneling. Each feels new and fresh, and displays exceptional craftsmanship—beveling, tongue-in-groove joinery, rounded corners—and impressive attention to detail. Each cabin has a queen bed (one is a waterbed), gas log fireplace, air-conditioning, commodious bathroom, folding bed for extra guests, and small kitchenette (refrigerator, microwave, toaster, coffee maker, sink, utensils). Two units have lofts, three have jetted bathtubs, and one is wheelchair-accessible. In keeping with the retreat atmosphere, there are no telephones in the cabins; a TV with VCR is available upon request.

A picnic table and kettle barbecue are provided for each unit. The Serenity's property also includes a restaurant. Open sporadically, it offers seasonally-

Serenity's well-crafted cabins

inspired multi-course gourmet fare. Another option is the summer season "barbecue system," wherein, for a fee, your hosts provide you with all the ingredients for your own private barbecue dinner. Ask about this when you reserve your room.

Getting There
Take Highway 141 north from White Salmon. You'll find Serenity's on the west side of Highway 141, just south of Trout Lake.

Hikes and Walks Nearby: Any in this section.

ADDITIONAL LODGINGS

These premises were not thoroughly reviewed by the author. See also Lodgings in *Section 4, Columbia Gorge*.

ADAMS HOUSE   (509) 395-2767
2299 Highway 141, Trout Lake, WA 98650
Adjacent to Time Out Pizza (see Dining, below), this private home, owned by Shelly and Bob Whitefield, has been renovated for use as a boarding house-style rental. It has 4 bedrooms, 2 with a private half bath, and 2 with shared baths. Full kitchen & living area. Rates to be determined; specials offered for parties renting entire house.

TROUT LAKE COUNTRY INN   (509) 395-2894
15 Guler Road, Trout Lake, WA 98650
Off the main highway, this rustic inn offers 2 rooms over a restaurant at $65 per night for two. An adjacent unit sleeps up to 4 for $85. Includes breakfast. Discounts for singles and for those not wishing breakfast.

TROUT LAKE GROCERY   (509) 395-2777
Highway 141, Trout Lake, WA 98650
Three simple rooms share 2 baths above the local grocery store; $30 each.

DINING
In Alphabetical Order
See also Hood River dining in Section 4, Columbia Gorge

THE LOGS
1258 Highway 141 • (BZ Corners) • White Salmon, WA 98672
(509) 493-1402
All roads lead to BZ Corners, and all the locals tell you to "eat at The Logs." This historic log cabin restaurant a few miles south of Trout Lake traces its history to the 1920s. Its checkered past includes life as a dance hall and moonshine parlor, complete with cock fighting, gambling, and beer brawling. In more recent years, its fame has centered around its broasted chicken and other family-style fare, although one side still functions as a tavern.

The Logs was purchased by Ramona and Steve Nybroten in 1992, and they continue a tradition of hearty (if heavy) fare, reasonably priced. Many dishes take their catchy names from logging terms. Would you eat a "Talkie-Tooter?" You might—it's a burger topped with mushrooms and Swiss, for $3.95. The "Choker Setter" doesn't require the Heimlich maneuver—that's their garden burger, $4.50. Other burgers and sandwiches, including the Pine Flat (Philly steak), Riggin' Slinger (fish sandwich), and Haywire (chili burger), run $3.65–$5.25; add fries for 75¢.

Besides the "secret recipe" chicken, other dinner choices include BBQ beef ribs ($7.95), breaded chicken gizzards ($6.25; $3.65 as an appetizer), and tavern battered cod & chips ($6.50). A passable pizza is also served, as well as a selection of desserts. (If it's huckleberry season, don't go home without a slice of huckleberry pie.)

You'll find BZ Corners and The Logs about 11 miles south of Trout Lake (19 miles southeast of Glenwood), halfway to White Salmon.

TIME OUT PIZZA
2295 Highway 141 • Trout Lake, WA 98650
(509) 395-2767

There's nothing like a really good, homemade pizza after an invigorating day of hiking. The sad fact is that there are very few dining choices around Trout Lake, so, in choosing Time Out Pizza, you might think you are settling for mediocre. The surprise is—you're not! These folks, Shelly & Bob Whitefield, make *great* pizza.

The soul of a perfect pizza is in the crust, and theirs is homemade and perfect: crispy, yet chewy, tender and flavorful. Standard toppings are generous and freshly prepared, and you have a choice of red sauce or pesto, 3-cheese blend or hot jalapeño cheese. Combinations are named after basketball catchphrases: Slam Dunk, Fast Break, Rebounder, etc., and the casual, family atmosphere with big-screen TV reflects a sports theme. Better than sitting inside, you can choose a spot on the deck for an out-of-this-world view of Mt. Adams.

Time Out also offers spaghetti, salad, hot Italian sandwiches, and ice cream. Located across the highway from the high school, just south of "town," Time Out is closed Mondays.

WALKS AND HIKES
Listed in approximate order of difficulty

PEELED-CEDAR LOOP
Barrier-free, old-growth interpretive loop.

Map:	Green Trails #366, "Mount Adams West" (access only)
Distance:	650 feet
Elevation Gain:	none
Estimated Time:	15 minutes

This 5-foot-wide barrier-free path through a small stand of old-growth trees is also an interpretive trail, with signs explaining how cedar trees were peeled for basket material, the ways in which animals use trees, the location of a Native American trail, how old-growth forests work, and the function of nurse logs and stumps.

Getting There

From Trout Lake, follow Highway 141 north through town (coming into Trout Lake from the south, Highway 141 is the left fork of the Y as you enter town). Pass the ranger station (0.9 mile from the Y), and continue to the junction of Road 88 (1.7 miles from the Y). Turn right on Road 88 and travel 12.8 miles. Turn left into a gravel parking area signed HISTORIC MARKER SITE. If you reach Big Tire Junction (that's the one with…uh…the big TIRE in the middle of the intersection…), you've gone 0.2 mile too far.

Coming from Big Tire Junction or Langfield Falls, go 0.2 mile past Big Tire and turn right into the parking area.

The Walk

Begin at the west end of the parking area, where you'll see a HISTORIC SITE sign. Twenty feet up the trail, the first sign explains the many uses Native Americans found for "The Giving Tree"—the Western red cedar. Its bark could be harvested and used as weaving material while leaving the tree alive. A giant cedar here bears the scar from careful peeling centuries ago.

Other signs along the wide, flat, loop path provide more information about this site and the old-growth forest remaining.

Be sure to visit Langfield Falls (below), another short walk just a quarter-mile up the road.

Nearest Lodgings: Any of the lodgings in this section, or any in *Section 4, Columbia Gorge.*

LANGFIELD FALLS

Waterfall drama and old-growth, easily attained.

Map:	Green Trails #366, "Mount Adams West"
Distance:	0.4 miles round-trip
Elevation Loss:	150´
Estimated Time:	30 minutes

This is a very easy and very pretty trail down a ravine framed with old-growth to an impressive waterfall.

Langfield Falls is just past Peeled-Cedar Loop (above); combine the two into one outing.

Getting There

From Trout Lake, follow Highway 141 north through town (coming into Trout Lake from the south, Highway 141 is the left fork of the Y as you enter town).

Pass the ranger station (0.9 mile from the Y), and continue to the junction of Road 88 (1.7 miles from the Y). Turn right on Road 88 and travel 13.0 miles to aptly-named Big Tire Junction. Turn right at the big tire, following the sign to Langfield Falls. A signed parking lot on your right about 200 feet from the turn has room for about 10 cars.

The Hike

From the trailhead sign, LANGFIELD FALLS TRAIL 8, descend on a wide, needle-carpeted path through a cool, shady, forested draw. The sound of rushing water meets you almost immediately; after just a few hundred feet, you can begin to see the falls on your right. The path continues along the rim of the gorge, then turns into an observation area. A plaque here commemorates K.C. Langfield, Mt. Adams Ranger from 1933 to 1956. Benches here offer a chance to sit and view the wide, sprawling falls as they cascade dramatically over an ancient lava cliff.

While this marked observation area is the best photographic vantage point, most will want to continue another 200 feet down the hill to another bench, and even a few dozen feet beyond, where the path peters out at the spray-flecked edge of the falls' pond.

Nearest Lodgings: Any of the lodgings in this section, or any in *Section 4, Columbia Gorge.*

TAKHLAKH LAKE LOOP

Picture-perfect lake at base of Mt. Adams.

Map:	Green Trails #334, "Blue Lake;" US Forest Service "Gifford Pinchot National Forest" or "Mt. Adams Wilderness"
Distance:	1.1 mile loop
Elevation Gain:	Negligible
Estimated Time:	30 minutes

Stroll the shore of a picturesque, nearly circular lake at the base of Mt. Adams. A wide, well-graded path takes you around the circumference of this scenic, justifiably popular lake. Only people-powered or electric-motor boats are allowed on the lake, which helps preserve its wilderness ambience. This short loop also connects with a loop through Takh Takh Meadow, to form a figure 8 about 2.5 total miles in length.

The Takhlakh Lake Loop trail is considered barrier-free, but presents a challenge to many wheelchair users due to its dirt surface and a few steep pitches around the back part of the loop, one of which reaches 15%. Check with the forest service for current surface conditions.

Getting There

From the gas station Y at the south end of Trout Lake, take the east fork (that's the right fork as you head north toward "downtown"). At 1.1 miles, take the first left fork opportunity, Highway 23 toward Randle. Follow this paved two-lane for 19 miles, to its forked junction with Road 90. Take the right fork to stay on

Road 23; the road turns to gravel in a few hundred feet. After 4.2 miles from the Road 90 junction, take Road 2329 to the right. Curiously, this road is paved. Follow signs toward Takhlakh Lake. After 1.5 miles, turn right into the Takhlakh Lake Campground. Stay right when the driveway into the park forks. You'll come to an information signboard just before the campground entrance. The day use area, with picnic tables, pit toilets, and parking for hikers, is just across the road from this signboard.

From Randle, take Road 25 south. After 1.0 mile, veer left at a fork, onto Road 23. After about 32 miles, turn left on Road 2329. Turn right into the Takhlakh Lake Campground after 1.5 miles.

From Cougar, take Road 90 east to its junction with Road 23. Take Road 23 north toward Randle. Turn right on Road 2329 after 4.2 miles. After 1.5 miles, turn right into the Takhlakh Lake Campground.

The Hike

From the day use parking area, walk past the toilets to a bridged inlet crossing. This is our starting point for a counterclockwise loop.

Approaching the loop in this direction, you will first walk through the campground. Many side trails criss-cross between campsites and the lakeshore for the first 0.2 mile; pick the widest trail, stay near the lake, and keep wending your way to the right.

Pass through dense thickets of beargrass and huckleberry on a wide, well-graded path of smooth dirt topped with sand.

After about 0.3 mile, you have left the campground behind and you approach a meadow. Several social trails veer off to the left toward the lake and into the

Takhlakh Lake's picture-perfect reflection of Mt. Adams

meadow, but stay right on the widest path, which will take you away from the lake, along the right-hand side of a small meadow, and into the woods.

Just before 0.5 mile, you come to a Y. A spur trail leads some 200 feet to the left, to a viewpoint at the lakeshore. The main trail (marked TRAIL, with an arrow), goes to the right, away from the lake.

Cross a wetland drainage area on a series of boardwalks before coming to another junction. This is the access point for Takh Takh Meadow Trail 136, another loop just over a mile in length. Turn right to take this additional loop, resulting in a hike of about 2.5 miles; stay left (straight ahead) to continue on the 1.1 mile Takhlakh Lake Loop.

The remainder of the loop follows the lakeshore back to the parking area. Just before reaching your car, pause and savor the views of Mt. Adams reflected in the lake. This side of the lake presents the best photo opportunities.

Nearest Lodgings: Any of the lodgings in this section, or St. Helens Manorhouse or Eagles Cliff Resort, *Section 2, Mount St. Helens.*

NATURAL BRIDGES
Explore a forested, partially-collapsed lava tube.

Map:	Green Trails #398, "Willard" (access only)
Distance:	Up to 2.0 miles
Elevation Gain:	negligible
Estimated Time:	15 minutes to 1 hour, 30 minutes

The area between Mt. Adams and Mount St. Helens is known for its lava tubes, underground channels formed by flowing, then cooling lava (see *Ape Cave,* Section 2). Natural "bridges" are formed when such tubes, lying beneath the surface of the ground, partially collapse. The collapsed areas become trenches, and the intact areas become bridges across the top of the trenches. The area called Natural Bridges is a particularly dramatic example. Here, a mile-long tube collapsed in several places, leaving a series of bridges. The area has grown over with maple trees and other deciduous foliage, and a network of paths connects the various bridges. The result is a striking geologic park which can be observed by walking 50 feet from one's car, or by strolling any or all of the approximately 2 miles of paths along both sides of the trench and across the bridges. For a special treat, visit in the fall, when the changing leaves turn the area into a flaming gully of color.

Getting There
From Trout Lake, follow Highway 141 north through town (coming into Trout Lake from the south, Highway 141 is the left fork of the Y as you enter town). Pass the ranger station (0.9 mile from the Y) and reset your odometer; stay on Highway 141. Highway 141 turns into Forest Road 24 at the Skamania County Line, 4.5 miles past the ranger station.

Natural bridges are created by partially collapsed lava tubes

After 6.2 miles from the ranger station, turn left, following a sign for NATUR-
AL BRIDGES AND MCCLELLAN'S TRAIL. Continue to follow the signs 0.7 mile down
this rough road to a parking area.

The Walk
Walk from the parking area up the short rise to the edge of the gully. To the right
is one of the most dramatic bridges. You may walk in either direction; trails
follow both sides of the tube and cross each bridge. Most of the tube and its
paths lie to your right.

Nearest Lodgings: Any of the lodgings in this section, or any in *Section 4,
Columbia Gorge.*

SLEEPING BEAUTY
Incredible views; short but steep.

Map:	Green Trails #366, "Mt. Adams West"
Distance:	3.0 miles round-trip
Elevation Gain:	1400′
Estimated Time:	2 hours, 30 minutes

A justifiably popular, albeit steep, hike, this trail charges up the side of 4900-foot
Sleeping Beauty, a bald, rocky peak 10 as-the-crow-flies miles from Mt. Adams.
The first mile of the route is under the cover of sparse forest, while the final half-
mile is open. Avoid doing this trail in the midday heat, but, by all means, do it.
And choose a clear day, because the views of the major Cascade peaks are the
whole point of this hike—and they are astounding. The final 0.3 mile travels
over loose, crumbly rock surfaces with precipitous drop-offs—not a problem for
most hikers, but I wouldn't recommend this one for kids. Most wouldn't enjoy

the steep climb, anyway. Bring bug repellent or a bandanna to shoo away pesky flies often present on this trail.

Getting There
From the Y at the south end of Trout Lake, go west (the left fork), taking Highway 141 through town. Pass the ranger station after 0.9 mile. After 1.7 miles (0.8 from the ranger station), turn right on Road 88.

Take Road 88 4.5 miles, then turn right onto Road 8810, a good gravel road. Stay on Road 8810 when, after 1.1 miles, it makes a hairpin turn and Spur Road 010 goes off to the right to TROUT CREEK CAMPGROUND.

After 6.1 miles on Road 8810, turn right on Spur Road 040. Follow the SLEEPING BEAUTY signs 0.3 mile up a narrow, gravel jeep trail to a trailhead on the left. Park alongside the road.

The Hike
Any trail that gains 1400 feet in 1.5 miles has to "get busy" from the get-go, and this one does. A hiker-only trail, Sleeping Beauty Trail 37 starts off steep and stays with it. The dirt path rises through sun-dappled Douglas and grand fir forest with an understory of wild berries, ferns, and vanilla leaf. Flowers, depending upon the season, include pipsissewa, wintergreen, and columbine. A symphony of crickets may accompany your ascent.

After 1.1 miles of unrelenting climbing, the canopy begins to open up. You find yourself surrounded by huckleberry bushes, with Mt. Adams in front of you and a rocky hillside covered with paintbrush beside you. Here, the path becomes rockier, and stays open for the short duration of the climb.

Fabulous view of Mt. Adams from the top of Sleeping Beauty

At 1.2 miles, begin switchbacking up through the shale mounds and protruding cornices of Sleeping Beauty herself, using hands and steady feet to climb the final 0.3 mile.

On top, you'll see why this is the first hike locals recommend to visitors. Quite simply, you can see it all: Mt. Hood, Mount St. Helens, Mt. Rainier, and, right in your face, the majesty of Mt. Adams. Savor the view—there are few like it.

Nearest Lodgings: Any of the lodgings in this section, or any in *Section 4, Columbia Gorge*.

BUCK CREEK
Three creek crossings on this cool, shady walk.

Map:	Green Trails #366, "Mt. Adams West"
Distance:	5.2 miles round-trip
Elevation Gain:	400´ but up-and-down
Estimated Time:	2 hours, 30 minutes

There's nothing like a deep, green forest walk to calm the soul. This trail follows the course of the White Salmon River, but is named for one of several tributaries you cross during the course of the hike. While the beginning and end of this trail is typical east-side—Ponderosa pine and Douglas-fir shading a dry and open understory—a 0.75-mile draw in the middle of the hike is a sheltered oasis of wildflowers and greenery.

The path, open to hikers, equestrians, and bicycles, is less popular than its showier cousins up the road, so it makes a great choice for a measure of solitude. It's also a good rainy or overcast day choice, as it is not a "view" hike. Bring insect repellent; the mosquitoes like this one, too.

Getting There
From the gas station Y at the south end of Trout Lake, take the east fork (that's the right fork as you head north toward "downtown"). At 1.1 miles, reach a fork: Road 23 goes west toward RANDLE; stay right, following signs toward MT. ADAMS RECREATION AREA.

At the next Y, take the left fork, marked SOUTH CLIMB–TRAIL 183. This road is one lane, paved, with pull-outs. Pass into Skamania County at 3.6 miles.

At 4.0 miles, turn left, following a sign for BUCK CREEK TRAIL 54. Drive 0.9 mile to the end of the road and the trailhead.

The Hike
From the signed trailhead, follow a path downhill for 0.25 mile to a T junction. There, follow the signed BUCK CREEK TRAIL 54 to the right.

Continue descending to the bank of the first stream, which you cross at 0.3 mile. As you walk through this Ponderosa pine and Douglas-fir forest, watch for occasional giants amongst the generally moderate-size trees.

At 0.75, rocky outcroppings invite you to walk carefully to their edges and peer down their sheer cliffs to the river gorge below. After a mile, drop down to a second creek crossing. The bridge may be out here, making the route impass-able for equestrians and requiring a portage for mountain bikers, but hikers can ford it readily.

You are now in a deep, sheltered draw, the floor of which is thick with vanil-la leaf, tiger lily, columbine, and wild rosebushes.

At 1.8 miles, you begin to ascend out of the valley, through a landscape of vine maple, lupine, and fern. A final plunge downward takes you to the cross-ing of Buck Creek at 2.2 miles.

The next 0.2-mile is a moderately steep ascent alongside Buck Creek, after which you veer to the left, away from the creek, and walk through forest, at a gen-tle ascent, to the other end of the trail, a much less-accessible trailhead, at 2.6 miles.

Nearest Lodgings: Any of the lodgings in this section, or any in *Section 4, Columbia Gorge.*

EAST CRATER
Wildflower meadows, streams, and lakes.

Map:	Green Trails #397 & #365, "Wind River" & "Lone Butte;" access on #366 & #398, "Mt. Adams West" & "Willard;" US Forest Service "Indian Heaven Wilderness"
Distance:	5.4 miles round-trip
Elevation Gain:	800′
Estimated Time:	2 hours, 45 minutes

East Crater is one of two featured hikes in Gifford Pinchot National Forest's magnificent Indian Heaven Wilderness (see also *Indian Heaven Loop,* below). This designated wilderness, established in 1984, encompasses 20,400 acres of bench-land, meadows, peaks, and craters. Once famous for its profusion of huckleber-ries, the landscape is now becoming more dominated by trees. Much of Indian Heaven Wilderness, with elevations ranging from 3500 feet to almost 6000 feet, remains snow-covered until mid-July or later. The East Crater trail ranges from 4000 to 4800 feet, and is one of the earlier trails to melt out.

Getting There
From Trout Lake, follow Highway 141 west through town (coming into Trout Lake from the south, Highway 141 is the left fork of the Y as you enter town). Pass the ranger station (0.9 mile from the Y) and reset your odometer; stay on Highway 141. Highway 141 turns into Forest Service Road 24 at the Skamania County Line, 4.5 miles past the ranger station. Pass the turnoffs to Ice Caves and Natural Bridges.

At 7.0 miles, where the road forks, take the left fork (more or less straight ahead—the right fork is the continuation of Road 24) onto Forest Service Road 60, signed GOOSE LAKE/CARSON, a one-lane, paved road with turnouts.

At 8.6 miles, come to another fork; pavement ends. Take the left fork, signed GOOSE LAKE/WILLARD/CARSON, continuing on Road 60.

At 8.8 miles, come to another fork. Take the right fork, signed GOOSE LAKE/CARSON, continuing on Road 60. (The left fork is Road 66, signed WILLARD.)

At 10.5 miles, turn right on Forest Service Road 6030, following the sign for EAST CRATER TRAIL 48. By staying left (straight) on this rough, potholed, gravel road, you will find yourself (probably without benefit of any signs) on Road 6035; Road 6030 is one of several roads which branch off to the right. Pass a signed junction with Road 6040, signed FORLORN LAKES, at 12.4 miles; continue on Road 6035, still signed EAST CRATER TRAIL.

At 13.6, at a fork where an unnamed road goes to the left, stay right. Drive through a miserable clearcut, then climb back into second-growth forest.

At 14.7 miles, just before the end of the maintained road, a pullout on the right affords room for 10–12 cars. The signed East Crater trailhead is on the left.

The Hike
Open to hikers and equestrians, this trail requires a self-issuing wilderness permit, available at the trailhead. It begins as a wide, needled path ascending gently through a majestic pine and fir forest. The understory is dominated by huckleberries (for which this area is famous) and beargrass.

At 0.3 mile, you find yourself alongside a seasonal runoff creek, then you cross it. Just after 0.5 mile, you pass officially into the Indian Heaven Wilderness. At 0.9, you begin to hear a larger creek to your left; at 1.0 mile, you see it, then cross it on a bridge.

At 1.4 miles, a small melt-out pond on your left may evaporate to meadow late in the season. This and other meadowed areas support a variety of seasonal wildflowers, from a profusion of avalanche lilies at the first snowmelt to the huge green false hellebore later in the season to the carpet of pink heather that dominates most of the summer.

Arrive at a more substantial pair of ponds at 1.7 miles. At 2.0 miles, a waterfall on your left feeds a creek that you cross on a bridge.

Slope gently downhill beginning at 2.4 miles. At 2.5 miles, arrive at Junction Lake. Walk 0.2 miles alongside the lake to the junction with the Pacific Crest Trail at the far end. If you followed the PCT about 1.5 miles to the north (a right turn), you would junction with the hike I call Indian Heaven Loop, detailed below. But, for a dayhike, the west end of Junction Lake makes a good turnaround point.

Nearest Lodgings: Any of the lodgings in this section, or any in *Section 4, Columbia Gorge*.

BIRD CREEK MEADOWS LOOP
Waterfalls, meadows, glacier, canyon overlook—it's all here!

Map:	"Yakama Nation Mt. Adams Recreational Area," Yakama Nation Department of Natural Resources Forest Development Program; US Forest Service "Mt. Adams Wilderness"
Distance:	5.8 mile loop
Elevation Gain:	900´
Estimated Time:	4 hours

Stroll at a mostly moderate but steady incline from the banks of Bird Lake up through meadows ablaze with color, crossing streams, viewing waterfalls, and listening to dozens of different birds en route to one of the most breathtaking viewpoints in the Cascades: the Hellroaring Meadows Overlook. The wildflowers, the streams and waterfalls, or the birds alone would be reason enough to do this hike; the Overlook makes it a "must." From your perch at the foot of Adams' southeast flank, you gaze up 5800 feet toward its summit and straight down 1000 feet over a precipice to the Eden of Hellroaring Meadows below.

Meadow fans interested in less of a hike may want to take the shorter, out-and-back route to Bird Creek Meadows. Follow the driving directions below as far as Mirror Lake, then continue straight ahead to the Bird Creek Meadows parking lot and follow the trail west to the meadow and picnic area. This will result in about a 1.5-mile round-trip hike, but will miss Bird Lake, Bluff Lake, and Crooked Creek Falls, all highlights of the loop hike. The Trail of the Flowers loop and the Hellroaring Overlook, included in the full loop hike detailed below, can be added to extend the shorter Bird Creek Meadows hike.

Whichever version you choose, be prepared for a tapestry of amazing color; every wildflower of the Cascades seems to bloom at Bird Creek Meadows. Birdwatchers will also appreciate the variety of species who call this area home: flycatchers, wrens, jays, flickers, and more. Plan extra time and lots of stopping on this trail; it's a five-star experience not to be rushed.

Getting There
The only viable route to Bird Creek Meadows and the other Mt. Adams hikes on the Yakama Reservation (see Bench Lake Loop and Heart Lake under Other Hike Notes) is through Trout Lake. A road exists between Glenwood and Bird Creek Meadows, but it's a deeply rutted, nasty trek even with a high-clearance four-wheel drive vehicle—the locals wisely advise going through Trout Lake. Even the route described here can be difficult and slow; be sure to check with the ranger station as to road conditions before embarking.

From the gas station Y in Trout Lake, take the east fork (that's the right fork as you head north toward "downtown"). At 1.1 miles, stay right at the fork, following the MT. ADAMS RECREATION AREA/BIRD CREEK MEADOWS sign. At 1.4, stay right again at another fork.

At 4.3 miles, you pass into the Gifford Pinchot National Forest, and a sign informs you that you are on Road 82. At 4.4 miles, the road narrows and turns

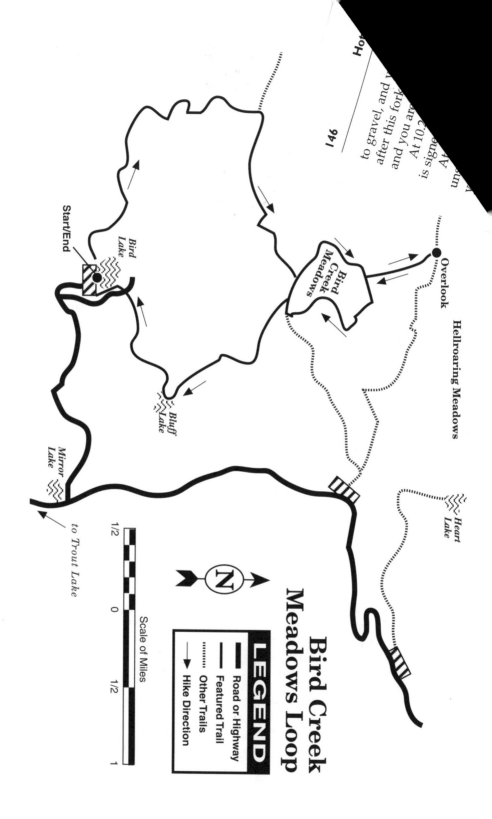

Bird Creek Meadows Loop

LEGEND

▬▬	Road or Highway
───	Featured Trail
·········	Other Trails
→	Hike Direction

Scale of Miles

1/2   0   1/2   1

Start/End

Bird Lake

Bluff Lake

Mirror Lake

to Trout Lake

Bird Creek Meadows

Overlook

Hellroaring Meadows

Heart Lake

ou come to a 3-way fork. Take the middle option. Immediately
, signs confirm you are still on your way to Bird Creek Meadows
still on Road 82.

miles, follow a sign left onto Road 8290. (This is the obvious route, and
d BIRD CREEK MEADOWS.)

10.7 miles, just after a sign warns "NARROW, ROUGH ROAD," you come to an
igned fork; stay left. (Indeed, if you thought the road had been rough so far,
ou're in for some really rugged surprises on the ensuing gravel one-lane.)

Pass through a gate at 11.7 miles, then another at 12.9. Immediately following
the second gate, you cross over Bird Creek. At 14.7 miles, you come to Mirror
Lake; you can see the lake on your left. Continue just past the lake to a large
intersection. A sign indicates that Bird Creek Meadows is straight ahead, and,
indeed, a parking area in that direction provides the shortest in-and-out route to
the meadow. For the loop detailed below, however, turn left, following the sign
toward Bird Lake.

Follow this hairy little road for 1.0 mile, passing the right-hand turn to Bird
Lake Forest Camp, and parking at the end of the road. You'll see some trailers
parked to your left; someone in the trailer area will take your $5.00 day use fee
and give you a permit/receipt. If no one is around, don't worry—you can pay
after your hike.

The Hike

Take a moment to enjoy Bird Lake from the parking area; you won't see it again
until the hike's end. Walk through the administrative (i.e. trailer) area to the left
of the parking area and stay left for the Bird Lake Trail 100 trailhead (the lake is
at your back as you face the trailhead). Two A-frame pit toilets are provided 100
feet up the trail.

The trail inclines gradually through stands of young trees; clearings filled
with lupine, beargrass, and mountain daisies give you a foretaste of the glorious
meadows to come. It's hard to imagine a better beginning to a hike than this
gradual ascent, with Mt. Adams looming ahead.

The trail winds back and forth across Crooked Creek, making bridged crossings at 0.25, 0.5, and 0.75 mile. The creek's banks are lined with moss and a profusion of wildflowers. At 1.1 miles, arrive at Crooked Creek Falls, a pretty waterfall that would be a destination by itself were there not so many delights ahead.

Cross through the first of many bench meadows just after the falls: lupine,
paintbrush, daisies, butterweed, meadow parsley, and more flowers greet you.
More creek crossings, more tapestries of color, then you arrive at the junction
with Round-the-Mountain Trail 9 at 1.4 miles; turn right.

As you wind your way north and uphill toward Mt. Adams, don't forget to
look behind you, to the south, to catch a view of Mt. Hood—a particularly fine
vista occurs in an open meadow at 2.0 miles.

At 2.1, turn to your left to take the Trail of the Flowers loop, a popular trail
around Bird Creek Meadows accessed by hikers from both directions. At 2.5,
stop on a rocky, flat viewpoint and turn again to look at Mt. Hood. On a clear
day, you can see the peak of Mt. Jefferson to its left. In front of both, the

Columbia Gorge yawns. On a crowded day, this might serve as a good picnic spot, an alternative to the crowds at the Bird Creek Meadows picnic area and the Hellroaring Meadows Overlook.

About 150 feet past this viewpoint is the left turn to the Overlook, signed HELLROARING VIEWPOINT. This out-and-back 0.9-mile round-trip spur is not to be missed. Climb a creekfed meadow, taking care to stay on the trail as it crosses rock slabs and, much of the season, snow patches.

Just before 3.0 miles, reach the top. Words nor photos can do justice to the view that awaits you at this Mother Of All Picnic Spots. You stand at the foot of the Klickitat and Mazama glaciers, the glory of Mt. Adams' southeast flank stretching up, your view of it unimpeded. In front of you is a rather sheer 1000-foot drop-off, with the lush basin of Hellroaring Meadows at the bottom. Find a rock, sit, and just try not to be awed.

When you've had your fill of Hellroaring views, retrace your steps downhill and rejoin Trail of the Flowers at 3.4 miles; turn left to complete the loop. Trail of the Flowers ends at the Bird Creek Meadows picnic area. Here, at 4.0 miles, you reach a T-junction with Round-the-Mountain Trail 9; the alternate Bird Creek Meadows parking area is to the left; you go right, following the sign toward Timberline Camp.

At 4.2 miles, turn left on Bluff Lake Trail 105. Drop down into a damp, mossy draw, heading south. Creeklet waterfalls cascade down the side of the draw to your right; stay to the left side of the draw to stay on the trail. Wind gently down the mountainside through the shadiest part of the hike. Another waterfall awaits you just after 4.6 miles, just before a stream fording.

Arrive at Bluff Lake just after 5.0 miles. Ignore Dry Creek Trail 90 where it intersects your trail from the east, on the north side of the lake. Stay to the right of the lake, where you'll find a couple of small, rocky beaches from which to enjoy this pretty, isolated lake.

Leaving the main lake, you will walk around a backwater lakelet adjacent to the main body of the lake; stay right at every opportunity, avoiding social trails that tend to draw you left. Climb a short hill back toward the north as you leave the lake.

The next half mile of the trail is subject to washouts; you may encounter a tricky stream fording or two.

Emerge at Bird Lake Campground at 5.6 miles. Go left along the road through the campground until it intersects with the road on which you drove in; turn right to find your car. Alternately, as you walk along the road, you will see social trails leading to your right down to the shore of Bird Lake. Follow these and work your way right along the lakeshore to the parking area where you left your car. Either way, it's about 5.8 miles total.

Nearest Lodgings: Any of the lodgings in this section, or any in *Section 4, Columbia Gorge.*

FALLS CREEK FALLS LOOP
Beautiful forest; outstanding waterfall.

Map:	Green Trails #397, "Wind River" (shows as 2 separate trails, not as a loop)
Distance:	4.7 mile loop (or 3.6 miles round-trip on lower trail)
Elevation Gain:	950′ (700′ on lower trail)
Estimated Time:	3 hours (or 2 hours, 15 minutes for out-and-back round-trip on lower trail)

This hike combines Lower Falls Creek Falls and Upper Falls Creek Falls trails to form a loop. The result is a deep-green walk along a creek through partial ancient-growth forest to a shimmering waterfall, then an uphill climb to an alternate return trail. Those who wish a less challenging hike can return via the easier Lower Falls Creek Falls trail on which they came in.

Getting There
From Highway 14 at the Columbia Gorge, take Road 30/Wind River Road north through Carson; follow the signs for Mount St. Helens. After 10.0 miles, you will pass through Stabler. After 15.0 miles, you will pass the national fish hatchery. At 15.2 miles, you come to a Y. Take the right fork, continuing on Wind River Road and following the sign toward Mount St. Helens. At 16.0 miles, turn right onto a gravel road signed FALLS CREEK TRAIL 152 & 152A. Continue following signs toward the trail, passing and ignoring right-forking roads at 0.5 and 1.0 mile. After 1.9 miles on this road, take the right fork, Road 057, to the Lower Falls Creek trailhead. Continue until the road dead ends at the trailhead and a parking loop at 2.4 miles.

To reach Falls Creek Falls trail from Trout Lake, it's best to drive south to White Salmon, then east to Carson, and come up as described. Backroads do connect more directly, but the condition of these roads is dubious at best.

The Hike
Begin on the trail signed LOWER FALLS CREEK TRAIL 152A. A soft, pine-needled path leads to almost immediate adjacency with the creek. The surrounding partial-old-growth forest is lush, with a complex understory of vine maple, salal, and a host of other plants growing from nurse logs and the thick, humus soil.

Walk at a gradual incline along the creek to a bridged crossing at 0.4 mile. Continue up the other side of the creek for the remainder of the first mile, the path undulating gently up and down, gaining altitude overall. After the first mile, the trail gets a bit steeper, dipping in and out of draws created by tributary creeks as it ascends.

Giant Douglas-firs tower over a forest that also includes healthy specimens of Western red cedar and Western hemlock.

At 1.7 miles, a craggy cliff on your left and the increasingly loud sound of rushing water on your right announce your approach to the falls. Pick your way down the rocky path to a falls overlook area at 1.8 miles. The multi-tiered cascade above you plunges down into a deep pool below you, then spills into Falls Creek, along which you have been walking.

Linger in the cedar-ringed grotto of the falls until ~
views, then retrace your steps up the trail, past the cr~
gentle decline. When the falls are about 0.5-mile behin~
unmarked singletrack trail ascending on your right. ~
path is the connector route to Upper Falls Creek Trail.

At the top of the rise, you reach the junction with the upper ~
the loop, turn left. (If you turned right, you could walk about a mile
nice camp/picnic sites along upper Falls Creek, but no exceptional views o~ ~
falls themselves. This is not part of the measured loop route.)

The dramatic plunge of Falls Creek Falls

turn route along Upper Falls Creek Trail is a pleasant, gentle downhill. 2 miles on this path (1.9 miles from the falls, 3.7 total miles on the route), ome back to Falls Creek. In another half-mile, you come to a fork. Take the fork to work your way back to the Lower Falls Creek Falls trailhead. Cross bridge over the creek, then reach a signed junction; follow the sign left toward LOWER FALLS CREEK TRAIL 152A.

Walk along at creek level for awhile; several toe-dipping opportunities. At 2.1 miles (2.8 from the falls, 4.6 total), intersect with the Lower Falls Creek Trail. No sign at this junction, but you can't miss the wide, flat trail when you T into it. Turn right and proceed the final 0.1 mile back to the parking lot.

Nearest Lodgings: Any in this section or *Section 4, Columbia Gorge*; also Eagles Cliff and Monfort's B&B in *Section 2, Mount St. Helens*

INDIAN HEAVEN LOOP
Pristine wilderness featuring lake after lake.

Map:	US Forest Service "Gifford Pinchot National Forest" or "Indian Heaven & Trapper Creek Wilderness"
Distance:	6.7 miles round trip
Elevation Gain:	1600′
Estimated Time:	4 hours

This is a sample of the best of Indian Heaven Wilderness. Three connecting trails form a scenic loop beginning and ending at Cultus Creek Campground. En route, you pass several lakes, circle a mountain, and descend through a meadow. Don't be surprised to spot wildlife (or evidence thereof); my trip included deer tracks, bear scat, a timid snake, a friendly frog, and at least a dozen species of birds. The route is well-maintained, and the scenery is varied, with many opportunities to pause and reflect on the beauty of a few of this 20,400-acre wilderness' 175 lakes.

If you enjoy this trail, see also East Crater, above, another featured trail within the Indian Heaven Wilderness.

Getting There
From Trout Lake, follow Highway 141 west. (If you're coming into Trout Lake from the south, you'll take the left fork at the gas station Y.) Pass the ranger station on the left side of the highway 0.9 mile past the Y; reset your odometer. Proceed 7.0 miles past the ranger station on this road, passing the signed turnoffs for Ice Cave and Natural Bridges (see above). (Note that 4.5 miles past the ranger station, Highway 141 becomes Forest Service Road 24.)

At 7.0 miles, reach a signed junction. Road 60 continues straight ahead; turn right to continue on gravel Road 24. A sign informs you that Cultus Campground, your destination, is 9 miles away, which is pretty accurate. Pass the first CULTUS CREEK CAMPGROUND sign without turning; turn left at the sign INDIAN HEAVEN TRAIL 33. (If you were to continue a very short distance on the main road, you would come to the trailhead at which you will exit upon finishing your loop. You will then walk back to your vehicle via the route you are now driving into the campground.)

Enter the campground. Bear right at the information signboard. Wind around through the campground about a quarter mile, until you find the signed INDIAN HEAVEN TRAIL 33 PARKING AREA. Turn right, around the pit toilet, to this parking area; if full, you may park on the road across from the toilet, just don't park in or block any campsites.

The Hike

This trail is part of the Indian Heaven Wilderness; fill out a permit at the trailhead. It is open to hikers, pets on leashes, and stock when surfaces are dry.

Begin on an attractive, medium-wide trail with a soft duff surface. You will cross your first stream within a few hundred feet, after which you begin ascending through a mixed coniferous forest. Vanilla leaf, beargrass, and huckleberry plants crowd the understory.

Ascend steadily for the first two miles, gaining about 1300 feet. After the first mile, watch for stunning views of Mt. Adams to your left. To its left (north) is Mt. Rainier. The jagged, snow-kissed peaks of Goat Rocks Wilderness fall between the two.

View of Mt. Adams from Indian Heaven Loop

Lupine flank the trail as you near Cultus Lake; tall, green stalks of hellebore let you know you're nearing water. Just after 2.1 miles, you arrive at the lake. Social paths lead down to its marshy margins, and square-topped Lemei Rock looms a mile beyond its far shore, to the southeast.

Continuing past Cultus Lake, you reach a signed junction with Lemei Trail 34 just past 2.3 miles. Lemei Trail goes to the left; you continue straight ahead. The trail begins a descent.

At 2.7 miles, Lemei Lake Trail 179 intersects on the left. Again, stay right. (Don't be confused by the sign telling you that a left turn will take you to the Pacific Crest Trail in 1.5 miles. This is true, but our PCT junction is straight ahead, via Trail 33.)

Continue descending; Clear Lake appears on your left at about 2.8 miles. Little trails lead to picnic/campsites along the lake shore. This is the optimum stop-and-have-lunch spot on the loop, in terms of both timing and scenery.

Trail 33 reaches a T-junction with the PCT just after 3.0 miles; straight ahead, through the trees, is Deer Lake. Turn right.

Follow the PCT north, contouring around the west side of Bird Mountain. Small, marshy lakes lie downhill to your left as the bulk of Bird Mountain rises to your right.

At 4.0 miles, Placid Lake Trail 29 intersects on the left. At 4.8, arrive at a four-way junction. Wood Lake Trail intersects on the left (a pleasant out-and-back excursion that adds a total of a mile to your hike) and Cultus Creek Trail 108 intersects on the right; PCT continues straight ahead. Turn right on Cultus Creek Trail, following the sign uphill toward Cultus Creek Campground.

Just before 5.0 miles, watch for a little, overgrown spur trail intersecting on the left. Take a moment to poke through the grasses and branches; within 30 feet, your reward is a breathtaking view of Mt. Adams.

After the spur, the main trail begins its descent. Adams is visible much of the way, as is Rainier. Sawtooth is the bare, rocky mountain in the near distance, directly north (appearing to the right of Mt. Rainier). The descent is steep in places, and the terrain is much more open, consisting of meadows dotted with small conifers and scattered deciduous trees.

At 6.6 miles, you emerge at the Cultus Creek trailhead. Turn right on the road to find your way back to the Indian Heaven trailhead, following the route you drove when you originally entered the campground. The complete loop is 6.7 miles.

Nearest Lodgings: Any of the lodgings in this section; the "South Side" lodgings from *Section 2, Mount St. Helens*; any of the lodgings from *Section 4, Columbia Gorge.*

DIVIDE CAMP
In-your-face look at Mt. Adams.

Map:	Green Trails #334 & #366, "Blue Lake" & "Mt. Adams West;" US Forest Service "Gifford Pinchot National Forest" or "Mt. Adams Wilderness"
Distance:	5.6 miles round trip
Elevation Gain:	1300´
Estimated Time:	3 hours, 30 minutes

High-altitude payoffs await you for fairly modest efforts on this hike. Expect a pretty steady, viewless uphill for the first 2.0 miles, then big rewards as the massive northwest face of Mt. Adams draws you like a piper across meadows and up to your final destination, an intersection with the Pacific Crest Trail/Round-the-Mountain trail.

Getting There
Follow directions to Takhlakh Lake, above. From Road 2329, instead of turning right into Takhlakh Campground, continue on 2329 past Takh Takh Meadow and up a hill. After a total of 3.4 miles on Road 2329, you will see a parking area on your right, signed DIVIDE CAMP TRAIL 112. This area, immediately adjacent to the road, has room for about a dozen cars. On the opposite side of this parking area, you will see two dirt roads. Walk (or, if surfaces are not too wet or rutted, drive) down the left-hand road another 0.1 mile to a signed trailhead. Parking is available for another 6 or 8 cars here.

Divide Camp Trail leads to breathtaking views of Mt. Adams

The Hike

Issue yourself a permit at the signed trailhead; this trail is part of the Mt. Adams Wilderness. It is open to hikers, leashed dogs, and stock when the surfaces are dry.

Enter a young forest, where mosses and lichens dominate an otherwise largely open understory. The path is wide and needle carpeted.

The hike begins flat, but doesn't stay that way for long. After about 0.3 mile, begin an ascent that will continue for the next 2.5 miles. The grade is sometimes moderate, sometimes gentle, and sometimes pretty steep, but it never lets up.

From the 0.6-mile point, you begin to hear Adams Creek to your left. This ebullient creek pours directly from Adams Glacier, and will be your more-or-less constant companion to the top.

As you gain altitude, the understory changes, becoming crowded with lupine and huckleberries. A few meadowed clearings let the sun through, but the views you seek remain hidden until nearly 2.0 miles. When you finally see it, baby, you *see* it. And it's *big*. Rising between tall trees and over the meadow in front of you, Mt. Adams' bulk pulls you like a siren's song for the remaining 0.8 mile.

At 2.1 miles, you can almost miss the narrow, often overgrown path to your right. This path leads 0.3 miles to Divide Camp, a sheltered, idyllic little site with its own spring and campsites, but no views. Unless you're seeking a spot for an elaborate picnic, it's a side trip not worth taking for the dayhiker.

Just beyond the Divide Camp junction, pass a helicopter landing site on your left. Continue through this open meadow, resplendent with lupine, mountain daisy, meadow parsley, hellebore, and paintbrush; late in the season, the deep indigo mountain bog gentian dominates.

Your best look at milky-white Adams Creek occurs at 2.6 miles, when the trail is immediately adjacent to the creek.

At 2.8 miles, Divide Camp Trail ends at its junction with Pacific Crest Trail/Round-the-Mountain Trail. Standing at the foot of Adams Glacier, you are just over 3.0 linear miles from Mt. Adams' summit; the mountain's broad northwest face fills your field of vision. As a bonus, turn 180° for an unimpeded view of the King of the Cascades, Mt. Rainier, directly to the north. Restless souls can wander left or right on the PCT, but the views don't get much better than right here at the junction. Enjoy them before retracing your steps back down the mountain.

Nearest Lodgings: Any of the lodgings in this section, or St. Helens Manorhouse or Eagles Cliff Resort, *Section 2, Mount St. Helens.*

OTHER HIKE NOTES
These hikes not personally reviewed or not as highly recommended as the above hikes.

Round-the-Mountain
This misnamed trail doesn't circumscribe the mountain at all, but stretches along its west and south flanks from the Pacific Crest Trail along the west side of the mountain to a south terminus at the Bird Creek Meadows access parking lot on the Yakama Indian Reservation. Unlike Mt. Rainier's Wonderland Trail, Mount St. Helens' Loowit Trail, and Mt. Hood's Timberline Trail, no maintained trail circles Mt. Adams.

Bench Lake Loop and Heart Lake (Yakama nation area)
While visiting the Yakama Nation Mt. Adams Recreation area (see *Bird Creek Meadows Loop*, above), you may also choose to hike these other short, developed trails. Follow the directions to Bird Creek Meadows as far as the junction just past Mirror Lake. Instead of turning left toward Bird Lake, continue straight. Pass the Bird Creek Meadows parking area and, after about 2 miles from Mirror Lake, you'll see the Heart Lake trailhead on the left. This is a short, fairly flat 1.5-mile round trip into a small lake in the Hellroaring Meadows basin. Continuing along the road past the Heart Lake trailhead another half mile, you come to a loop road around Bench Lake. The Bench Lake Trail is a 3.25-mile loop with moderate elevation changes. One trailhead is on the north side of the lake across from the boat launch, and the other is on the east end of the lake.

Lewis River Falls
The Lewis River Falls trail, detailed in *Section 2*, "Mount St. Helens," is also within daytrip distance of the Mt. Adams area and the lodgings listed in this section. Take Road 23 north out of Trout Lake toward Randle for 19 miles to its junction with Road 90. Turn left on Road 90, and follow it to the Lower Falls Campground and the trailhead as described in *Section 2*.

Ice Caves
These caves are not a hike, but they are interesting to see while you're out and about with your hiking boots on. See directions to East Crater or Natural Bridges; the turnoff is 5.5 miles past the ranger station, and the parking area is 0.25 mile down the road from the turnoff. Drop down a staircase to see the stalagmites and stalactites of ice in caves that were once an ice source for the community of Hood River. Bring warm clothes, a flashlight, sturdy shoes, a hard hat, and a flash camera. Of the caves' 650 feet of passages, the most accessible part is the 120-foot section that slopes southeastward from the ladder. The floor can be wet, icy, and extremely slippery. Use caution and check with the Trout Lake Ranger District before exploring the caves.

	THE FARM B&B	FLYING L RANCH	LLAMA RANCH B&B	SERENITY'S
PRICE (1997 SUMMER RATES, PRE-TAX, 2 PERSON)	$70–$80	Rooms $80–$110; Cabins $110–$140	$79–$99	$72–$125
EXTRA PERSON	$10	$10–$15	$10	included
PAYMENT METHODS	Checks, Cash	VISA, MC, AmEx, Checks, Cash	VISA, MC, Disc, Checks, Cash	VISA, MC, AmEx, Checks, Cash
# OF UNITS	2	10 rooms; 3 cabins	7	4
PRIVATE BATH	No	Yes	Yes, 2 rooms; No, 5 rooms	Yes
BREAKFAST INCLUDED	Yes	Yes	Yes	No
COOKING FACILITIES	No	Yes	Yes	Yes, kitchenettes
POOL	No	No	No	No
HOT TUB	No	Yes	No	No; jetted bathtubs in 3
CHILDREN	By arrangement	OK	OK	OK
PETS	No	No	OK	No
HANDICAPPED ACCESSIBLE	No	Yes	No	Yes

Table 6. Lodgings in the Mt. Adams vicinity

Canadian dogwood, a common trailside plant

Section 4—
Columbia Gorge

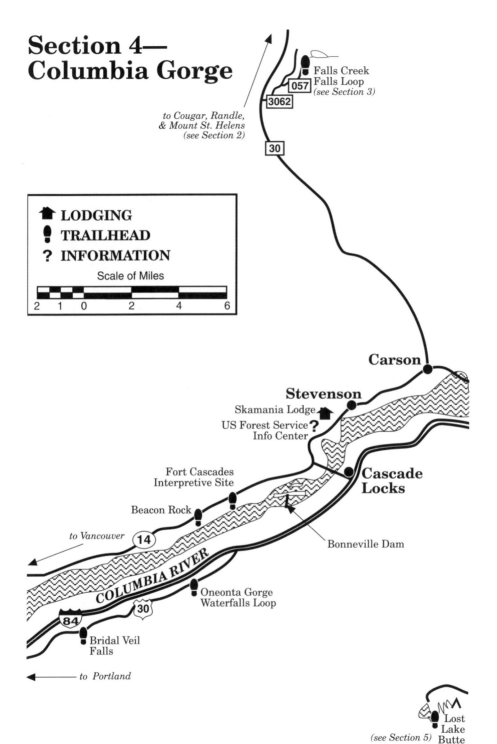

Falls Creek
Falls Loop
(see Section 3)

057

3062

*to Cougar, Randle,
& Mount St. Helens
(see Section 2)*

30

🏠 **LODGING**

🚶 **TRAILHEAD**

? **INFORMATION**

Scale of Miles

2 1 0 2 4 6

Carson

Stevenson

Skamania Lodge

US Forest Service ?
Info Center

Fort Cascades
Interpretive Site

**Cascade
Locks**

Beacon Rock

to Vancouver (14)

Bonneville Dam

COLUMBIA RIVER

Oneonta Gorge
Waterfalls Loop

(84) (30)

Bridal Veil
Falls

to Portland

Lost
Lake
(see Section 5) Butte

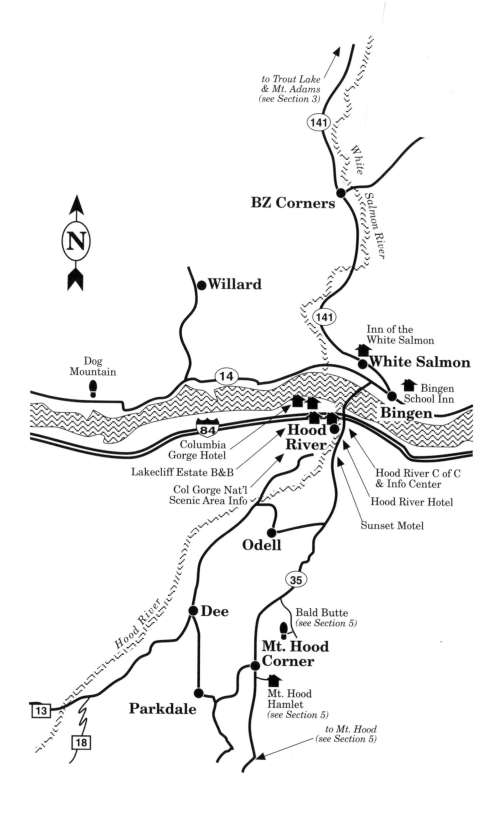

N

to Trout Lake
& Mt. Adams
(see Section 3)

141

BZ Corners

White Salmon River

Willard

141

Dog
Mountain

Inn of the
White Salmon

14

White Salmon

Bingen
School Inn

84

**Hood
River**

Bingen

Columbia
Gorge Hotel

Hood River C of C
& Info Center

Lakecliff Estate B&B

Hood River Hotel

Col Gorge Nat'l
Scenic Area Info

Sunset Motel

Odell

35

Hood River

Bald Butte
(see Section 5)

Dee

**Mt. Hood
Corner**

Mt. Hood
Hamlet
(see Section 5)

13

Parkdale

to Mt. Hood
(see Section 5)

18

Columbia Gorge

OVERVIEW

The Columbia Gorge, where the mighty Columbia River cuts through the ridge of the Cascade Mountains and forms part of the border between Washington and Oregon states, has been designated a National Scenic Area, but you don't need the US Government to tell you that. The area is rich in scenic beauty—towering cliffs, plummeting waterfalls, the majesty of the Columbia River.

Since the Columbia Gorge lies at a lower elevation than the rest of the central Cascades, many of its trails are accessible year-round, or at least much longer than the nearby mountain trails of St. Helens, Adams, and Hood. While those trails are still under a thick blanket of snow, early season hikers are barreling up the side of Dog Mountain to see the wildflowers.

Non-hikers will find plenty to do in the Columbia Gorge, too: a scenic railroad ride, a sternwheeler trip on the river, a trip through the Bonneville Dam visitor center. This well-developed tourist corridor also has an assortment of museums, galleries, and shopping venues.

For some, the Columbia Gorge means only one thing: world-class windsurfing. Strong winds funnel through the canyon, sucked by the atmospheric variation between the cool, wet, west side of the Cascades and the warmer, dry east side. As the only low-elevation route through the Cascades, the Gorge is a magnet for wind and for windsurfers, who enjoy the waves created by the west-flowing Columbia and the east-flowing wind. Whether you join in or just watch, windsurfing is a fun part of the local color in the Gorge.

The lodgings and the hikes featured in this section are reached via the highways flanking the Columbia River: swift and efficient Interstate 84 on the south (Oregon) side and scenic Highway 14 on the north (Washington) side. Also on the Oregon side, Highway 30, the historic Columbia River Highway, parallels Interstate 84 along part of its route. This gem of a road is also known as The Waterfall Highway, as it provides access to several exceptional falls.

As a major east-west traffic corridor, the Columbia Gorge is particularly well-endowed with lodgings and restaurants. On the Washington side, you have Skamania Lodge, a first-class conference center and self-contained mountain retreat; Inn of the White Salmon, a gracious European-style hotel with a fabulous breakfast; and the Bingen School Inn, a funky, casual, hostel-type budget lodging. On the Oregon side, I have concentrated on lodgings in Hood River, a growing community with a well-developed sense of serving tourists. The small sampling of Hood River lodgings featured includes two distinctive historic hotels (Columbia Gorge Hotel and Hood River Hotel), a noteworthy B&B (Lakecliff Estate), and a standard, reliable motel (Sunset Motel).

With over 70 different waterfalls in all, the Columbia Gorge is particularly rich in waterfall hikes, as the many streams and creeks make their final plunge to the Columbia River. These hikes are especially rewarding in late spring, when runoff is high and the falls are at their mightiest. Two waterfall hikes, including one with three separate falls, are featured in this section.

The Gorge presents a different ecosystem than that of the mountain hikes. Poison oak and ticks can be a problem here; learn to recognize both. Rattlesnakes may also be present, particularly on Dog Mountain.

Columbia River Gorge National Scenic Area trails, including Dog Mountain, Oneonta Gorge Waterfall Loop, and the other waterfall trails along the historic Columbia River Highway, allow dogs on leashes. Columbia River Gorge National Scenic Area participates in the Trail Park Pass system; vehicles parked at these trailheads must display a pass. See *Trail Park Pass System*, in the *Introduction*.

The Beacon Rock and Bridal Veil Falls trails are under the jurisdiction of the Washington and Oregon state park systems, respectively, and the Fort Cascades Interpretive Trail is maintained by the US Army Corps of Engineers. At this time, no fees or permits are required for these trails.

The hikes and restaurants listed in this section can be readily accessed from the lodgings in *Section 3*, "Mt. Adams," and some of the lodgings in *Section 5*, "Mt. Hood," and even some of the lodgings in *Section 2*, "Mount St. Helens." Likewise, the lodgings in this section are close to many of the dayhikes in the adjoining sections.

LODGINGS
In Alphabetical Order

BINGEN SCHOOL INN
P.O. Box 155 • Humboldt & Cedar Streets • Bingen, WA 98605
(509) 493-3363
www.gorge.net/lodging/cgoc • e-mail cgoc@gorge.net

A snobby guidebook might not include the Bingen School Inn, but I can't resist its funky, youthful charm. Originally an elementary school built by the CCC in 1938, the long-abandoned school was purchased by John Newman in 1988 and renovated into a casual inn and hostel for the active crowd.

BINGEN SCHOOL INN
Budget, hostel-style lodging

Three large, high-ceilinged hostel rooms sleep 12 to 18 in bunkbeds. Rent a 12-bed room for $100 a night, an 18-bed room for $150, or an individual bunk for $11. Partitions provide a modicum of privacy. Linens are available for an additional $3, or bring your own sleeping bag.

The old school also offers six private rooms, each with 2 queen beds (linens provided), a small fridge, and room for a couple more bunkbeds, for a total capacity of up to 8 people. Rates are $29 for two, or $40 for four. John and his wife, Patti, have left the school's chalkboards in place for atmosphere and amusement.

Many of the school's other fixtures are still in place as well—you may find yourself flashing back to your youth as you stroll the hallways en route to the shared European-style toilet and shower facilities. Bring a lock, and you may secure your valuables in one of the hallway lockers. Unsecured hallway storage is available for outdoor recreation equipment.

A lounge area on the lower level has cable TV, a kitchen, and a coin laundry. (Kitchen may not be available to guests during July and August, when food service may be offered. Inexpensive meals are available for purchase at these times. A microwave is provided for guest use at all times.) The adjacent gymnasium retains a basketball/volleyball court and stage; a weight room and rock-climbing wall has been added. Sports equipment, including windsurfing boards, mountain bikes, and fishing gear, is available for rent; outdoor recreation tips and advice are free.

Getting There
You'll find the Bingen School Inn one block north of Highway 14 as it passes through Bingen. Turn north on Cedar, and proceed uphill to the corner of Humboldt; the old school is on your right.

Hikes and Walks Nearby: Anything in this section; most hikes in *Section 3,* "Mt. Adams;" Lost Lake Butte and Bald Butte in *Section 5,* "Mt. Hood."

COLUMBIA GORGE HOTEL
4000 Westcliff Drive • Hood River, OR 97031-9970
(800) 345-1921 • (541) 386-5566
www.gorge.net/lodging/cghotel • e-mail cghotel@gorge.net

From the carved-apple rose that greets you in your room to the incongruous lobby cat to the eye-popping four-course breakfast, the Columbia Gorge Hotel is a Pacific Northwest original. About an hour east of Portland, the stately, pale yellow Mediterranean structure rises majestically on the north side of the road between the highway and the mighty Columbia River.

COLUMBIA GORGE HOTEL

Elegant old-world styling and a breakfast fit for royalty

The hotel was built by lumber baron Simon Benson in 1921, serving as a highly fashionable upper-class retreat from its breathtaking location over Wah-Gwin-Gwin falls. With the Depression, the grand old dame fell into disuse, then disrepair, eventually serving as a rest home until its rescue in the late 1970s.

Hospitality industry veterans Boyd and Halla Graves have owned and operated the historic hotel since 1978. Their uncompromising dedication to old-world elegance is everywhere, from the manicured formal gardens to the Victorian/French Renaissance furnishings. They maintain a property designed to be a respite from the world, a place of relaxation and romance. You'll find no hot tub at the Columbia Gorge Hotel, no pool or exercise room. Those who visit the Gorge will find ample diversion by day, whether hiking, windsurfing, or golfing. The Columbia Gorge Hotel concentrates its efforts on the lodging and dining experience—the guests' oasis at day's end.

As with many historic hotels, the guest rooms at the Columbia Gorge are not large, but each has a walk-in closet (complete with plush terry robes), full bath with tub, and gilt-edged decor befitting a grand, historic hotel. The bath is stocked with plenty of thick, oversized towels, European soaps, and cotton balls, along with the expected amenities.

Rates for two persons range from $150 for a Garden View queen or double on a weeknight to $365 for a Riverside Family Room on a weekend, with extra persons $30 (including breakfast) apiece. Each room at the hotel is unique: some have garden views, some river or waterfall views; some have fireplaces; some are two-bedroom units. Children under 12 are not allowed, but well-mannered pets are cheerfully accommodated.

Perhaps the most memorable aspect of staying at the Columbia Gorge Hotel is "The World Famous Farm Breakfast," a four-course extravaganza served with panache in the elegant dining room overlooking the Columbia River. Don't plan to rush through it—a properly relaxed sitting takes about 90 minutes. Schedule your hiking for late in the morning, and come with an appetite for life's good things—and plenty of them. (For details, see *Dining,* below.) The breakfast is included with the price of your room, but you'll want to leave a little something extra for the presenters, whose job goes beyond waiting tables.

The deluxe Columbia Gorge Hotel

Getting There
Take Interstate 84 to Exit 62, at the far west end of Hood River. Go north, toward the Columbia River. At the T, turn left. The Columbia Gorge Hotel is the grand, yellow, Mediterranean-style edifice just ahead; turn right into its driveway.

Hikes and Walks Nearby: Anything in this section; most hikes in *Section 3,* "Mt. Adams," and *Section 5,* "Mt. Hood."

HOOD RIVER HOTEL
102 Oak Ave. • Hood River, OR 97031
(800) 386-1859 • (541) 386-1900
www.gorge.net/business/hrhotel • e-mail hrhotel@gorge.net
How did the unassuming little burg of Hood River get lucky enough to fall heir to two of the finest restored old hotels in the Northwest?

The fact is that today's Hood River Hotel has nothing to do with luck. Just ask Jacquie Brown-Barone and her husband, Pasquale Barone. This young Canadian couple's success with the Hood River Hotel is the product of years of hard work, and more than a little vision and tenacity.

The building that houses the Hood River Hotel was built in 1910. Formerly known as the Mt. Hood Hotel (and listed as such with the National Registry of Historic Places), the name was changed to clarify its location.

Before Jacquie and Pasquale purchased it in 1989, the building had fallen victim to neglect and had, in fact, stood vacant for years. The

> **HOOD RIVER HOTEL**
>
> Lovingly restored grand hotel in downtown Hood River

new owners' care and skill did more than restore the property to its former glory. As a before-and-after photo album in the lobby shows, the Barones' remodeling was extensive, opening up spaces formerly closed, enclosing ductwork, forging bathrooms from closets. Each of the 41 units now has a private bath (nearly half with tubs). Nine of the units are multi-room suites with full kitchens, including stove, oven, refrigerator, microwave, coffee maker, and all utensils.

While the hotel still bears the quirks of its age—slanting floors here and there, steam heat throughout—the remodel has been a class act, preserving the best of the old while adding many modern touches. Woodwork has been lovingly restored and embellished with millwork of local craftsmen; art glass produced by local artisans has been added. Tile, marble, slate, and brick are used throughout. No two rooms are alike, and the furnishings vary as well. Armoires are used extensively to compensate for lack of closets. Beds are a beautiful assortment of 4-poster, sleigh, canopy, and other period pieces.

The hotel encompasses four stories, and includes an elevator. The top 26 rooms offer air-conditioning. Room rates range from $69 to $99; suites from $85 to $145. Seasonal discounts available November–March. Kids under 10 stay free, and pets are allowed ($15 fee charged). Guests receive a $3.95 voucher for use at the hotel restaurant (see *Pasquale's* under *Dining,* below); this purchases a continental breakfast or can be applied to any breakfast entrée. Use of an on-premises exercise facility (extensive selection of weight and aerobic machines, spa tub, and sauna) is included.

Hood River Hotel's restored lobby

Getting There
From I-84, take Exit 63. Come into downtown Hood River. Turn left onto Oak Avenue; proceed one block to the hotel.

Hikes and Walks Nearby: Anything in this section; most hikes in *Section 3*, "Mt. Adams," and *Section 5*, "Mt. Hood."

INN OF THE WHITE SALMON
P.O. Box 1549 • 172 West Jewett • White Salmon, WA 98672
(800) 972-5226 • (509) 493-2335
www.gorge.net/lodging/iws/ • email innkeeper@gorge.net
   A beautiful brick hotel that has housed travelers since 1937, Inn of the White Salmon is a delightful lodging experience. It's off the main highway, yet conveniently located for not only all the hikes in this section, but everything in *Section 3*, "Mt. Adams" as well. Owners Janet and Roger Holen, who purchased the property in 1990, are active community members with a good sense of local goings-on. They, and their friendly, competent staff, go out of their way to ensure your stay is comfortable.

> **INN OF THE WHITE SALMON**
> Old World elegance; fabulous breakfast

   Rooms, while somewhat dim and not overlarge, are comfortable, clean, and tastefully furnished with antiques. Each has a private bath, cable TV,

Delightful Inn of the White Salmon

telephone, steam heat, and window-unit air-conditioning. A basic room runs $89 for two ($75 single occupancy), and a two-room suite (larger and brighter than the standard rooms) runs $99–$115 for two. These prices include a fabulous breakfast. Extra persons age 13 and over sharing a suite are $20 each; children 12 and under are $1 per year of age.

Breakfasts at the inn are a memorable treat, served in an elegant, sunny dining room at individual tables reminiscent of a European café. The staff serves your choice of juice and hot beverage, then takes your entrée order—artichoke frittata, broccoli quiche, chile relleno, Italian frittata, Hungarian flauf, or diced ham and eggs. While your main course is being prepared, serve yourself from a sumptuous buffet of fresh fruits and over twenty pastries, tarts, cakes, and rolls. You'll want to linger over this special meal.

The inn's common areas are works of art. You'll feel as though you've stepped back in time as you walk down halls richly decorated with brocades and gilt-framed antique photos and painting reproductions. A comfortable sitting room is exquisitely furnished, and supplied with games, reading material, and helpful binders of Things To Do, Places To Eat, and Thank You Notes from previous guests. Outside, the wildflower gardens are lovely to walk through or to look at as you relax in the hot tub. Beer, wine, and soft drinks are available for purchase; a menu is provided in your room.

Getting There

From Highway 14 at Bingen, go north on Highway 141, following signs to WHITE SALMON, which is just up the hill. Drive through town on the sleepy little two-lane highway, and watch for the attractive brick inn on the right.

Hikes and Walks Nearby: Anything in this section; most hikes in *Section 3,* "Mt. Adams;" Lost Lake Butte and Bald Butte in *Section 5,* "Mt. Hood."

LAKECLIFF ESTATE B&B
P.O. Box 1220 • Westcliff Drive • Hood River, OR 97031
(541) 386-7000

Situated atop a 175-foot cliff overlooking Columbia River Gorge is a very special B&B. The property now known as Lakecliff Estate was designed by prominent turn-of-the-century architect Albert Doyle, whose credits include Multnomah Falls Lodge, Portland's Public Library, and the Benson Hotel. One of very few private residences he designed, this stately summer home was built in 1908 and is listed in the National Register of Historic Places.

LAKECLIFF ESTATE B&B
Historic home perched on a 175-foot cliff

Your hosts, owners Bruce and Judy Thesenga, offer 4 guest rooms, all upstairs. Wendy's Room and Lynn's Room each have a queen bed, stone fireplace, washbasin, and a view of the Columbia River and the woods. They share a bath, and rent for $85/night for two. Emily's Room and the Garden Room each have a private bath and rent for $100/night for two. The Garden Room has a queen bed, fireplace, and garden view. A rollaway bed is available for this large room; extra persons are $15 each. Emily's Room has a river view and twin beds that can be made into a king. All guest rooms and common areas of the home are attractively furnished with unique and tasteful items Judy has spent a lifetime collecting.

Spend your evening relaxing on the deck or in the downstairs rumpus room, where you'll find a big television with a video library, and a selection of games. Or peruse brochures from the literature rack, and plan your next day's adventures. In the morning, coffee is served upstairs beginning around 7 A.M. Then join Bruce, Judy, and your fellow guests for a full farm breakfast downstairs in the sunroom at 9 A.M.

Lakecliff Estate only operates as a B&B from Memorial Day to Labor Day, and this popular place fills up fast, so make your reservations well ahead, especially if you plan to visit over a weekend.

Getting There
From Interstate 84, take Exit 62 at the far west end of Hood River. Go north, toward the Columbia River. At the T, turn right on Westcliff. (This is the same exit you take to get to the Columbia Gorge Hotel, see above.) Turn left at the stone-and-timber fronted drive with the Lakecliff sign.

Hikes and Walks Nearby: Anything in this section; most hikes in *Section 3,* "Mt. Adams," and *Section 5,* "Mt. Hood."

SKAMANIA LODGE
P.O. Box 189 • 1131 Skamania Lodge Way • Stevenson, WA 98648
(800) 221-7117 • (888) SKAMANIA • (509) 427-7700

Hundred-year old timber. Montana slate. Andesite rock. Native American accents. Skamania Lodge is definitely a place of the Northwest—clean lines, warm wood, elegant simplicity. The conference center/resort was opened just a few years ago, in 1993, but its bold design and extensive use of antique and recycled materials give it a feeling of mass, history, and permanence.

SKAMANIA LODGE

First-class mountain lodge overlooking Columbia Gorge

The 195 rooms at Skamania Lodge are understated and well-appointed, decorated with original artwork and Pendleton fabrics. Televisions nestle unobtrusively in armoires. Small coffee makers with supplies of coffee, tea, cocoa, and cider mix are provided, as are complimentary *USA Today* newspapers in the morning. Other amenities include plush terry robes, hair dryers, honor bars, and air-conditioning. Get a room with a river view if you can—the sunrise over the Columbia is exquisite.

During peak season (mid-June through mid-October), rooms start at $135 for a Forest Guest Room, a comfortable room facing the forest with one king or two double beds. A River Guest Room is the same, but has a view of the river, for $170. A Fireplace Guest Room, at $210, is slightly larger, and includes a gas fireplace and a hideabed couch; each has a river view. A Family Guest Room (with separate bedroom and living room) or a Parlor Suite (1600 sq. ft. junior suite including Murphy bed) is $240. A VIP suite is also available for $350; it has a kitchen, dining room that seats 8, bath with jetted tub, and a Murphy bed.

Skamania Lodge

Outside your room, many more amenities await. It's hard to resist lounging in the massive, 3-story great room off the lobby, where stylish and comfortable chairs offer spots to sit, play cards, read the newspaper, or stare at the stone fireplace on one wall or the awe-inspiring view out the other. A fitness center includes a spa and swimming pool. The restaurant is excellent (see *Dining*, below). A permanent US Forest Service Information Center is located in the lobby—hikers can't beat *that* for convenience! Outside, you'll find tennis courts, an 18-hole golf course, and 4 miles of trails (see *Other Hike Notes*, near the end of this section).

Getting There

From Oregon, take Interstate 84 to the Cascade Locks/Bridge of the Gods exit. Take the Bridge of the Gods across the Columbia River (75¢ toll), then turn right (east) on Highway 14. Just before entering the town of Stevenson, turn left on Rock Creek Drive; the Columbia Gorge Interpretive Center and Skamania Lodge are up this road. Turn left into the drive leading up to the lodge.

From Vancouver, take Highway 14 east. From Seattle, take Interstate 5 to Interstate 205, which will in turn take you to Highway 14, bypassing Vancouver. From eastern Washington, you may take Highway 14 all the way, passing through Stevenson before you turn right on Rock Creek Drive.

Hikes and Walks Nearby: Anything in this section; Falls Creek Falls Loop and other hikes in *Section 3*, "Mt. Adams;" hikes in the South Approach and East Approach subsections of *Section 2*, "Mount St. Helens."

SUNSET MOTEL
2300 Cascade Ave. • Hood River, OR 97031
(541) 386-6027

When Lee and Norma Curtis opened their 14-unit motel in 1995, they decided to provide a clean place, as nearly allergen-free as possible. As a result, you can count on not only getting a non-smoking room at the Sunset Motel, you can rest assured that your room has *never* been smoked in. All rooms are non-smoking/no pets.

The result is a motel that is clean, tidy, and fresh, with nearly new decor and fixtures. All rooms have queen beds, TVs, telephones (free local calls) and full baths with tubs (except the handicapped-accessible unit, which has an extra-large shower). Many rooms have a view of Mt. Adams. A room with one queen bed rents for $55; a room with two queens is $65.

SUNSET MOTEL
Clean, smoke-free motel

Coffee, tea, and, sometimes, fresh fruit are available in the lobby, which also functions as an antique shop. The property also includes an RV park and a laundromat.

Sunset Motel is located on Cascade Avenue, near the west side of the town of Hood River. This newer section of town includes strip-mall shopping and fast-food restaurants, so it's not as "atmospheric" as downtown, but the location is convenient for freeway access and all basic shopping and services a traveler might need.

Getting There
Coming from the west on Interstate 84, take Exit 62; go southwest into Hood River. You will be on Cascade Avenue, which is also Highway 30. Watch for the motel on the north side of the street. Coming from the east you may take exit 63 to downtown. From downtown, proceed west on Oak or Cascade; these join just west of 13th Street. Stay on Cascade to the motel.

Hikes and Walks Nearby: Anything in this section; most hikes in *Section 3*, "Mt. Adams," and *Section 5*, "Mt. Hood."

ADDITIONAL LODGINGS

There are many other lodgings in the Columbia Gorge area: B&B's, resorts, motels, cabins, and other overnight accommodations. Contact the Hood River County Chamber of Commerce (including lodgings in Hood River and Cascade Locks) at (800) 366-3530 or (541) 386-2000; Skamania County Chamber of Commerce (including the Stevenson area) at (509) 427-8911; or the Mt. Adams Chamber of Commerce (including the White Salmon/Bingen area) at (509) 493-3630.

DINING
In Alphabetical Order

BIG CITY CHICKS
1302 - 13th Street • Hood River, OR 97031
(541) 387-3811
Billing itself as a purveyor of "Healthy Foods of the World," Big City Chicks does indeed bring a slice of the big city to the Columbia River Gorge. Located in the south part of Hood River in a big old house on 13th Street, Big City Chicks serves up a unique menu that draws inspiration from the Caribbean, South America, Asia, the Mediterranean, and the Pacific.

Entrées at Big City Chicks emphasize seafood, vegetables, and, of course, chicken (hence, the name). One lonely beef tenderloin graces the dinner menu as the sole nod to red-meat-eaters. Adventurous eaters fond of lighter flesh will love choosing from such wild-and-woolly creations as pistachio-crusted salmon (Cuban, $12.95), coconut curried chicken (Indonesian, $10.95), blackened tequila snapper (Mexican, $11.95), and herb-crusted chicken dijon (Mediterranean, $10.95). Vegetarians will sigh with relief at not one or two, but *eleven* veggie entrées, including gorgonzola-spinach ravioli with 3 sauces (Italian, $10.95), herbed polenta cakes with chile sauce (Peruvian, $9.95), and blackened tofu (Cajun, $9.95).

The accompaniments to each meal are every bit as groovy as the main course, and each entrée comes with diner's choice of salad: Mediterranean (leaf lettuce with tomatoes, olives, feta, and balsamic vinaigrette), Asian (greens with cucumbers, carrots, and ginger with sesame-soy dressing), or Caesar (a garlicky rendition with homemade croutons).

COLUMBIA GORGE HOTEL
4000 Westcliff Drive • Hood River, OR 97031-9970
(800) 345-0931 • (541) 387-5414
www.gorge.net/lodging/cghotel • e-mail cghotel@gorge.net

Guests at this classic hotel know about its "World Famous Farm Breakfast," a four-course extravaganza included in the price of their room. Non-guests can purchase the same feast for $22.95 per person. Reservations are suggested, and hours are 8 A.M.–11 A.M. Monday through Friday, 8 A.M.–Noon Saturday, and 8 A.M.–2 P.M. Sunday.

The parade of delicacies begins with a selection of seasonal and exotic fruits, artfully presented, along with a baked cinnamon apple and a miniature apple fritter. This is followed by a second course of old-fashioned oatmeal, served with berries, brown sugar, and cream. Next comes the egg and meat course, with three eggs prepared to your specifications, hash browns, and your choice of breakfast meat (bacon, smoked pork chop, apple-maple sausage) or fresh grilled trout. (See why the Columbia Gorge Hotel suggests allowing 90 minutes for breakfast?) While you are working your way through your perfectly poached eggs, your hostess will ask if you want honey on your biscuits. Say yes. This is where the server becomes a performer, drizzling the honey down onto your biscuits from high above your table in a ceremony designed to commemorate Wah-Gwin-Gwin, the waterfall behind the hotel. Hokey? A tad, but why not enjoy it? This fabulous breakfast, reviled by some snobby travel writers and uptight waist-watchers, is a delightful extravagance, and should be embraced as such. Finally, a tiny stack of buttermilk pancakes ends the meal. Cocktails and champagne are available for purchase.

The hotel serves a fine dinner as well. The menu is on the heavy side, emphasizing meat and fish, although a gorgonzola-walnut ravioli is available for vegetarians, and special requests are gracefully accommodated. The dungeness crab cakes, one of five appetizers, are a delicate, flavorful rendition. Other entrées include a rich honey-orange glazed duckling and broiled rack of Oregon lamb. All are presented with artfully-prepared accompaniments and the flair one would expect from a fine Continental restaurant. Expect to spend about $40 per person.

FIDEL'S
Highway 14 • Bingen, WA 98605
(509) 493-1017

When on the Washington side of the Gorge—or if you get a hankering for serious Mexican food—come to Fidel's. South-of-the-border standards and specialties are served up in a colorful, lively atmosphere that is a gathering place for Bingen and White Salmon residents and tourists alike. Come for a refreshing Margarita, and stay for lunch or dinner.

Hearty two-item combinations—your choice from six items and seven fillings—run $7.95 or $8.95. Specialties include machaca (shredded meat of your choice scrambled with eggs, veggies, and spices), $7.95; fish taco, $6.95; and a mountainous tostada suprema (taco salad with beans and meat in a deep-fried flour shell), $6.75. The vegetable casserole (steamed broccoli, cauliflower, and potatoes served over rice and topped with cheese sauce, marinated tomatoes, and onions), a tasty alternative to the usual fare, is just $4.95.

A children's menu, complete with fun mocktails, is also available. Good food, lively atmosphere, and fair prices all make Fidel's a hit.

PASQUALE'S
102 Oak Avenue • Hood River, OR 97031
(541) 386-1900

Adjacent to the Hood River Hotel on Oak Avenue in downtown Hood River, Pasquale's Ristorante offers fresh, carefully prepared northern Italian cuisine in an upscale but comfortable atmosphere. Dine inside or on the patio, watching the world go by on historic Oak Avenue.

Start your dinner at Pasquale's with an appetizer—the simplicity of a whole roasted head of garlic, buttery-soft and nutty, or a rich house pâté with Port wine and capers. Soups and salad dressings are made fresh on the premises. Whether you dine on pasta or choose a main course from their extensive selection of meat, fish, and poultry, the careful choice of ingredients and preparation shows. This restaurant knows its pancetta from its prosciutto. The vegetarian lasagna fresca, at $11.95, is indeed fresh, its layers of roasted eggplant, summer squash, porta-bellos, spinach, and bell peppers distinct between al denté pasta and just the right amount of mozzarella and ricotta. Topped with a slightly zippy marinara, this is not your standard veggie lasagna. The rack of New Zealand lamb, pre-pared in a flavorful rosemary-garlic sauce, is $17.95. It's melt-in-your-mouth ten-der and served complete with soup or salad, lightly steamed fresh vegetable, and roasted red potatoes. Other pastas range from $7.95 to $13.50, and main dishes from $9.95 to $17.95.

Pasquale's also serves breakfast and lunch, both of which are delightful and reasonably priced, with choices from standard (omelette, pancakes, Reuben, clubhouse) to exotic (eggs Florentine, chicken sausage and artichoke frittata, roasted veggie sandwich).

SAGE'S CAFÉ & COFFEE HOUSE
202 Cascade Street, Suite H • Hood River, OR 97031
(541) 386-9404

An outstanding lunch spot, this bright, high-ceilinged café is freshly decorat-ed in pale teal and rose tones, and located in a funky little mall that bears brows-ing. Former proprietors of Hood River's Riverview Deli, Sherry and Bill Bohn opened Sage's in 1997, with an inspired menu of deli sandwiches, espresso drinks, and salads.

Regular deli sandwiches are generous and a bargain at $4.25 ($2.25 for a half). Over a dozen specialty sandwiches include the Californian (hot chicken with melted cheddar, avocado, hot peppers, and all the trimmings, $5.15), the Fat Pig (sausage, bacon, egg, and cheddar on a muffin with tomatoes and sprouts, priced at a slim $3.25), and a dandy Tuna Melt ($4.50). Sage's also offers three vegetarian sandwiches—one fairly standard, one with hummus, and one with pesto cream cheese—and a freshly prepared veggie burrito.

Breakfasts are served all day at Sage's. Choices include the Riverview Sunrise Special (two scrambled eggs, fresh fruit, meat choice, and toast choice, $3.95), quiche of the day ($3.50), a breakfast burrito ($2.75), or one of five breakfast sandwiches.

Odds and ends at Sage's include green salad, pasta salad, fruit salad, muffins, cookies, pie, ice cream, and well-turned-out espresso drinks.

6TH STREET BISTRO & LOFT
P.O. Box 352 • 6th and Cascade • Hood River, OR 97031
(541) 386-5737

The brainchild of improbably named Maui Meyer, this pub and eatery combines the airiness and casual atmosphere of a California beachfront bar with the quality cuisine of a Continental bistro, all with a dash of Boston's "Cheers" atmosphere. The result is a nice mix of white-tablecloth elegance and no-dress-code friendliness.

The menu is a trendy mix of cultures, with appetizers alone spanning the globe: Thai chicken satay, quesadilla a la Parrilla, hummus with pita, baked French onion soup. Dinner entrées range in price from a teriyaki vegetable stir-fry at $6.95 to an aged T-bone steak with mushroom burgundy sauce at $14.95. Each is preceded by a yummy herbed loaf they call their "famous loft bread;" a dinner salad is $2.25 extra. Other choices include a perfectly spiced pad thai with chicken ($7.95) or shrimp ($9.95), also available without meat. A curried chicken takes on a Northwest flair, topped with Oregon pears and raisins, and served over seasoned rice, for $10.25, while that Northwest standard—salmon—is anything but typical, roasted with cumin and served with tomato-lime salsa for $11.25.

Lunchtime at 6th Street Bistro & Loft offers salads (grilled sesame chicken, Caesar, organic spinach with gorgonzola), sandwiches, and bounteous burgers, complete with fries, for $6.50 to $7.95.

SKAMANIA LODGE DINING ROOM
P.O. Box 189 • 1131 Skamania Lodge Way • Stevenson, WA 98648
(800) 221-7117 • (888) SKAMANIA • (509) 427-7700

Dine overlooking the sprawling lawn of this mountain lodge, with its artfully strewn boulders, and the Columbia Gorge yawning below. The dining room has a high, beamed ceiling, lots of glass, and the warmth of red-gold wood.

Lodge guests and visitors will appreciate the breakfasts and lunches offered—a wide selection of standard and more unusual fare.

Dinners are especially elegant at Skamania Lodge. Entrées have a decidedly Pacific Northwest flair, in keeping with the lodge itself. Salmon, venison, and sturgeon are specialties; excellent pastas, steaks, and vegetarian choices are also available, as well as chicken, duck, pork, and lamb dishes. Your meal is preceded by a basket of assorted breads and your choice of soup or a salad of velvety mixed greens, shredded carrots, and delicately crunchy, lightly curried pumpkin seed hearts. The extensive wine list includes many fine Washington and Oregon labels.

A dessert bar concludes the meal. Choose from among a dozen treats, from a humble cookie to a multi-layered torte, or sample a bit of each.

Prices and choices vary; both reflect a first-class dining experience.

WY'EAST
110 - 5th Street • Hood River, OR 97031
(541) 386-6181

This outrageous, everything-you-need wholefood grocer and deli is a must-stop for the health-conscious. Swing by the "juice & java" bar for a fresh-squeezed glass of your favorite fruit or vegetable juice or any espresso concoction. Browse the bulk food section, where hearty trail mixes are just one of many offerings. Choose some organic produce from the fresh section, or just grab some chips and a six-pack of microbrew. You can even get freshly-ground peanut butter at Wy'East; team it with local apiary honey on a slab of homemade bread, and you're set for lunch! Or let the deli folks make you up a sandwich for the road.

Other offerings include a health and beauty section (forget your vitamins? sunscreen? bug repellent? no problem!), magazines (national titles plus hip Northwest fare), dairy and beverage cooler, and a large selection of nutrient-dense trail-ready products such as PowerBars.

Wy'East has its own off-site bakery as well, so bagels, breads, and mysterious confections are at hand. Why buy a packaged PowerBar when a buck will get you a honey-sweet millet-oat puck made fresh by Wy'East? Some items are prepared vegan-conscious.

For the uninitiated, "Wy'East" is the Native American name for Mt. Hood. The business has been here since 1984, under its current ownership since 1994. The proprietor, Jamie Greenan, takes pride in being both a year-round full-service organic grocer to locals and a tourist-friendly store where everyone is welcome.

WALKS AND HIKES
Listed in approximate order of difficulty

FORT CASCADES INTERPRETIVE SITE
Pleasant historic walk near the Columbia River.

Map:	US Army Corps of Engineers map, available at trailhead or nearby Bonneville Dam visitor center
Distance:	1.1 mile loop
Elevation Gain:	negligible
Estimated Time:	45 minutes

Just over a mile west of Bonneville Dam, along the banks of the mighty Columbia River on the Washington side, sits an interpretive trail that tells the story of a little plot of ground with a rich history. The US Army built a fort here in 1850, which was later abandoned. The buildings on the site became the town of Cascades. Most traces of Cascades were destroyed in a flood in 1894, but some artifacts remain.

A peaceful, nearly level walk appropriate for all ages, this trail is both historically and aesthetically significant. It's a great leg-stretcher for anyone traveling along Highway 14. For more information, contact the Bonneville Dam visitor center at (541) 374-8820.

Getting There

On Highway 14, just over a mile west of Bonneville Dam, turn south on DAM ACCESS ROAD. Follow the signs for FORT CASCADES HISTORIC SITE to a parking lot, where you'll find portable toilets and room for about 15 cars.

The Walk

Begin at the interpretive kiosk just off the southwest end of the parking lot. Information placards explain this riverside site's relationship to the Lewis and Clark and Oregon trails, to Beacon Rock (see related trail, below), to the fishing and transportation industries, to those who have lived on this site, including Native Americans, early white settlers, and the US military. Brochures, available at the trailhead, further explain numbered interpretive sites along the trail.

Drop down to the bank of the Columbia, where you can look back to see Bonneville Dam. Love them or hate them, the dams of the Columbia River changed the face of the Pacific Northwest forever.

Continue straight ahead, ignoring a right turn at 0.3 mile (turning here, then right again in 0.1 mile, would result in a 0.7-mile loop). After a total of about 0.4 mile, you arrive at the old Cascades townsite. No buildings remain, but the

Indian petroglyph replica at Fort Cascades Interpretive Site

Corps of Engineers brochure explains what was here. Pass a replica of an Indian petroglyph (the original has been relocated to the Skamania County Courthouse, 6 miles east) and the site of a former hotel and stable before reaching a meadow, at which you will turn right. (An alternate path continues ahead into the meadow, looping back to add 0.3 mile to the total loop, but there's nothing to see.)

The return loop has a few more artifacts to view, including some blacksmith shop remnants, a piece of the Cascade Portage Railroad (narrow-gauge track with a small railcar), and the grave of one of Cascade's founding citizens.

Nearest Lodgings: Skamania Lodge; any lodging in this section.

BRIDAL VEIL FALLS
Short walk to a two-tiered waterfall.

Map:	None Needed; trail does not show on most maps; falls are indicated on Green Trails #428, "Bridal Veil"
Distance:	1.0 mile round trip
Elevation Loss:	approx. 400´
Estimated Time:	45 minutes

A short stroll down a ferny path to a full-throttle waterfall, this walk is appropriate for all ages, but folks with unstable footing or slick footwear might find the combination of loose gravel and moderately steep descent a bit treacherous.

Getting There
This is an easy hike to reach from the Portland or Hood River area. Take Exit 28 off Interstate 84 to the scenic alternate known as the Columbia River Highway. After traveling a quarter mile east, you come to an intersection: Columbia River Highway east, to Multnomah Falls, is straight ahead; Columbia River Highway west, to Bridal Veil Falls, is to your right. Turn right and proceed about a mile to the large Bridal Veil Falls State Park parking lot. Restrooms are provided at this trailhead.

The Walk
Proceed past the restrooms (at the east end of the parking lot), along a well-marked, extra-wide asphalt path. The path soon turns to gravel, and you begin descending into an area lined with vine maple, ivy, and ferns.

At 0.4 mile, cross a little footbridge, then continue descending to a second bridge just before 0.5 miles. After crossing the second bridge (over Bridal Veil Creek), ascend to the falls viewing platform and a satisfying look at two-tiered Bridal Veil Falls.

Nearest Lodgings: Skamania Lodge, Columbia Gorge Hotel, Lakecliff Estate, Sunset Motel, Hood River Hotel; any lodging in this section.

Bridal Veil Falls

BEACON ROCK

World's 2nd-highest monolith; great views.

Map:	None needed; Beacon Rock State Park shows on most highway, forest service, or recreation maps
Distance:	1.8 miles round-trip
Elevation Gain:	848'
Estimated Time:	1 hour

Thanks to Henry J. Biddle, folks like you and I can see what it's like to go where rock-climbers go: up the face of a sheer basalt monolith. Biddle owned this chunk of geology in 1915, and, with the help of friends, built a zigzagging trail with handrails up the side of it. His family later deeded it to the state as a park. The combination of natural stone surfaces and cantilevered boardwalks makes this climb fairly easy and safe for anyone without mobility impairment; children will love it. Those not wishing to climb the 15% grades can enjoy pleasant views from adjacent Beacon Rock State Park.

The cantilevered trail up Beacon Rock

At 848 feet high, Beacon Rock is the world's second tallest monolith, after Gibraltar. The trail is open during daylight hours, and leashed pets are OK.

Getting There
The parking lot for Beacon Rock is right on Washington's Highway 14 along the Columbia Gorge, 4.5 miles west of Bonneville Dam (7.0 miles west of Bridge of the Gods. You need not drive down the access road to Beacon Rock State Park, just park in the lot on the south side of the road. Restrooms are provided.

The Hike
You'll find the trailhead on the west side of the parking area. Follow the path 0.2 mile through a mossy, ivied glen shaded by a lush mixture of trees. Emerging from the trees, you'll pass through a gateway and start switchbacking up the west side of the rock.

About halfway up, the trail contours around to the east side of the rock, ascending steadily until it reaches the two viewpoint areas at the top. The vista, as expected, is grand: the sweep of the Columbia east and west, the wall of the Oregon side of the gorge, Bonneville Dam to the east. Railings make you feel safe and secure.

Nearest Lodgings: Skamania Lodge; any lodging in this section.

ONEONTA GORGE WATERFALLS LOOP

A walk-under falls, a triple waterfall, and a deep, scenic canyon.

Map:	Green Trails #428, "Bridal Veil"
Distance:	4.4 mile loop
Elevation Gain:	700´
Estimated Time:	3 hours

This rousing hiker-only climb (no bikes or horses) passes multiple waterfalls and a box canyon overlook, providing enough exercise for an active adult, yet enough visual interest to keep sturdy kids and bored teenagers going. While the hike can be undertaken as an out-and-back, turning at Ponytail Falls (1.2 miles round-trip), Oneonta Gorge overlook (about 2.3 miles round-trip), or Triple Falls (about 4.1 miles round-trip), the route described is a loop, including a 0.6-mile walk along the shoulder of the scenic Columbia River Highway to view the mouth of the Oneonta Gorge.

Don't let the trailhead crowds discourage you. This is a popular trail (particularly the first half of the loop), but not nearly as popular as the Disneyland

Triple Falls seen from the Oneonta Gorge Waterfalls Loop

atmosphere of the parking lot might lead you to believe. Because Horsetail Falls is clearly visible from the trailhead, most souls never leave the parking and picnic areas.

No restrooms are available at the trailhead; the nearest are a short drive east on the Columbia River Highway.

Getting There

From Interstate 84, take Exit 35, the Ainsworth State Park exit. Follow the scenic Columbia River Highway 1.3 miles west to large, well-marked parking lot at Horsetail Falls. A beautiful picnic area is situated across the road at the base of Horsetail Falls, making this an excellent trailhead for your non-hiking friends and family members.

The Hike

After appreciating the 176-foot plunge of Horsetail Falls, repair to the signed trailhead ("ONEONTA TRAIL JCT 1.3") at the south end of the picnic area. A wide, well-graded, crushed gravel path with stone retaining walls takes you on a switchbacking ascent steep enough to discourage some sandal-footed hikers. Within 200 yards, you can turn to see the Columbia River through the trees below.

At 0.2 mile, your access path connects with Trail 400. Follow the sign to the right, toward PONYTAIL FALLS, ONEONTA GORGE, and TRIPLE FALLS. Continue ascending until you reach Ponytail Falls at 0.6 miles. Ponytail is a walk-under waterfall; the path follows a deep cleft in the rock behind the falls. Many turn here and retrace their steps to the picnic area. Some of the best views and photo angles, however, are on the short, steep ascent just beyond the falls.

Predictably, the path deteriorates after Ponytail Falls, giving the hike a bit more of a wilderness character. After a brief ascent, it turns due west, remaining fairly level for a quarter mile as it hugs the hillside between the Horsetail Creek draw and that of Oneonta Creek. At about 0.9 mile, a marked scenic viewpoint on the right provides an overlook of the Columbia River Gorge.

The path bends left and, leaving the Columbia River behind, moves up a draw created by Oneonta Creek. At 1.1 miles, as the trail begins a switchbacking descent, note the little wooden sign for ONEONTA GORGE; this is an overlook point for the narrow-walled canyon, now below.

Descend and cross the bridge over Oneonta Creek and its gorge. In warm weather, you will see folks splashing their way up the gorge from an access point along the Columbia River Highway that you will pass toward the end of the hike.

Climb uphill from the bridge to a signed junction; you have hiked 1.3 miles. TRAIL 400 goes to the right; you will take that to complete your loop when you return from viewing Triple Falls. To see the falls, turn left on ONEONTA TRAIL 424.

After another three-quarters of a mile, the three graceful streams of Triple Falls can be seen. A 50-foot path forks off to your left, ending in a flat, sunny landing perfect for picnicking and enjoying the falls. Watch your footing, especially with small children—the drop-off is steep. The main path continues to the right along the shady canyon walls, affording more views of the falls, none better than that from the sunny landing, which makes a good turnaround point, at just over 2.0 miles.

Return to the junction of Trails 424 and 400, this time continuing straight on Trail 400.

After 0.2 mile on Trail 400, you come to a fork; the main path proceeds to your left, a slightly narrower path descends to the right. I recommend the right fork; it is a slightly longer loop that rejoins the main trail after 0.25 mile and several Columbia Gorge viewpoints. After a total of 0.75 mile on Trail 400 (3.5 miles from the beginning of the hike), turn right at a signed intersection, following Oneonta Trail 424 0.3 mile back to the scenic highway.

Turn right at the highway to return the 0.6 mile to your car. Please exercise caution; drivers on this historic Columbia River Highway are looking at the scenery, not you.

Halfway back to the Horsetail Falls parking lot, you will come to the Oneonta Gorge parking area. This is an access point for those wishing to walk up the creek into Oneonta Gorge, or simply play in the water at the mouth of the creek. Stop here to dip your toes, read the interpretive sign, or simply gaze up canyon to the site of your earlier crossing.

Nearest Lodgings: Skamania Lodge, Columbia Gorge Hotel, Lakecliff Estate, Sunset Motel, Hood River Hotel; any lodging in this section.

DOG MOUNTAIN
Steep trail with great Gorge views and wildflowers.

Map:	US Forest Service "Gifford Pinchot National Forest"
Distance:	7.0-mile double loop
Elevation Gain:	2900′
Estimated Time:	4 hours

It seems that all Columbia Gorge promotional materials feature the Dog Mountain trail. There are many good reasons for this, but it's certainly not a hike for everyone. At worst, it's a steep struggle up a dry, viewless trail to an exposed knoll buffeted by severe winds. At best, it's a shady climb to an exceptional lookout point and color-packed meadows above the Columbia Gorge. (Hey, wind is just part of the package. This is The Gorge.) Both versions can be true; it's a matter of attitude.

Wildflower buffs take Dog Mountain early in the season to make the most of the blooms before the wind and sun suck the life out of them (the blooms, that is). But for viewhounds who don't mind a steep climb, it's a good trek virtually year-round.

As with most Gorge hikes, hazards on this trail include ticks, poison oak, and rattlesnakes. With its south-facing, sun-warmed slopes, Dog Mountain can be a particular favorite of the sun-loving rattler. If you see one (and you probably won't, especially if you make a little noise as you walk), just let it pass.

In case it's not yet abundantly clear, leave the kiddies home this time. If you want them to see a fantastic Gorge view, do Beacon Rock, above.

So why, you may be asking, do Dog Mountain at all? Mostly, "because it's there." This big old hulk of a hill can be seen for miles coming up or down the Gorge, and you just *know* the views will be killer if you climb it. And everyone else you run into at Happy Hour will have done it, so you might as well. Thump your chest a few times when you reach the top, take some aspirin for your burning quads, and head for town.

Getting There

The Dog Mountain trailhead is on the north side of Washington's Highway 14, 9.0 miles east of Stevenson, 4.4 miles east of the Carson turnoff, and 11.5 miles west of Bingen/White Salmon. It is marked with a formal COLUMBIA RIVER GORGE NATIONAL SCENIC AREA TRAILHEAD sign. The gravel parking area has room for about two dozen cars, and pit toilets are located about 200 feet up the trail.

The Hike

This is also the parking area for the Augspurger Trail, a 7.5-mile-each-way trek to the northwest; its trailhead is on the north side of the parking area. Walk to the east end of the parking lot for the Dog Mountain trailhead.

The Dog Mountain Trail is a double-loop, sort of a figure-8. The lower loop goes up through the woods to a former lookout site; the upper loop circles an

open meadow on the south face of the mountaintop. This description takes you up the steeper western sides of each loop first, then back down their eastern sides, in favor of a more rapid ascent and a more leisurely descent.

Head up the trail, past the toilets, and onto a steep, rocky-dusty path lined with lovely thickets of poison oak. The switchbacking ascent is so steep that good views back down into the Gorge begin within the first quarter mile. You'll have no more views until the old fire lookout site at 2.7 miles, so enjoy these.

At 0.75 miles, you come to a fork. A sign describes the left fork as OLD ROUTE and the right fork as SCENIC. More accurate signs might call them EXTREMELY STEEP and PRETTY DARN STEEP. To do the recommended loop, take the left fork. (Note there is a hard left—an older, overgrown path that has been blocked off—and a "more straight ahead" left; take the latter.) Ascend a wide, shady path up a protected draw canopied with mixed deciduous and coniferous trees.

At 1.9 miles, the path narrows and bends to the east, toward its junction with the "scenic" path at 2.1 miles. Turn left at the junction and continue uphill. And I mean *uphill*. The next 0.3 mile should be signed NO WHINERS—it's an unholy butt-kicker.

At 2.4 miles, you know you're nearing a summit: the canopy thins and the sun breaks through. Views of the Gorge open up below as you contour along the side of the mountain, through open meadow, toward the former lookout site at 2.7 miles. Don't be surprised when the wind smacks you in the face up here—not only are you right next to Wind Mountain and the Wind River, you are hiking above one of the world's most renowned windsurfing areas! A commanding view of the Gorge awaits you at the lookout site. Note the striking contrast between the brown hills to the east and the green forests to the west.

Turning and facing uphill, take the path to your left up through the meadow. This 1.1-mile loop is the part wildflower enthusiasts come for—showy blooms include penstemon, balsamroot, phlox, mountain daisy, lupine, and many others.

Just past 3.0 miles, you come to a junction with the Augspurger Mountain Trail; continue straight ahead toward the Dog Mountain summit. At 3.2 miles, as you crest the summit of the meadow loop, an unsigned spur to the left leads up and into a grove of trees. You would think the views north from that grove of trees would be fabulous, but they really aren't—just disappointing, tree-blocked glimpses of Mount St. Helens and Mt. Adams. Ignore the spur and continue straight ahead on the loop, which will take you down a more wooded route back to the lookout site at 3.8 miles.

Retrace your steps back down the mountain to the junction at 4.4 miles, and take a left on the SCENIC trail, so named because of its occasional breaks in foliage that allow you to see the Gorge as you descend.

Reach the junction of the SCENIC and OLD ROUTE trails at 6.3 miles, where you turn left and descend the final 0.7 mile to the parking area.

Nearest Lodgings: Skamania Lodge, Bingen School Inn, Inn of the White Salmon; any lodging in this section.

OTHER HIKE NOTES
These hikes not personally reviewed or not as highly recommended as the above hikes.

Skamania Lodge On-Site Hikes
Guests at Skamania Lodge (see under *Lodgings,* above) can stretch their hiking legs without ever leaving the property. The grounds of the lodge include three pleasant loop trails, ranging from 1.0 mile to 1.75 mile in length. The Creek Loop, Lake Loop, and Gorge Loop meander through the wooded and meadowed grounds and the Skamania Lodge's scenic 18-hole golf course. A map is available at the front desk of the lodge. There are even restrooms along the way.

Multnomah Falls
This extremely popular waterfall is surrounded by trails that have long suffered from overuse. With its Disneyland-like parking pullout on Interstate 84, and much of its 620-foot cascade clearly visible from the highway, it stops hordes of tourists. Trails surround the falls, but they are not easy and would not be my first choice, due to overcrowding.

Falls Creek Falls Loop
The Falls Creek Falls Loop trail in the Mt. Adams section is easily accessed from any lodging in this section. To reach the trailhead from the Columbia Gorge area, take Highway 14 (on the Washington side) to Carson. Go north out of Carson on Road 30, also known as Wind River Road. Follow the directions explained for the hike in *Section 3,* "Mt. Adams."

Lewis River Falls
See also the Lewis River Falls trail in *Section 2,* "Mount St. Helens." As with Falls Creek Falls Loop (above), go north out of Carson on Road 30/Wind River Road. Continue north, past the Falls Creek Falls turnoff, until you reach Road 51. Take 51 northwest to Road 90, then turn right on 90 and proceed about 9 miles to the Lower Falls Campground.

Lost Lake and Lost Lake Butte
Directions to Lost Lake and the Lost Lake Butte hike are in *Section 5,* "Mt. Hood." The scenic, all-paved drive gives you a good look at the Hood River Valley and better views of Mt. Hood than you get from the Gorge or Hood River. Not far from Hood River.

Table 7.
Lodgings in the Columbia Gorge vicinity

	COLUMBIA GORGE HOTEL	HOOD RIVER HOTEL	LAKECLIFF ESTATE	SUNSET MOTEL	BINGEN SCHOOL INN	INN OF THE WHITE SALMON	SKAMANIA LODGE
PRICE (1997 SUMMER RATES, PRE-TAX, 2 PERSON)	$150–$270 (family rooms $295–$365)	$69–$99 (suites $85–$145)	$85–$100	$55–$65	$29 (Hostel bed $11 pp)	$89 (suites $99–$115)	$135–$240 (one $350 suite)
EXTRA PERSON	$30	$10	$15	included	see listing	$20 over 12; age 1–12 $1/yr. of age	$15 over 11
PAYMENT METHODS	Visa, MC, AmEx, Disc, Checks, Cash	Visa, MC, AmEx, Disc, Checks, Cash	Checks, Cash	VISA, MC, AmEx, Checks, Cash	VISA, MC, checks, cash	VISA, MC, AmEx, Disc, Checks, Cash	VISA, MC, AmEx, Disc, Checks, Cash
# OF UNITS	46	41	4	14	9	16	195
PRIVATE BATH	Yes	Yes	Yes, 2 rooms; No, 2 rooms	Yes	No	Yes	Yes
BREAKFAST INCLUDED	Yes	Yes, continental	Yes	No	No	Yes	No
COOKING FACILITIES	No	Yes, 9 units	No	No	Some; see listing	No	No
POOL	No	No	No	No	No	No	Yes
HOT TUB	No	Yes	No	No	No	Yes	Yes
CHILDREN	OK, 12 & over	OK, under 10 free	OK	OK	OK	OK	OK
PETS	OK	OK, w/ $15 fee	No	No	Call	OK	No
HANDICAPPED ACCESSIBLE	Yes	Yes	No	Yes	No	No	Yes

Section 5—Mt. Hood

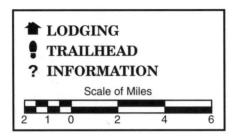

LODGING
TRAILHEAD
? INFORMATION

Scale of Miles

2 1 0   2   4   6

to Gresham & Portland

Sandy River

Sandy

Brightwood

Brightwood Guest House

Brookside B&B

26

Mt. Hood Information Center ?

Castle Canyon

Wemme

Resort at the Mountain

Welches

Old Welches Inn

Zigzag

Rhodo-dendron

Salmon River

Old Salmon River

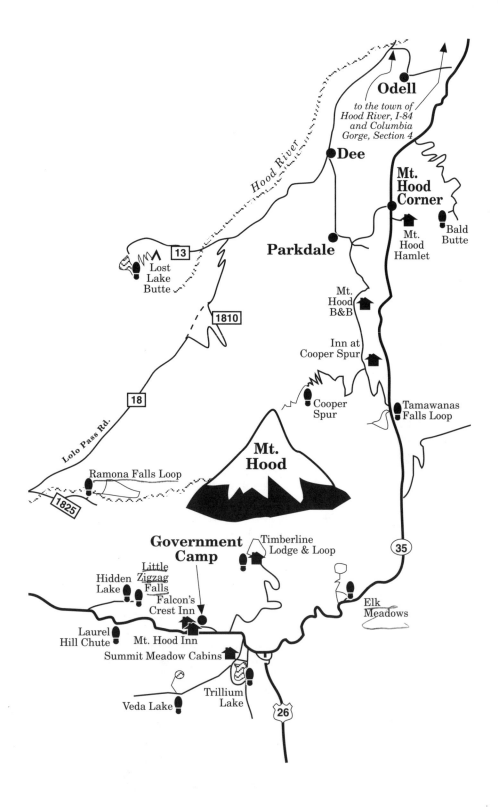

Odell

to the town of Hood River, I-84 and Columbia Gorge, Section 4

Hood River

Dee

Mt. Hood Corner

Mt. Hood Hamlet

Bald Butte

13

Lost Lake Butte

Parkdale

Mt. Hood B&B

1810

Inn at Cooper Spur

18

Cooper Spur

Tamawanas Falls Loop

Lolo Pass Rd.

Ramona Falls Loop

Mt. Hood

1825

Government Camp

Timberline Lodge & Loop

35

Little Zigzag Falls

Hidden Lake

Falcon's Crest Inn

Elk Meadows

Laurel Hill Chute

Mt. Hood Inn

Summit Meadow Cabins

Veda Lake

Trillium Lake

26

Mt. Hood

OVERVIEW

Mt. Hood, Oregon's northernmost Cascade peak, is surrounded by a well-developed recreation area with a wide range of dayhike, lodging, and dining opportunities. This section includes the area east of Mt. Hood known as the Hood River Valley, which stretches south from the town of Hood River along Highway 35, and the corridor south of Mt. Hood along Highway 26, including the communities of Welches, Brightwood, Zigzag, and Government Camp, and the historic Timberline Lodge. As highways 35 and 26 intersect a few miles east of Government Camp, any of the dayhikes in this section can be reached from any of the lodgings.

While I have listed the town of Hood River in *Section 4*, "Columbia River Gorge," it actually lies at the junction of Highway 35 and Interstate 84, and is as much a part of Mt. Hood and the Hood River Valley as it is a part of the Columbia Gorge. Those staying along Mt. Hood's east side (Mt. Hood Hamlet, Mt. Hood B&B, Inn at Cooper Spur) will find a wide variety of dining choices in nearby Hood River; please review *Section 4* as well.

The Hood River Valley is home to thousands of acres of orchards, and is a popular scenic drive. From Interstate 84 along the Columbia Gorge, turn south on Highway 35 at Hood River to reach the valley. Soon, rows of apple and pear trees fill the near distance, with pristine, ever-snowcapped Mt. Hood rising above them. Mt. Hood Hamlet is at the heart of the valley, 14 miles south of Hood River. The two other east side lodgings are located on Cooper Spur Road, a loop road off Highway 35. Mt. Hood B&B is about 18 miles from Hood River, at the edge of the valley, where farm country meets foothills and forest. Inn at Cooper Spur is about 24 miles south of Hood River, at higher altitude, and close to several popular hiking trails.

Continuing south on Highway 35—and many do, just for the scenery—you will intersect Highway 26 at Barlow Pass, about 40 miles south of Hood River. From here, Highway 26 proceeds west, roughly along the route Samuel Barlow pioneered as an alternative to finishing the Oregon Trail by rafting down the Columbia. His arduous but less-life-threatening route through the mountains, known as Barlow Trail or Barlow Toll Road, became the favored route after 1846. The remaining lodgings in this section, and all of the featured dining establishments, are located along this corridor south of the mountain.

Those approaching the south Mt. Hood corridor from Portland will leave Portland via SE Powell Boulevard, which is also Highway 26 East. From Portland, you pass through Gresham, then Sandy. You will pass the turnoff for Brightwood about 12 miles out of Sandy. The Mt. Hood Information Center at

Mt. Hood Village, an excellent resource for up-to-date trail and road information, is on your right about 14 miles east of Sandy. The village of Wemme, including the Rendezvous Grill and Wy'East Bookstore, is 15.5 miles east of Sandy. The stoplight and turnoff to Welches is 16 miles east of Sandy. Welches offers an array of services, including a full-sized grocery store, to serve the needs of anyone staying along the south corridor.

Continuing east, the next village is Zigzag, just over a mile east of the Welches Road/Highway 26 stoplight junction. This is followed by Rhododendron a mile or two later. Government Camp is about 8.5 miles east of Rhododendron, and the turnoff to Timberline Lodge is just past Government Camp. The junction of highways 26 and 35 is 2.5 miles past the Timberline turnoff.

LODGINGS
In Alphabetical Order
See also Hood River lodgings in Section 4, Columbia Gorge

BRIGHTWOOD GUEST HOUSE
P.O. Box 189 • 64725 E. Barlow Trail • Brightwood, OR 97011
(888) 503-5783 • (503) 622-5783

I can think of no more romantic place for a couple to spend a few days along Mt. Hood's south corridor than Brightwood Guest House. This single unit guest house, separate from the owner's home, is a self-contained retreat offering the best of both B&B-style and cabin-style accommodations. The property is situated on two wooded acres that include an honest-to-goodness segment of the historic Barlow Trail.

BRIGHTWOOD GUEST HOUSE
Intimate, Japanese-theme cabin with excellent breakfast

Essentially a one-room cabin with a sleeping loft, the guest house has a living area, kitchen, dining area, and full bath. Outside, guests have a private deck and Koi pond. With a futon in the living room as well as a featherbed in the loft, it could sleep four, but the setting invites intimacy, making it best-suited as a private haven for two.

The decor is an effortless and charming mix of eastern cultures, with Japanese the predominant theme. Aromatic cedar paneling enhances the warmth. Your hostess, Jan Colgan, has furnished the guest house with an amazing array of convenience items—you truly need only the clothes on your back and a sense of adventure when you visit Brightwood Guest House. You won't find a better-stocked bathroom or kitchen anywhere.

The kitchen is a bit of a surprise, with no oven or stove top, but the combination of appliances—microwave, hot plate, electric wok, toaster oven—provide enough heat sources for the creative chef to produce almost anything. And the cupboards are filled with utensils and condiments, making food preparation a pleasure. Best of all—you don't do the dishes! Leave them, and Jan will see that they are washed before you return from your next outing. Of course, if you'd rather not cook, a helpful binder of local menus is provided for your perusal, as is a telephone to call in your reservation.

Other amenities include books, videos (not your average "first-run" variety—*good* stuff!), VCR, games, puzzles, art supplies (including brush calligraphy set), iron and board, tea and coffee, washer and dryer, daily newspaper, food for the fish, slippers, and kimonos. Bicycles are available for guest use.

Rates are $95 per couple, with a two night minimum on weekends ($125 if a single weekend night is available); extra persons $15. Full breakfast, served in your cabin or on your deck, is included. Jan's breakfasts are a harmonious celebration of fresh tastes—abundant, hearty, and complex. Each morning includes fresh fruit, juice, hot beverage of choice, and both savory and sweet dishes—frittatas, brioche, scrapple, waffles, muesli. Special diets (as well as simpler palates) are graciously accommodated with advance notice.

Not everyone will be comfortable in this unique, artistic, smoke-free environment. If you must have a mattress and box springs, and aren't impressed by 30 varieties of herbal tea, you may want to check out the resort at Welches or the motel at Government Camp. But if you like the idea of a hostess who embodies warmth and generosity of spirit, surroundings that promote harmony and intimacy, and a gourmet breakfast that's off-the-beaten path but out-of-this-world, call Jan at the Brightwood Guest House.

Getting There

Coming from the west, you will see the turnoff for Brightwood about 12 miles east of Sandy; turn left. Turn left again at the Brightwood Store and Brightwood Tavern. (From the east, turn right on Brightwood Loop Road, right across Highway 26 from Mt. Hood RV Village. Then turn *right* at Brightwood Store and Brightwood Tavern.) This road crosses the Sandy River and ends in a T inter-

Romantic Brightwood Guest House

section with East Barlow Trail Road. Turn right and go one mile. Turn in at the sign with Japanese characters, the second driveway on the left after you pass Sandy River Lane on the right.

Hikes and Walks Nearby: Ramona Falls Loop, Castle Canyon, Old Salmon River, Laurel Hill Chute, Hidden Lake, Little Zigzag Falls.

BROOKSIDE B&B
P.O. Box 1112 • 45232 SE Paha Loop • Sandy, OR 97055
(503) 668-4766

Here's a casual, family-style B&B in the European tradition. Staying at Brookside is really like staying with family, because you *are* staying with the family—sharing their spacious living quarters and sprawling yard. Children are more than welcome at Brookside, and they'll love it. The grounds house peacocks, hummingbirds, exotic fowl, llamas, and pygmy goats. In keeping with the exuberant atmosphere, your well-mannered pet is also welcome.

BROOKSIDE B&B
Family-friendly, affordable B&B with Mt. Hood view

"Brookside" is a play on words—not only are your hosts Barbara and Jack Brooks, but a brook runs through the property; be sure to take a walk through their private woods and visit its peaceful banks. Rascal, the farm dog, will lead you through the cedars. Barbara and Jack bought the house and grounds in 1988, and have operated it as a B&B since 1989.

The house itself is a rambling, unpretentious two-story affair, built in 1948, with five guest rooms. Downstairs, a double room ($50) and a queen room ($55) share a bath. Upstairs, a deluxe king room (which also includes a daybed and a sitting area, for $60) and a single room ($35) share a bath, while a spacious queen room ($65) has a private bath, view of Mt. Hood, and a whimsical (and large) collection of teddy bears.

Guests are invited and encouraged to use common areas of the house. A kitchenette and sitting area is provided upstairs, and other TV and sitting areas throughout the house are yours to use. A breezeway/smoking area is decorated with artifacts collected by the Brooks' sons during their travels in Europe and Africa. The rest of the house is non-smoking. A large deck with porch swing on the upper level provides great views and a comfortable place to relax at the end of the day. Take time to get to know your hosts—they are a fount of information about the area, including the hiking trails ("Been on all of 'em!").

A hearty breakfast is served each morning. If you need an early start, the Brookses are happy to accommodate your schedule.

Brookside is farther west than the other featured lodgings, but still offers good access to the trails along the southern corridor. Uniquely affordable and family-friendly, it is a worthy inclusion in a list of lodging options for Mt. Hood.

Getting There
Coming from the west, take a right turn on Paha Loop Road about 3.5 miles east of Sandy. Coming from Mt. Hood, turn left at the first Paha Loop Road sign.

Brookside is a family-friendly, in-home B&B

Watch for the BROOKSIDE B&B sign and turn uphill into their driveway. Drive past the llamas and watch for the tail-wagging welcoming committee.

Hikes and Walks Nearby: Ramona Falls Loop, Castle Canyon, Old Salmon River, Laurel Hill Chute, Hidden Lake, Little Zigzag Falls.

FALCON'S CREST INN

P.O. Box 185 • 87287 E. Government Camp Loop • Government Camp, OR 97028
(800) 624-7384 • (503) 272-3403

At the west edge of Government Camp, a ratty little burg known mostly for hosting hordes of youngsters for its summer ski camps, is an unlikely find: an exceptional bed and breakfast. Not only is Falcon's Crest Inn one of the most pleasant lodgings on the mountain, it is a fully licensed restaurant, offering the most extravagant dinner experience on the south corridor (see *Dining, below*).

FALCON'S CREST INN
Outstanding B&B also offers fabulous full course dinners

Your well-connected hosts, BJ and Melody Johnson, have their fingers on the pulse of all the local and nearby goings-on; they can provide any information you might need for recreation, shopping, or entertainment. The Johnsons purchased the property in 1987 and began operating it as an inn almost immediately, marshalling their considerable combined energies to turn it into the standard by which all other B&B's on the south corridor seem to be measured.

The 6500-square foot mountain chalet is perfectly suited for use as a B&B, with open-plan architecture that gives the interior a marvelous, airy feeling, yet offers ample opportunity for privacy in any one of several indoor and outdoor sitting areas.

The inn offers five themed guest rooms, two of which are suites. Each room has a private bath and telephone. Television and stereo system are available in an upstairs sitting area. The Safari Room, at $95, is decorated with rattan furniture, stuffed (toy) animals, and has a queen canopy bed. The Sophia Room, at $99, is ideal for those wishing two twin beds and separate vanity areas; it is decorated with 1920s heirlooms. The Cat Ballou Room, also $99, has a romantic old west theme and a king bed. The Master Suite, at $169, has its own exercise room, private deck, outdoor hot tub, and queen four-poster bed. The spacious and newly remodeled Mexicalli Suite, at $179, boasts a luxurious bathroom with double spa tub, a queen bed, and vibrant Southwest decor. Rates are for one or two persons in a room, and include breakfast. Ask about discounts for multi-night stays. Rooms at Falcon's Crest are not designed to accommodate more than two persons under most circumstances.

The inn is licensed as a restaurant, so cocktails, wine, beer, and non-alcoholic beverages are available, and are typically offered in the second level lounge/lobby adjacent to the dining room in the late afternoon/early evening

One of Falcon's Crest Inn's several sitting areas

upon check-in. (Because of the restaurant license, no personal food or beverages may be brought into the inn.)

Do consider making a reservation for dinner. Starting at $37.95 per person, these six-course extravaganzas are a delight for the senses. (For details, see *Dining*, below.) If you're staying more than one night, why not do dinner every night if it's available? It's a fabulous meal and a good time.

The inn also hosts a number of popular events from mystery theater dinners to Christmas events to spiritual retreats to wine-tastings; call for a current calendar.

Your morning at Falcon's Crest begins with a unique wake-up service at the time you have pre-selected with your hosts upon check-in the night before. A knock on your door is followed by delivery of a basket of freshly baked muffins and your hot beverage of choice. This is not breakfast, but a little "eye-opener" service to help you get started and dressed for breakfast, which is served 7 A.M. to 9:30 A.M. in the dining room.

Call well in advance to make lodging and/or dining reservations at this absolutely top-notch B&B.

Getting There

From Highway 26, take the west entrance to Government Camp (Government Camp Loop road). Across from a gas station, and just before the Mt. Hood Brewing Company, turn left on East Ski Haus Lane. There it is, immediately, on your right. Park where you can, or, better yet, let the engine idle and trot up to the door. BJ or Melody will direct you to a good and convenient spot.

Hikes and Walks Nearby: Castle Canyon, Hidden Lake, Little Zigzag Falls, Laurel Hill Chute, Trillium Lake, Veda Lake, Timberline Mountaineer Loop.

INN AT COOPER SPUR
10755 Cooper Spur Road • Mt. Hood, OR 97041
(541) 352-6692

The Inn at Cooper Spur is a collection of nine cabins and seven motel-style rooms at the junction of Cooper Spur Road and Cloud Cap Road, off Highway 35 east of Mt. Hood. Its location is excellent for all hikes in this section, especially Cooper Spur and Tamawanas Falls.

The cabins each provide 1280 square feet of living space, two bedrooms, loft, complete kitchen, fireplace, and a bathroom and a half. Detached cabins start at $129 for two or three people, with extra persons $10 apiece. "Cabin suites" are similarly appointed units within the motel, starting at $119. A special cabin, known as the Little Cabin, is a recently renovated CCC-built cabin with its own private hot tub and a gas fireplace.

INN AT COOPER SPUR
Kitchen-equipped cabins, great location

The motel-style rooms run $65 for one bed, two people; $75 for two beds, up to four people. Each unit has a coffee maker.

Cooper Spur Inn is an excellent property for families or groups. The kitchens enable longer, more economical stays, yet, when you'd rather not cook, you can enjoy the Cooper Spur Inn Restaurant,

Inn at Cooper Spur

located immediately adjacent to the inn. And, at day's end, the hot tubs—there are eight of them, though not all are open at all times—are a great gathering spot. As you soak, you may see deer pass through the grounds, or at least watch some of the resident bunnies hopping around. (The presence of wildlife explains the "no pets" policy.)

Getting There
If you're coming from the west, take Highway 26 east to its junction with Highway 35, then 35 north toward Hood River. North of Robinhood and Sherwood campgrounds, and across the highway from the Polallie Trailhead, turn left (west) on Cooper Spur Road. From Hood River, take Highway 35 south 24 miles to Cooper Spur Road; turn right (west). Take Cooper Spur Road 2.3 miles; the inn is on your right at the junction of Cooper Spur Road and Forest Service Road 3512, also known as Cloud Cap Road.

Hikes and Walks Nearby: Cooper Spur, Tamawanas Fall.

MT. HOOD B&B
8885 Cooper Spur Road • Parkdale, OR 97041
(800) 557-8885 • (541) 352-6885

Arriving at Mt. Hood B&B is like coming home. You are likely to be greeted by a tail-wagging welcome committee and a home-baked snack. Unless you're phobic about animals or just plain uptight, you can't help but get comfortable here. The sprawling farm setting, complete with an assortment of pettable livestock that may include piglets, calves, lambs, horses, cats, and dogs, will charm anyone who loves coun-

MT. HOOD B&B
Warm hospitality on a real farm

try living, while the gardens, food, and hospitality are enough to make Martha Stewart envious.

Your hosts, Mike and Jackie Rice, purchased the pastoral 42 acres and farm-house in 1994, subsequently turning it into a successful lodging for skiers and hikers, as well as a destination in its own right for those wanting to "get away from it all" for a country experience. The location, 18 miles south of Hood River and 18 miles northeast of Mt. Hood Meadows, makes for an ideal, central location for hikes in the Hood River valley and along the south corridor. It is close enough for easy access to town for dinner, yet isolated enough for real rural relaxation.

Mike, Jackie, and family offer three guest rooms in the main farmhouse and a rustic suite in a separate building. The cozy and antique-filled Meadow Room and the light and airy Mt. Adams Room share a convenient bath. Each has a queen feather bed. The larger Mt. Hood Room has a full view of the mountain, private bath with spa tub, and comfy four-poster bed. Each room has a TV and VCR.

The fourth unit is a treasure, with all the comforts of the other rooms, yet spacious and private, with the feeling of your own private, rustic fort. Known as the Homestead, this detached cabin unit has a king bed and three twins, making it equally appropriate for a romantic honeymoon retreat or a longer stay with a family. It has a kitchenette for simple meal preparation, as well as TV/VCR, wood stove, built-in cupboards, and private bath.

Amenities available to all guests include an extensive video library, an indoor tennis/basketball court, pool table, sauna, deck with hot tub and porch swing, gazebo, and beautiful grounds inviting horseshoes or croquet. (Also great for weddings and other gatherings.) In short, there's plenty to do here, whether your idea of relaxation is active or idle. It's hard to say which we enjoyed more—

Pastoral Mt. Hood B&B

the frenzy of an impromptu cattle round-up with the family, or a quiet hour we spent reading in the gazebo as the sun set behind Mt. Hood.

And the breakfast...! Goodness gracious, put on the feed bag and plan a serious day of hiking to work this one off! You won't know when to quit when everything on the table is so delicious. Your ebullient hostess is a wizard in the kitchen. Prepared to your tastes and dietary requirements, the fare may include fresh rolled oats, seasonal and home-preserved fruits, fresh pastries and breakfast breads, and traditional egg and potato dishes, all prepared and presented with the warmth and country flair that typifies this wonderful establishment.

Getting There

Mt. Hood B&B is located where the idyllic orchards of the Hood River valley meet the forested foothills of sparkling Mt. Hood. Coming from the south or west, take Highway 26 east to its junction with Highway 35, then 35 north toward Hood River. North of Robinhood and Sherwood campgrounds, and across the highway from the Polallie Trailhead, turn left (west) on Cooper Spur Road. Pass the Inn at Cooper Spur and continue a few miles north until the woods open up and you begin descending into the open valley. You will see the farmhouse and barns as you descend the hill. Turn right, through the archway entrance, into the long driveway.

From the north, proceed south on Highway 35 to Mt. Hood Corner, about 14 miles south of Hood River. Turn right (west) at the corner market, following the signs COOPER SPUR and PARKDALE. After a couple of miles, you will come to a four-way intersection: Parkdale is to your right and Cooper Spur is straight ahead. Continue straight ahead. After a total of 4.9 miles from Mt. Hood Corner, watch for a sign, driveway, and archway entrance on your left.

Hikes and Walks Nearby: Cooper Spur, Tamawanas Falls, Bald Butte, Lost Lake Butte.

MT. HOOD HAMLET
6741 Highway 35 • Mt. Hood, OR 97041
(800) 407-0570 • (541) 352-3574
www.site-works.com/hoodhamlet

One of Mt. Hood's newest B&B's, Mt. Hood Hamlet is also one of its most delightful surprises. Their brochure summarizes it best: "Eighteenth Century New England Colonial elegance and pastoral charm, with Twentieth Century comfort and amenities."

Paul and Diane Romans opened their B&B in August 1996. Designed to replicate an ancestral home in Rhode Island, the Hamlet was built with exceptional craftsmanship throughout. The use of open space, painted and natural woodwork, and beautiful hardwood flooring (much of it black oak, which, for the uninitiated, isn't black), results in a home that is both elegant and inviting. The decor, furnishings, and amenities throughout the guest rooms and common areas are strictly top-drawer as well.

MT. HOOD HAMLET

Elegant new reproduction of 18th Century Colonial home

Mt. Hood Hamlet offers three guest rooms, each with a private bath and a view. The Klickitat room has a queen bed and a view of Mt. Adams (known to Native Americans as "Klickitat"), for $95/night. The spacious Cloud Cap room has a king bed and exceptional view of Mt. Hood, for $110. And the Vista Ridge room has a queen bed with antique Amish quilt, a view of Mt. Adams, a small sitting area, and a roomy bath with Jacuzzi tub, for $125. Discounts are extended for multi-night stays and parties taking more than one room. (Parties wishing to rent the whole house receive a 10% discount, plus have the option of a hideabed in the library, expanding the sleeping capacity.) All rooms come with TV, VCR, and air conditioning. Chilled beverages are available at all times, and the innkeepers maintain a library of books, magazines, and area maps for your use. Other amenities, such as laundry facilities, wine glasses/ice bucket, iron and board, are available for the asking.

Breakfast, included in the price of your room, is served in beautiful surroundings. The dining area looks out across the patio, Paul and Diane's sprawling, lovingly tended flower gardens, the farms of the Hood River valley, and Mt. Hood itself. Our fare featured a delicate array of fresh fruits, local and exotic, ripened to perfection and served with a yogurt sauce on the side. This was accompanied by a choice of locally roasted coffee (regular and decaf) or teas. The entrée was a tasty French toast with ginger-peach compote and an array of syrups.

Paul and Diane's main concern is the comfort of their guests. For this reason, both pets and children are welcome if arrangements can be made in advance, and depending upon other guests in the inn. Alternately, they will make boarding arrangements for your pet in a nearby kennel if you wish. These two former schoolteachers have created a respite from the cares of your workaday world,

Mt. Hood Hamlet's sunny dining area

combining the best of modern, high-tech amenities and well-engineered facilities with old-fashioned hospitality.

Getting There
You'll find Mt. Hood Hamlet off Highway 35 just south of Mt. Hood Corner (the turnoff from Highway 35 to Parkdale). Just south of the junction, look for the MT. HOOD HAMLET sign on the east side of the road and turn down the driveway.

Hikes and Walks Nearby: Bald Butte, Lost Lake Butte, Cooper Spur, Tamawanas Falls Loop; also hikes in *Section 4,* "Columbia Gorge."

MT. HOOD INN
87450 E. Government Camp Loop • Government Camp, OR 97028
(800) 443-7777 • (503) 272-3205

An affiliate of Val-U Inn Motels, Mt. Hood Inn provides a reliable, clean, modern alternative for those who prefer a predictable environment over the adventure of a B&B or private cabin. The inn has 56 rooms, all modern, with private baths. Their basic room ("deluxe") has two queen beds, for $105; the larger "superior," also with two queen beds, is $115. Mini-suites, with king bed, fold-out couch, microwave, refrigerator, and sink, are $125, and king room with a private spa and no fold-out couch is

MT. HOOD INN
Clean, modern, deluxe motel-style lodging

$145. All rooms have satellite TV. All guests have access to a large indoor spa, coin-operated laundry facilities, and a complimentary continental breakfast in the lobby. The inn is especially attractive during ski season because of its indoor parking, ski lockers, and ski-tuning facilities.

Mt. Hood Inn is conveniently located in Government Camp, providing excellent access to all south corridor trails. It is adjacent to Mt. Hood Brewing Company, a microbrewery and family restaurant.

Getting There
Mt. Hood Inn, clearly visible from Highway 26, is located on the main drag (Government Camp Loop) at the west end of Government Camp.

Hikes and Walks Nearby: Castle Canyon, Hidden Lake, Little Zigzag Falls, Laurel Hill Chute, Trillium Lake, Veda Lake, Timberline Mountaineer Loop.

OLD WELCHES INN
26401 East Welches Road • Welches, OR 97067
(503) 622-3754
www.innsandouts.com/property/old_welches_inn.html

Here's your chance to participate in a slice of Hoodland history, while enjoying the comforts of a traditional B&B. Sure, Timberline Lodge has been around since the '30s, but the Old Welches Inn was built in *1890*. It's said to be the oldest home on this side of the mountain. Built by Samuel Welch and his son Billy as Mt. Hood's first summer resort and hotel, it operated as a guest lodging until the late 1930s, when it became a

OLD WELCHES INN
Traditional B&B built in 1890, plus cottage

single-family home. Later, it fell victim of disrepair and the vicissitudes of age. Rescued by current owners Judith and Ted Mondun in 1987, Old Welches Inn survived to be one of the finest lodgings on the south Mt. Hood corridor.

Judi and Ted undertook a restoration of amazing proportions to bring us the inn you see today. The result of their loving labor is a warm, bright, yet cozy-feeling home reminiscent of the Old South. Natural decorators, the Monduns chose every piece of wallpaper, every moulding, every ceiling treatment with care. The premises are graced by antiques, yet are not fussy or overdone. Guest rooms and common areas are comfortable by modern standards, yet retain a distinct historical feeling. Particularly delightful is the sunroom, a cheerful sitting and TV area (video library provided) with windows on three sides. It is adjacent to a cozy, more enclosed sitting room with two loveseats, a stone fireplace, and bookcases. Take a moment to browse the scrapbooks and learn about the history of this unique property, and the Herculean efforts the Monduns put forth to rescue it.

Outside, the park-like, groomed yard and gardens extend down to the banks of the Salmon River. Book your stay late August through early October, and you're likely to catch the salmon spawning.

The inn's three original rooms, Sweet Briar, Columbine, and Trillium, share two spacious full bathrooms; they rent for $75, $85, and $95. A new upstairs room, Forget-Me-Not, has twin beds, a private bath, and its own TV, for $110. A separate unit, Lutie's Cottage, is also available for rent, at $130–$175, depending upon the number of guests. Located adjacent to the B&B, this two-bedroom,

Restored Old Welches Inn, built in 1890

one-bath home has a full kitchen and river rock fireplace. It, too, was part of the original resort, and was built in 1901.

Breakfast, included in the price of the room for guests inside the main inn, is a special treat. (Breakfast not included for cottage guests.) Served elegantly with antique tableware in an inviting, sunny breakfast area, the multi-course extravaganza might include French toast, quiche, pastries, fresh fruit, and an array of other delights. (I must say, Judi, the flaky pumpkin pastries were to die for!)

The innkeepers request a minimum two-night stay most of the hiking season. Call for specific reservation and cancellation policies.

Getting There
Go south on Welches Road from its stoplight intersection with Highway 26. Pass Fairway Avenue and the other entrances to Resort at the Mountain. After 1.0 mile, watch for the sign and the white picket fence on your right. Turn in and park just past the inn.

Hikes and Walks Nearby: Old Salmon River, Ramona Falls Loop, Castle Canyon, Old Salmon River, Laurel Hill Chute, Hidden Lake, Little Zigzag Falls.

RESORT AT THE MOUNTAIN
68010 East Fairway • Welches, OR 97067
(800) 669-7666 • (503) 622-3101
www.theresort.com

A sprawling, 300-acre resort and conference center, Resort at the Mountain offers 160 guest rooms and a wide variety of amenities. Three nine-hole golf courses are the centerpiece for a complex that includes two restaurants, regulation croquet and lawn bowling, tennis, volleyball, a fitness center, a pool and spa, and three gift shops. (A word about "regulation croquet"—it's not that humble child's game involving wire wickets poked randomly in a suburban lawn. This game is a challenging one, with fixed wickets on a special, smooth-as-a-putting-green laser-groomed surface. Give it a try!)

RESORT AT THE MOUNTAIN

160 rooms on a 300-acre, 27-hole golf resort

The Resort at the Mountain traces its heritage back to the same resort as Old Welches Inn (see above), the turn-of-the-century campground and hotel started by Samuel and Billy Welch. The first nine-hole golf course was built on the property in 1928, followed by another in the 1950s, and a third in the 1980s, when the property was known as Rippling River Resort.

Current owners Ed and Janice Hopper took over the resort in 1989, and began implementing a Scottish theme, playing off the resort's location in the "highlands" of Oregon. Today, tartan plaids, and images of thistles, pinecones, foxglove, and, of course, golf, predominate.

Each room at the resort has a patio or deck, TV and VCR, and a view of the forest, the fairways, or the pool. Many rooms are handicapped-accessible. Summer rates begin at $109 for a room with two double beds. Rooms with two queen beds, wet bar, and a small refrigerator rent for $140. Fireside studio rooms have a king bed, fireplace, double sofa sleeper, and a kitchenette, for $169. One and two-bedroom suites have full kitchens, a living room with double sofa sleeper, towel warmer, pant presser, and fairway views, plus separate bedrooms, each with two queen beds. One-bedroom suites are $199; two-bedroom suites are $240. Rates are for two persons, and children under 18 stay free with a parent. Each extra adult 18 and over costs $20.

Several extra touches make your stay especially comfortable: fireplace logs, bottled water, microwave popcorn (in rooms with microwaves), morning *USA Today*. The large bathrooms are complete with hair dryers, tubs, and extra towels. (The resort participates in the eco-conscious optional-linen-washing program.) Nightly turndown service is provided, and daily maid service. Room service is available, and the kitchenette units are very complete (including coffeemaker with coffee and tea, mini-dishwasher, microwave, stovetop, cooking and eating utensils) if you wish to prepare your own meals. Full kitchen units (the suites) also include an oven. Or visit one of the two restaurants on-site, The Highlands and The Tartans Inn (see *Dining,* below).

Getting There
From the stoplight intersection of Welches Road and Highway 26, proceed 0.75 miles south on Welches to Fairway Avenue. Turn right into the resort property. The main lodge, with parking and guest registration, is on your left as you enter.

Hikes and Walks Nearby: Old Salmon River, Ramona Falls Loop, Castle Canyon, Old Salmon River, Laurel Hill Chute, Hidden Lake, Little Zigzag Falls.

Overlooking two of the golf courses at Resort at the Mountain

SUMMIT MEADOW CABINS
Box 235 • Government Camp, OR 97028
(503) 272-3494

Once upon a time, Dave and Wendy built a cabin at Summit Meadow. They chose the spot carefully: 6 miles south of Mt. Hood, just north of Trillium Lake, near enough to the highway for easy access, but far enough from anything else to ensure privacy and a sense of wilderness.

SUMMIT MEADOW CABINS
Well-built, isolated (yet convenient) mountain cabins

Today, Dave, Wendy, and their son, Jeremy, share their wonderful location with others, by renting cabins on their exceptional property.

The cabins are fresh, new-feeling, and built with care and craftsmanship. The rustic, high-ceilinged, open architecture is designed for group and family use. Two chalet units (Meadow Chalet and Chimney Rock Chalet) include two bedrooms, a loft, two bathrooms, jacuzzi bathtub, oversized living area, dining room, and kitchen with dishwasher. With 1850 square feet of living space, these units sleep 8 to 12 persons, and rent for $325/weekend (Friday 4 P.M.–Sunday 1 P.M.), $685 for a week (excluding holidays), or $130/night weekdays with a two-night minimum. The Chimney Rock A-Frame unit (not to be confused with the Chimney Rock Chalet) is similarly appointed, with 1400 square feet and sleeping capacity of 5 to 10 persons. It rents for $275/weekend, $575/week, or $110/weeknight. The smallest unit, Mineral Creek Cabin, has one bedroom plus a loft, one bathroom, kitchen, and 1000 square feet. It sleeps two to six persons, and rents for $200/weekend, $455/week, or $90/weeknight. Each cabin has a wood or pellet stove, deck, picnic table, and barbecue. Ask about the new unit Dave and Wendy added in the fall of 1997; it's a dandy one, near a waterfall.

Summit Meadow cabins are stocked with pots and pans, tableware, can openers, popcorn poppers, toasters, coffee pots and coffee, dish soap, pillows, and towels. Guests need to bring sleeping bags or other bedding (linens can be arranged if necessary), food and beverages, amusement items (books, games, etc.), and, as their brochure says, "the energy and enthusiasm to enjoy a vacation away from…phone, traffic, television, and busy schedules."

The cabins are easily accessible via gravel roads during hiking season (a bit of x/c skiing is required in winter), and are close enough to Government Camp for dining out and restocking basic convenience items. But the beauty of these cabins is their rustic isolation. This is truly a place to get away from it all, yet with great access to every trail in this section. As the cabins are far enough apart to provide "elbow room" and privacy, each cabin is accessed slightly differently. Call for directions to the unit you choose.

Hikes and Walks Nearby: Trillium Lake, Veda Lake, Timberline Mountaineer Loop, Elk Meadows.

TIMBERLINE LODGE
Oregon 97028
(800) 547-1406 • (503) 272-3311 • From Portland (503) 231-7979
www.timberlinelodge.com

No visit to Mt. Hood's south corridor is complete without a visit to Timberline Lodge. To say this "Masterpiece of Mountain Lodges" is listed in the National Register of Historic Places is to understate its majesty. Like the Ahwahnee at Yosemite, the El Tovar at Grand Canyon, this is a historic lodge of epic proportions.

> **TIMBERLINE LODGE**
>
> Classic mountain lodge built by WPA in 1936

Built in 1936–37 with funds from President Roosevelt's Works Progress Administration (WPA) and the labor of over 500 previously unemployed men and women, Timberline Lodge is a monument to American strength and craftsmanship. Its labor-intensive construction included wood, stone, iron, and textile work fashioned by hand from the simplest of tools. Three themes were used in the project's design: early pioneers (shown in the hand-hewn timbers and hand-crafted furnishings); Native Americans (shown in wood and ironwork designs throughout the lodge); and Mt. Hood's wildlife (shown in carvings and paintings of indigenous animals and plants).

Reflecting the period of its design and construction, the lodge's common areas are majestic and spacious, while the guest rooms are small, but comfortable. The rooms include wonderfully nostalgic period furniture, such as old wood-and-metal writing desks. The use of wood is exceptional throughout the lodge. The builders used whatever species of tree was handy, useful, and appropriate for the job—it is, in the end, the very hands-on practicality of this lodging that makes it so marvelous.

The lodge has 71 rooms, most with private baths. Eleven rooms, referred to as Chalet Rooms, are private bunkrooms with shared bath facilities, at $65 per night for one or two persons. Of the remaining 60 rooms, all with private baths,

Timberline Lodge—quintessential mountain lodge, at the base of Mt. Hood

the most numerous type is the Timberline Room, each of which has a queen or a queen and a twin bed, for $125/night. A more spacious room, of which there are only two, known as the Large Corner Rooms, rents for $150/night. The eight Fireplace Rooms each have two queens or a king and a queen, and can accommodate a rollaway bed; these run $170/night, if you can get one. Rates are for one or two persons in a room; extra persons are $15. Children 11 and under stay free with an adult.

For all its historic heritage, the lodge participates in the very 1990s concept of environmentally friendly optional linen washing—the WPAs and CCCs would have approved. Other decidedly modern features include updated bathrooms and in-room TVs.

You'll want to eat at the wonderful Cascade Dining Room (see *Dining*, below), one of the top culinary destinations on the mountain. When a lighter appetite calls, choose the Ram's Head Bar or, if you're fortunate to catch it open, the historic Blue Ox Bar. As Mt. Hood is a year-round ski destination, snacks are available at the Wy'East Day Lodge and Silcox Hut if the lift is open. If it's sunny, you can take advantage of the Palmer Junction barbecue set up at the top of the Magic Mile Chairlift (see *Timberline Mountaineer Trail*, below).

Getting There

From Highway 26, go north on the clearly signed TIMBERLINE ROAD, just east of Government Camp and about 2.5 miles west of the Highway 26/Highway 35 junction. The lodge is about 6.0 miles up, at the end of the road.

Hikes and Walks Nearby: Timberline Mountaineer Loop, Elk Meadows, Hidden Lake, Little Zigzag Falls, Laurel Hill Chute, Trillium Lake, Veda Lake.

DINING
In Alphabetical Order

These restaurants serve the south corridor, along Highway 26. Those staying along Highway 35 should see Hood River dining in *Section 4*, "Columbia Gorge."

BARLOW TRAIL INN RESTAURANT
69580 E. Highway 26 • Zigzag, OR 97049
(503) 622-3112

Established in 1927, the Barlow Trail Inn was named for the historic Barlow Trail. This well-preserved segment of the Oregon Trail has many access points along Highway 26. Today, the Barlow Trail Inn Restaurant is a kitschy log-cabin family establishment owned and operated by Wayne and Judi Graf.

Fare isn't fancy, but what they do, they do well. Breakfasts include bountiful three-egg omelets starting at $4.75, and all the usual egg and griddle dishes, from a $2.95 short stack to the House Special (three eggs, sirloin steak, hash browns, and toast) at $7.25. As the restaurant is licensed, you can even order up a Bloody Mary or Screwdriver with your biscuits and gravy.

Lunch centers around burgers and sandwiches, including a $5.75 genuine buffalo burger. These range from $3.75 to $6.25, complete with choice of fries, tater tots, potato salad, soup, or salad. Dinner entrées include pork chops, Hawaiian chicken, and steaks; most complete dinners are between $7.95 and $13.95. A few meal-sized salads are also offered, and vegetarians can go with a gardenburger or veggie sandwich. Children's menu starts at $2.95.

The restaurant is located 0.75 mile east of the Welches Road/Highway 26 junction, on the south side of Highway 26.

CASCADE DINING ROOM
Timberline Lodge • Oregon 97028
(503) 272-3311

The Cascade Dining Room at Timberline Lodge is the quintessential Pacific Northwest dining experience. Located in the majestic, historic Timberline Lodge (see *Lodgings,* above) at the base of Mt. Hood, the dining room serves three meals a day. And, just in case you've forgotten where you are, salmon is available at all three: as hash, with eggs, for breakfast; pan-seared over spinach salad for lunch; roasted on cedar for dinner.

No meal at the Cascade Dining Room need be ordinary. Even the lowliest pancake is offered up with hazelnut praline butter (a stack of three is $5.75). Or start your day with hot 10-grain cereal or a freshly made pecan sticky bun, each $3.95. Inspired egg dishes also available. Lunch offerings are innovative and delightful, including two tempting vegetarian selections (a Mediterranean wrap with baba ghanoush and tzatziki, and a grilled Portobello sandwich) as well as meatier fare. Full lunches range from $8.50 to $14.95, with lighter bites such as chili and salad available.

But dinner is the meal most folks will drive up the hill for. From the fresh mixed-Northwest-greens salad to the seasonally inspired desserts, dinner at Timberline Lodge is a celebration. If salmon isn't your thing, choose Pan-Seared Breast of Moulard Duckling (medium-rare with lingonberry balsamic demi-glace, $24.95), Chilean Sea Bass (first marinated, then roasted and wrapped in crispy potato "hay," $21.95), or Prime Rib of Midwest Pork (marinated in Calvados brandy and served with local apple/cranberry sauce, $23.95). To complement it all, an extensive wine selection is available.

The Cascade Dining Room's award-winning chef prides himself on offering fresh foods prepared in a healthful manner, and special needs are graciously accommodated. Be sure to call ahead to secure your reservation, and to check serving hours.

FALCON'S CREST INN
P.O. Box 185 • Government Camp, OR 97028
(800) 624-7384 • (503) 272-3403

Falcon's Crest Inn is a unique bed and breakfast establishment (see *Lodgings,* above), which also functions as a restaurant, serving special multi-course *prix fixe* dinners by advance reservation only. If space is available, non-guests are welcome to join the inn's guests for dinner; call at least 24 hours in advance to inquire. Prices start at $37.95, and the maximum seating is 16 (except for special events—call or write for calendar of these festivities).

Innkeeper Bob "BJ" Johnson is a chef *par excellence,* choosing a nightly entrée that might vary from signature prime rib to French 95 chicken to Cornish game hens to beef Wellington. (Some dietary restrictions or special entrée requests can be accommodated with advance notice.) There is only one seating, at 7:30 P.M., and don't make any other plans for the evening, because the meal is an event. The dining extravaganza begins with an entertaining and mouth-watering explanation of the menu by master storyteller, Melody Johnson. Before you know it, three hours have passed, you're enjoying dessert, and you don't know where the time went.

BJ, Melody, and their helpers prepare every ingredient for their dinners by hand, and everything is fresh, gourmet, and first-class, right down to the table settings and presentation. The premises are fully licensed; beer, wine, and cocktails are available. If you're visiting the south Mt. Hood corridor, treat yourself to this wonderful experience at least one night of your visit.

THE HIGHLANDS
Resort at the Mountain • 68010 East Fairway • Welches, OR 97067
(503) 622-3101
www.theresort.com

The Highlands is the Resort at the Mountain's formal dining room (see Resort at the Mountain under *Lodgings,* above), serving breakfast, lunch, and dinner year-round.

Breakfast choices include standard fare plus a few specialties like Highland's Prime Rib Hash, served with poached eggs, hashbrowns, and toast, for $5.95. Salmon fans can get their morning bagel and lox for $6.95, and those who prefer a lighter breakfast might try the Highland's signature scone, just $2.

Lunches range from excellent meal-sized salads ($5.25–$9.95) to a selection of scaled-down dinner entrées ($6.95–$10.95) to sandwiches, among them a heart-healthy and tasty grilled eggplant on sourdough ($5.95).

Dinners at The Highlands may begin with a selection from their extensive appetizer menu. Decadently rich crispy brie is served warm with roasted garlic, fresh pear, and baguette for $7.95; a Mediterranean sampler plate includes prosciutto ham, cheeses, and imported olives for $9.95; and the Hoodland Salad of mixed field greens with roasted hazelnuts, gorgonzola cheese, and raspberry vinaigrette is a delight at $5.95. Choose an entrée from the daily fresh sheet or one of the house specialties such as Highland's King Salmon (marinated in lemon and thyme, then glazed with soy sauce and white wine butter, $17.95) or Southwestern Rack of Lamb (marinated in chili-cilantro rub and served with jalapeño-mint jelly, $20.95). Dinners start at $13.95 and include salad or soup. Locally made desserts finish the menu.

The Highlands restaurant is located in the resort's main lodge. From the stoplight intersection of Welches Road and Highway 26, proceed 0.75 miles south on Welches to Fairway Avenue. Turn right into the resort property, then left into the main lodge and guest registration parking area.

MT. HOOD BREWING COMPANY
87304 E. Government Camp Loop • Government Camp, OR 97028
(503) 272-3724

Just off Highway 26 at the west entrance to Government Camp is the Mt. Hood Brewing Company and Brew Pub. Four microbrews—Ice Axe India Pale Ale, Cloud Cap Amber Ale, Pinnacle Extra Special Bitter Ale, and Hogsback Oatmeal Stout—complement a reasonably priced pub menu of sandwiches, chili, and pizza. Northwest wines are also available, all served in a fun, casual atmosphere.

MT. HOOD COFFEE ROASTERS
67411 E. Highway 26 • Welches, OR 97067
(503) 662-5153

OK, so coffee isn't "dining," but in the Pacific Northwest, it's almost mother's milk. So a local roaster with a fine product is worth knowing about. That's what you'll find at Mt. Hood Coffee Roasters. Founder and proprietor Serene Elliott-Graber has created quite a following for her boutique-roasted Arabica beans. Bulk beans, ground coffees, espresso drinks, and fun-loving coffee-related gift items are among the items available in their retail outlet on Highway 26. Stop in and browse, have a scone or a cookie, pick up some fresh-roasted Oregon hazelnuts, and, by all means, have a cup of coffee.

RENDEZVOUS GRILL & TAP ROOM
67149 E. Highway 26 • Welches, OR 97067
(503) 622-6837

For those staying toward the west end of the Highway 26 corridor, the Rendezvous Grill & Tap Room offers a nice pair of dining options. Two dining establishments in one, it's more innovative and "grown-up" than the diner fare at Barlow Trail Inn, yet not as elaborate as Falcon's Crest or Timberline's Cascade Room.

The Grill Room serves lunch and dinner. Lunches include fried Willapa Bay oysters ($8), rigatoni with alder-smoked chicken and toasted hazelnuts ($7.50), and a killer Cobb salad with Oregon bleu cheese dressing ($6.95). Dinners, including field greens salad or soup, range from an $11.95 sausage grill plate to an $18.95 twenty-ounce Porterhouse. Handcut vegetable and cheese raviolis are $12.95, and a special sake-glazed salmon with sesame asparagus is $16.95. A full wine list and boutique draft beers are available.

Next door in the Tap Room, you can choose from a Small Plates menu of mini-meals (sort of like tapas), or a Large Plates menu of casual full meals. The Small Plates include crab and shrimp cakes with beans for $6.50; spinach salad with pears, bleu cheese, and hazelnuts for $3.95; and marinated goat cheese with crostini, red peppers, and olives for $4.95. The Large Plates include a burger with Tillamook cheddar and fries for $6.95; salad and unlimited soup and bread for $5.95; and the same chicken rigatoni served next door, for $9.95.

You'll find Rendezvous Grill & Tap Room in a little shopping center on the north side of Highway 26 about half a mile west of the Welches Road stoplight intersection. The sign on the highway says WEMME, but the address is Welches.

THE TARTANS INN
Resort at the Mountain • 68010 East Fairway • Welches, OR 97067
(503) 622-3101
www.theresort.com

The Tartans Inn is Resort at the Mountain's casual dining room (see Resort at the Mountain under *Lodgings,* above), serving breakfasts, burgers, and sandwiches overlooking the fairways of the resort's three nine-hole golf courses.

Breakfasts are great, from whole wheat and honey griddle cakes at $3.95 to a spicy Mexican omelette with chorizo at $6.95. Enjoy biscuits with country gravy plus eggs and your choice of meat for $5.95, or scrambled eggs, Canadian bacon, and fresh tomato on a croissant for $5.25.

For lunch, hamburgers and sandwiches run $4.75 to $5.95 (unless you want to really pig out with a massive Double Bogey Burger at $7.50). Or choose halibut and chips ($6.95), a chef's salad ($5.50), or one of the tavern appetizers like buffalo wings ($5.25), jalapeño poppers ($4.95), or nachos ($5.25). Microbrewed beers are available on tap or by the bottle.

The Tartans Inn restaurant, open mornings and afternoons during the golf season, is located in the resort's east side complex. From the stoplight intersection of Welches Road and Highway 26, proceed 0.8 miles south on Welches, passing Fairway Avenue and the entrance to the main lodge without turning. Turn left toward the Three Nines Golf Shop and the sign for The Tartans Inn.

WALKS AND HIKES
Listed in approximate order of difficulty

Mt. Hood National Forest participates in the Trail Park Pass system. See *Trail Park Pass System,* in the Introduction.

LITTLE ZIGZAG FALLS
All-weather, all-ages stroll to small waterfall.

Map:	Green Trails #461, "Government Camp"
Distance:	0.6 mile round trip
Elevation Gain:	Negligible
Estimated Time:	30 minutes

This cool, green walk meanders along Little Zigzag Creek to a view of its waterfall, then continues briefly to the top of the falls. Suitable for the whole family, this makes a nice leg-stretcher for anyone buzzing down Highway 26 between Sandy and Government Camp or points east. Can be muddy in spring.

Getting There

A few miles west of Government Camp (4.0 miles west of the Rest Area at the east end of Government Camp) on Highway 26, turn north on Road 39 (also known as Road 2639, but the first sign you will see says 39). If you're coming from the west, this road is 7.4 miles east of the Welches Road/Highway 26 stoplight intersection. The road is signed MT. HOOD KIWANIS CAMP. Follow this paved but patched road 2.3 miles to its end, where a parking area provides room for two dozen cars.

The trailhead, at the far end of the parking lot, is marked LITTLE ZIGZAG FALLS, TRAIL 795C, FALLS 1/2 MI. (Either the Forest Service was being generous, or this refers to round-trip distance; the falls are actually only about 0.25 miles from the trailhead.)

The Walk

This immediately beautiful trail follows Little Zigzag Creek to a close-up view of its waterfall. The trail itself is medium wide and carpeted with pine needles; its flanks are lined with Canadian dogwood, vine maple, and the occasional rhododendron.

Snaking along the appropriately named Little Zigzag, the twisty trail is deeply shaded by noble old conifers, providing a beautiful respite on a hot and sunny day. Since the only view is that of the falls themselves, this short, sheltered jaunt is also a good pick on a rainy or overcast day.

At 0.25 mile, a viewing platform offers a look at the playful, two-story waterfall. Those wishing to expend a little more energy can continue, switchbacking to the left and up to the top of the little falls. The trail peters out shortly, at about 0.3 mile.

Little Zigzag Falls is a short, super trail for all ages

Nearest Lodgings: Falcon's Crest, Mt. Hood Inn, Brightwood Guest House, Old Welches Inn, Summit Meadow Cabins.

LAUREL HILL CHUTE

Charge up a hillside to an Oregon Trail historical site.

Map:	None Needed; Green Trails #461, "Government Camp" (access only)
Distance:	1.0 mile round-trip
Elevation Gain:	300′
Estimated Time:	45 minutes

Immediately adjacent to Highway 26, this historical walk takes hikers to the base, then the top, of the Laurel Hill "chute," one of many difficult passages along the Oregon Trail. Interpretive signs explain how pioneers had to lower their precious wagons with primitive rope winches down the too-steep hillside.

The walk to the top is short, but climbs steadily. The hill was named by early settlers who mistook the indigenous trees for laurel.

Getting There

Traveling either direction on Highway 26, watch for the HISTORIC TRAIL MARKER sign a few miles west of Government Camp. The historic marker, the trailhead, and a pullout for four or five cars are on the south side of the highway.

The Walk

Find the trailhead to the right of the LAUREL HILL historic marker. The hiker-only trail is marked LAUREL HILL CHUTE, TRAIL 795A.

Begin by ascending a few dozen stone steps to an old road, a section of the 1925 Mt. Hood Highway. Turn right, proceeding past the bottom of the rocky chute itself (marked with an interpretive plaque). After about 0.1 mile on the road, the clearly-marked trail leads uphill to your left.

From here, the walk is a moderate ascent for the remaining 0.4 mile. The trail is attractive, bordered with ferns and rhododendron. Birds fill the woods around you; nuthatches and peewees are among those seen and heard.

Two side paths intersect the main path en route to the top. Both are remnants of original Oregon Trail wagon routes. The first, at 0.25 mile, joins at an angle from behind, on the right. The second, at 0.4, is a 4-way intersection; the main path goes straight ahead. (Those wishing to explore the path to the right will traipse about 0.2 mile through the forest, over deadfall and under branches, eventually climbing to intersect with another segment of the old Mt. Hood Highway.)

Just before 0.5 miles, the path forks into a keyhole loop; either direction will take you to the viewpoint atop the rocky chute. A second interpretive plaque reminds you how the early settlers descended here, risking all their worldly possessions en route to the Promised Land of the Willamette Valley. Complete the loop and return down the hill the way you came.

Laurel Hill Chute is part of the historic Oregon Trail

Nearest Lodgings: Falcon's Crest, Mt. Hood Inn, Brightwood Guest House, Old Welches Inn, Summit Meadow Cabins.

BALD BUTTE
Views of Hood River Valley and Mt. Hood.

Map:	Green Trails #430, "Hood River" (access road 630 does not show)
Distance:	1.5 miles round-trip
Elevation Gain:	420′
Estimated Time:	1 hour

If you find yourself in the Hood River Valley at the beginning or end of the day with an hour or so to kill, romp up Bald Butte. The hike itself is nothing special—a dusty old road bed, basically—but the view is splendid. For a modicum of effort, you are rewarded with sweeping views of the Hood River Valley orchard-lands and Mt. Hood.

This three-quarter-mile segment is part of the 17-mile Surveyor's Ridge Trail, a scenic but dry ridgeline route that roughly parallels Highway 35 north-south along the valley. The trail may be accessed from several points, or hiked in its entirety. Contact the Hood River Ranger District for more information.

Getting There
From Hood River, take Highway 35 south for 10 miles to Pine Mont Drive, also Forest Service Road 17. Turn left. Ignore a right-hand turn at 1.6 miles that leads to another part of Surveyor's Ridge Trail 688. Continue on Road 17, which turns to gravel at 4.0 miles, then back to patchy asphalt at 4.8 miles. Cross a cattle guard, then pass a junction with Road 620, which forks to your left at 5.6 miles. At 6.0 miles, turn right onto Road 630, and follow it 0.4 miles to a gravel pull-out on the left, right under the powerlines.

From points south and west, take Highway 26 east, then Highway 35 north from the 35/26 junction. Continue just over 3.0 miles past the grocery store at Mt. Hood Corner, and turn right on Pine Mont, then follow the directions above.

A sign, SURVEYOR'S RIDGE TRAIL 688, marks the trailhead.

The Hike
From the trailhead sign, turn right and proceed up the rocky, rutted, four-wheel drive road, winding under the power lines. Immediate views of Mt. Hood com-pensate for the motley condition of the trail, which is shared by hikers, eques-trians, and mountain bikers.

After an initial ascent, the trail drops down through a stand of trees, then climbs to its final destination, Bald Butte, at 0.75 mile. From this open summit, popular with hang gliders, the 180°+ view sweeps from the Columbia Gorge to Mt. Hood.

Nearest Lodgings: Mt. Hood Hamlet, Mt. Hood B&B, Inn at Cooper Spur; lodg-ings in *Section 4*, "Columbia Gorge."

TRILLIUM LAKE LOOP
Stunning Mt. Hood and lake views; barrier-free.

Map:	None Needed; Green Trails #462, "Mt. Hood" (access only; shows lake but not trail)
Distance:	2.0 mile loop
Elevation Gain:	none
Estimated Time:	1 hour

A dead-flat, well-graded, scenic loop, this new 1997 trail is ideal for families, wheelchair hikers, birdwatchers and flower lovers. Boardwalk sections take you across delicate wetlands, and majestic Mt. Hood looms large at the north end of the lake.

Trillium Lake is a peaceful, family-oriented camping, swimming, picnicking, and fishing area. No motorized craft are allowed on the lake. Bicycles are allowed on the part of the loop trail adjacent to the campground and day use areas (the east shore), but are prohibited between the dam and the amphitheater (the north and west shores).

Getting There

From Highway 26, turn south on Road 56 (also known as 2656), following the highway signs for TRILLIUM LAKE CAMPGROUND. This turnoff is about a mile west of the junction of highways 26 and 35, or 1.8 miles east of the Government Camp public rest area (at the east end of Government Camp).

Follow the signs 1.7 miles to the Trillium Lake Campground day use area, where you will find toilet facilities and parking for about two dozen cars. A day use fee of $3.00 is charged. Interpretive walks are offered during peak use times.

The Walk

Begin from any one of several points along the lake shore. From the parking area or the fee collection booth, walk down asphalt paths through picnic areas to the lake, or begin at the day use boat launch. The following mileages are given from a starting point at the picturesque fishing dock just south of the boat launch, proceeding clockwise around the lake on Trail 761. If trailhead signs are not in place, simply follow the path closest to the lake shore, turning right as you leave the dock.

Stroll along the most populated section of trail first, passing picnic sites and a canoe beach. The path is medium wide and well graded, with boardwalk or finely crushed rock surfaces throughout the 2.0-mile loop.

At 0.25 mile, you reach the dam at the south end of the lake. Here, turn right and walk along the road 0.1 mile before dropping onto boardwalks. The next segment of the walk is a banquet for flower lovers: columbine, paintbrush, tiger

Scenic Trillium Lake Loop

lilies, yellow monkeyflowers, and, of course, trilliums peep from carpets of Canadian dogwood, fern, wild raspberries, and vanilla leaf as you walk under a canopy of fir and cedar. Emerge from shady glens to cross wetland sections on sturdy boardwalks. Here, skunk cabbage and cow parsnips dominate, with patches of lavender-and-yellow mountain daisies and dusky bluebells thrown in for color.

Near the halfway point, a 0.2-mile stretch of boardwalk crosses a large, damp meadow, in the midst of which is a sitting bench—a great place to regroup, share a snack, and take a can't-miss snapshot of Mt. Hood.

At 1.25 miles, a boardwalk spur trail leads a few hundred feet to the right, back out into the wetlands; stay left on the forest path to continue on the main trail. (As construction was new in 1997, trail specifics may change. Watch for signs.)

At 1.6 miles, reach the park amphitheater and the lake shore. From here, the path continues through the park's camping areas. Bicycles are allowed on this part of the path. When you reach the second boat launch, you will have come full-circle.

Nearest Lodgings: Summit Meadow Cabins, Timberline Lodge, Falcon's Crest Inn, Mt. Hood Inn.

CASTLE CANYON

Mysterious rock formations.

Map:	Green Trails #461, "Government Camp"
Distance:	2.0 miles round-trip
Elevation Gain:	800′
Estimated Time:	1.5 hours

The only drawback to this little gem is the lack of parking at the trailhead. Well, and the steepness. If your party is seeking an *easy* 2-mile hike, look to those listed above. This one is steep, gritty, and altogether too cool to miss. The reward for your at-first-gradual-then-steep climb through thick forest is a series of eerie rock formations reminiscent of ancient ruins.

Getting There

From Highway 26, turn north at the east end of the tiny hamlet of Rhododendron (3.0 miles east of the Welches Road/Highway 26 stoplight intersection). The road onto which you turn is marked E. LITTLEBROOK LN. at its intersection with the highway.

Immediately turn left, following the brown OREGON TRAIL historical sign onto a frontage road signed E. ARLIE MITCHELL RD. This paved, one-lane road parallels the highway northwest for a few hundred feet, then veers left into the woods and a residential area.

At 0.2 mile, where the main road curves to the right (becoming HENRY CREEK RD.), you will turn left, following another OREGON TRAIL sign onto a paved-but-potholed road marked BARLOW ROAD ROUTE. A sign informs you as you enter MT. HOOD NATIONAL FOREST.

Watch for a trailhead sign on your right, 0.4 miles from your turn onto the Barlow Road Route. A driveway on the left (southwest) side of the road enables you to turn around and park one or two cars in the slight pullout on the side of the road across from the trailhead. Please do not block driveways. Because parking is so tight, consider dropping hikers off at the trailhead and seeking other parking options down the road, or even in town—it's only 0.6 miles each way.

In the past, the Castle Canyon trailhead has been accessible from Road 18/Lolo Pass Road out of Zigzag. By turning north on Road 18 and proceeding 0.4 mile, you could access the east end of the trailhead road (sometimes signed ROAD 19), on which you would turn right. Proceed about 2 miles to the trailhead. In 1997, Road 19 was closed west of the trailhead, and plans for reopening it were uncertain.

The Hike

Begin at the trailhead sign: CASTLE CANYON, TR. 765. A lovely, narrow trail overhung with ferns and moss-draped vine maple takes you to a registration box a short distance up the trail. As part of the Mt. Hood Wilderness, this trail requires

One of the rock formations on Castle Canyon Trail

the self-issuing permits you will find in the box. This particular t
only—no stock or bicycles.

Continue through the thick, primeval growth. After 0.3 mile, the switchbacks
begin. Climbing past a profusion of Oregon grape and salal, you will notice the
canopy begins to thin after about 0.5 mile.

After 0.6 miles, watch for the first rock formation. We call this one "The
Sentry." It sits just to the left of the path, an ovate boulder topped by a larger,
blocky one. With a little imagination, you can see a face in the lower rock (especially in profile); the top one forms a Russian or British beefeater-style hat. From
here on, rock formations loom everywhere. As you climb (knee-to-chest in
places), watch for and explore the various little side paths, glimpsing views
across the Zigzag Valley and the draws created by its tributaries. Use caution
with children. Footing can be slippery, and dropoffs steep. This is no trail for
running or horseplay.

Just before a mile, you reach a summit. This saddle between two boulder formations is a good final destination and snack stop. Those wishing to explore further can drop down the backside of the outcropping to look back up (caution!
slippery footing) or step carefully along a shelf in front of the same outcropping
to peer through a rock "porthole" at the rocky spires beyond.

Nearest Lodgings: Brightwood Guest House, Resort at the Mountain, Old
Welches Inn, Brookside B&B, Falcon's Crest Inn, Mt. Hood Inn.

TIMBERLINE MOUNTAINEER LOOP
Steep loop with alpine meadows and views.

Map:	Green Trails #462, "Mt. Hood"
Distance:	2.75 miles round-trip
Elevation Gain:	1100′
Estimated Time:	2 hours, 15 minutes

This beautiful and popular loop from Timberline Lodge will take your breath
away—in every sense of the expression. It's an alpine flower paradise, and
views south toward Central Oregon are predictably expansive. It also gains 1100
feet in a mile, and tops out at 7000 feet elevation, so it's no walk in the park for
those unaccustomed to hill climbing or altitude. Those unsure of their ability to
climb can take the Magic Mile Chairlift up to the top (for a fee of around $6.00)
and the Silcox Hut and walk just over a mile back to the lodge, all downhill.
Whichever way you choose to get to the top, be sure to pick up a brochure at the
lodge for the interpretive trail that follows numbered markers down the hill.

Getting There
When you've found Timberline Lodge, you've found the trailhead. From
Highway 26, go north on Timberline Road, just east of Government Camp and
a little over 2.0 miles west of the Highway 35/Highway 26 junction. Follow the
road 5.2 miles to the lodge.

The Hike

From the Timberline Lodge parking lot, walk west on the service road about 200 feet. There, you will find the Magic Mile Chairlift. Just beyond the lift is the trailhead, signed MOUNTAINEER TRAIL 798. Wend your way west across treeline meadows and past a few scattered trees until you cross Timberline Trail 600 at 0.5 mile. (Alternately, if you start from the north side of the lodge instead of the parking lot, you can step onto Timberline Trail and turn left, heading west. When you intersect Mountaineer Trail, turn right and head uphill.)

Climb steadily up the lower flanks of Mt. Hood toward Palmer Glacier, where skiing takes place all year long (with a little help from snow brought down the mountain from another area). You'll want to take your time, enjoying the alpine meadow flowers all around you and views of Mt. Jefferson to the south. When in doubt about the trail, use the top of Magic Mile Chairlift as your guide.

The hike tops out at the chairlift, at about 1.5 miles. From here, work your way east to the Silcox Hut, built as a warming hut in the 1930s. Grab a snack or a beverage, if you like, then head down the hill. (On some sunny summer days, the Palmer Junction barbecue is set up at the top of the Magic Mile Chairlift—a fun place for lunch!) Descending from Silcox Hut, use the brochure you picked up at the lodge before your ascent to look up the numbered interpretive posts on the way down and learn about the plants, animals, and weather of the south slope of Mt. Hood.

Nearest Lodgings: Timberline Lodge, Summit Meadow Cabins, Mt. Hood Inn, Falcon's Crest Inn.

VEDA LAKE

Pretty, secluded 3-acre lake.

Map:	Green Trails #461, "Government Camp;" access on #462 & #493, "Mt. Hood" & "High Rock"
Distance:	2.5 miles round-trip
Elevation Loss:	500´
Estimated Time:	1 hour, 45 minutes

A pleasant, forested drop into a lovely cirque lake, Veda Lake has much to recommend it. The drive is rough (see below), but the trail is beautiful, and the difficult access increases your chance of solitude. Early in the season, enjoy a profusion of rhododendron and beargrass; in the fall, huckleberries are your reward. And, on any clear day, you'll enjoy views of Mt. Hood and the pretty little lake itself.

Getting There

The only bad thing about this hike is getting there. The road is awfully rough, to the point where forest service folks don't readily recommend it. For inclusion in this book, a trail must be reachable by passenger car (as opposed to requiring four-wheel drive); this one is borderline. That being said, if you have a reasonably high-clearance vehicle and plenty of time, go for it. Go slowly, expect the worst road you've ever driven, and you'll be OK.

From the west, take Highway 26 east 0.4 miles past Government Camp. Turn south on Road 2650, signed STILL CREEK CAMPGROUND. Drive through the campground, continuing for 1.0 mile (Road 2650 becomes 2650-131). Turn right on E. CHIMNEY ROCK RD., also known as Road 2612-126, at an A-frame cabin (this is one of the Summit Meadow Cabins, see *Lodging*, above). Continue 0.5 mile to a four-way intersection. Take the road ahead and to the left, Road 2613/Sherar Burn Road, which heads south. This very rough, one-lane road demands patience and caution, but affords stunning views of Mt. Jefferson to the south. After 3.5 miles, arrive at Fir Tree Campground. Veda Lake Trailhead is on the right side of the road, across from the campground. Park in the campground (not in a campsite) or alongside the road.

From the east, you can take Highway 26 about a mile west of the Highway 35/Highway 26 junction, then turn south on Road 2656, signed TRILLIUM LAKE. Take this road past Trillium Lake Campground. Stay right when the road forks at 1.7 miles. Go around the south end of Trillium Lake (great views of Mt. Hood!), after which the road turns to gravel. Continue for a total of 3.1 miles from Highway 26 to the four-way intersection described above. Take a hard left onto Road 2613/Sherar Burn Road, and proceed as above.

The Hike
Across the road from the campground, take the narrow, rocky, rooty singletrack signed VEDA LAKE TR. 673. The trail begins with a moderate ascent through woods thick with huckleberries and beargrass.

After 0.3 mile, the grade flattens out, and you walk along a deeply shaded, needle-carpeted, flat path until you begin descending at 0.5 mile. Within 0.2

Huckleberries, abundant throughout much of the central Cascades, bear fruit in late August–September

mile, you can see Mt. Hood shining like a beacon just 10 miles to the north, and the little round button of Veda Lake below.

Switchback down the verdant hillside, where rhododendrons take over the understory.

Reach the lake at 1.25 miles, then continue as far as you wish around the north side, where a defined trail continues another 0.2 mile. Depending upon the water level, a trail of sorts goes pretty much all the way around the lake, but the best spots to hang out are on the north side.

Nearest Lodgings: Summit Meadow Cabins, Timberline Lodge, Mt. Hood Inn, Falcon's Crest Inn.

HIDDEN LAKE

Easy hike to a marshy mountain lake.

Map:	Green Trails #461, "Government Camp"
Distance:	3.2 miles round-trip
Elevation Gain:	740′
Estimated Time:	2 hours, 15 minutes

Climb a moderate grade along a ridge, then plunge down to a little lakelet. More suitable for viewing than bathing, marshy little Hidden Lake is surrounded by rhododendron and huckleberry bushes, the former more exciting in spring, the latter in fall. A few campsites at the lake provide suitable picnic spots. Bring the mosquito juice, or you won't be staying long.

Most sources call this a 4.0-mile round-trip, but I think 3.2 is more accurate.

If you are fortunate enough to catch the rhododendrons in bloom, this trail is a riot of color. Otherwise, the native plant's broad, glossy leaves blend with the salal, beargrass, and moss-hung trees to create a lush understory en route to the tiny lake.

Getting There

A few miles west of Government Camp (4.0 miles west of the Rest Area at the east end of Government Camp) on Highway 26, turn north on Road 39 (also known as Road 2639, but the first sign you will see says 39). If you're coming from the west, this road is 7.4 miles east of the Welches Road/Highway 26 stoplight intersection. The road is signed MT. HOOD KIWANIS CAMP. (This is the same road you take to reach the Little Zigzag Falls walk, above).

Follow this road for 2.1 miles. Park at the pullout on the left, signed HIDDEN LAKE TR. 779. There is room for about a dozen cars.

The Hike

From the trailhead sign, climb about 50′ to the Mt. Hood Wilderness information and self-registration signboard. The trail is open to hikers, horses, and leashed dogs, with group size limited to no more than 12 heartbeats.

Continue ascending the wide, needle-carpeted trail, which is closely shaded by mixed conifers and a profusion of rhododendron bushes.

The canopy thins after the first 0.25 mile and the third or fourth switchback; you are coming to the crest of the ridge. Views open up across the valley; the highway is visible below.

Just before 0.5 mile, climb a short, steep 0.1 mile. About 1.4 miles, the canopy opens up, and huckleberries crowd the trail. Just before 1.5 miles, the trail plunges down abruptly, switchbacking to the banks of a stream thick with skunk cabbage. If you crossed the stream and continued up the other bank, you would reach the Pacific Crest Trail after another 2.5 miles. Instead, turn right at the streambank and follow a little bootbeaten path along the stream, which takes you to the lake in just about 200 feet. Some of the best access is off to the left, about a quarter of the way around the lake.

Nearest Lodgings: Falcon's Crest, Mt. Hood Inn, Brightwood Guest House, Old Welches Inn, Summit Meadow Cabins.

OLD SALMON RIVER
Easy trail, beautiful river, old-growth trees.

Map:	Green Trails #461, "Government Camp"
Distance:	4.8 miles round-trip (2.4 miles with shuttle car)
Elevation Gain:	negligible
Estimated Time:	2 hours, 15 minutes

This nearly flat trail takes you along the banks of the Salmon River under a canopy of majestic old-growth. Both the river, where salmon spawn each fall, and the surrounding woods are gorgeous. The Salmon River Trail in its entirety is a long one; the segment described here is an easy piece of the older part of the trail.

Getting There
Turn south off Highway 26 at the stoplight intersection with Welches Road. You will follow this road a total of 4.9 miles to the campground from which you will begin. En route, pass the Resort at the Mountain entrance at 0.75 miles, Old Welches Inn at 1.0 mile, a reverse Y-junction with the road to Zigzag at 2.3 miles, and a pullout for the other end of the Old Salmon River Trail at 3.0 miles. (One could leave a shuttle car at this 8-car pullout for a 2.4-mile one-way walk.) Continue to the MT. HOOD NATIONAL FOREST GREEN CANYONS CAMPGROUND sign after 4.9 miles and turn right into the campground. Park in the day use area (if unsure, a campground host should be on duty in the first camping spot; just ask). Toilets are provided in the campground.

The Hike
From the campground day use area, work your way down to the riverbank via any one of a number of social trails until you come to the main path paralleling the river. The trail is open to mountain bikes as well as hikers.

Walk along a wide, fragrant, needle-carpeted path amongst old-growth timber. At first, the campground is to your right. Always, the melodic and photogenic Salmon River flows to your left.

At one point, where a tributary flows into the river and the riverbank all but disappears, the trail veers to the right and goes along the shoulder of the road briefly before descending again into forest.

This idyllic path offers a close-up, easily-accessible look at giant trees and an old-growth environment. Nurse logs decay and provide food and root medium for new growth; mushrooms sprout in the damp, humus soil.

After 2.3 miles, you come to the first real incline. The remaining 0.1-mile climb to the other trailhead is relatively viewless and featureless, so, unless you are doing the hike as a 2.4-mile point-to-point shuttle, you could turn around here, especially if you don't like walking uphill. The resulting 4.6-mile walk is nice and flat and appropriate for almost anyone. For those who want to finish the 2.4 miles, continue uphill to the trail's end at the parking pullout along the road.

If you do the round-trip, the walk is just as beautiful on the way back, and the shifting light over the river makes it a joy in both directions. Be sure to keep your eyes peeled for your turnoff to the campground, as the trail keeps going past it.

Nearest Lodgings: Old Welches Inn, Resort at the Mountain.

TAMAWANAS FALLS/EAST FORK LOOP
Postcard-perfect waterfall and a loop hike through varied terrain.

Map:	Green Trails #462, "Mt. Hood"
Distance:	4.0 mile loop
Elevation Gain:	700′
Estimated Time:	2.5 hours

This is a satisfying hike through varied terrain to view one of the most beautiful waterfalls in the Cascades. In June, when runoff is high, Tamawanas Falls is a vision of epic proportions. A churning curtain of water in a moss-lined grotto, it plunges about 100 feet into a deep pool and sends up a spray that fills the natural amphitheater around it.

This loop trail is a variation that adds a pleasant ridgetop climb and a return along a less-traveled route. Tamawanas Falls can also be reached from the Tamawanas Falls trailhead, just north of Sherwood Campground on Highway 35.

Getting There
Begin the loop from the POLALLIE TRAILHEAD, just south of the intersection of Cooper Spur Road and Highway 35. You'll find parking for 8 or 10 cars at this marked trailhead on the east side of the highway. The route begins across the highway at the sign for EAST FORK TRAIL 650.

The Hike

This is a hiker-only trail. From the EAST FORK TRAIL 650/ELK MEADOWS JCT. sign, climb briefly and steeply up an access trail, switchbacking once, then intersecting at an angle with the main East Fork Trail 650. Proceed straight ahead (to the left, or south), following the sign to TAMAWANAS FALLS 2.25 MI. (The other direction, marked LAMBERSON TRAIL, BLUE GRASS RIDGE TRAIL, ELK MEADOWS, is the trail on which you will return.)

The first tenth of a mile of this trail is a pretty steep climb, then it settles into an undulating up-and-down as it parallels Highway 35 and, after half a mile, the East Fork Hood River. Climb through a young pine, cedar, and vine maple forest, your path lined with vanilla leaf, queen's cup and trillium in the early season, as well as lupine, paintbrush, ferns, and salmonberry bushes.

Tamawanas Falls makes a great picnic destination

At 0.7 mile, you come to the confluence of Cold Spring Creek and East Fork Hood River, and the trail turns right (west) to run alongside Cold Spring Creek, which it will continue to do most of the way to the falls.

At 0.8 mile, cross a bridge over Cold Spring Creek and enter a boulder field, apparently the remains of a mudslide or long-ago glacial event.

Just after 1.0 mile, you reach a signed intersection. To your left is the continuation of EAST FORK TRAIL 650 toward Sherwood Campground. Take the trail to your right, marked TAMAWANAS FALLS 650A.

Cross Cold Spring Creek again, continuing through a variety of closed and open areas, always flanking the creek. Arrive at the junction with TAMAWANAS FALLS TIE 650B at about 2.0 miles. This trail, which you will take on your return trip, goes uphill and to the right. To reach the falls, stay left, following the sign.

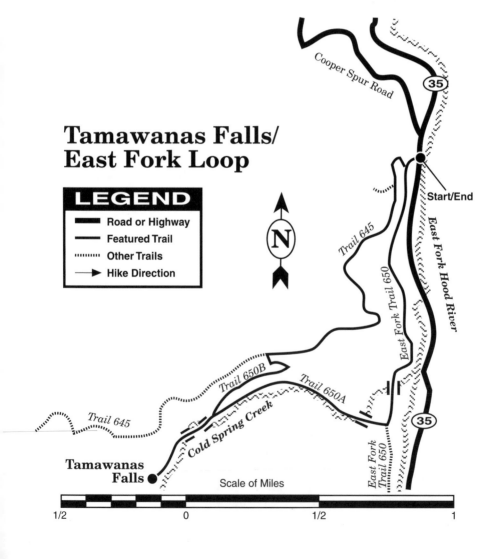

Tamawanas Falls/ East Fork Loop

LEGEND

▬▬ Road or Highway
— Featured Trail
▪▪▪▪▪ Other Trails
—➤ Hike Direction

N

Cooper Spur Road

35

Start/End

East Fork Hood River

Trail 645

East Fork Trail 650

Trail 650B

Trail 650A

Trail 645

Cold Spring Creek

East Fork Trail 650

35

Tamawanas Falls ●

Scale of Miles

1/2   0   1/2   1

Cross Cold Spring Creek twice more, each time on sturdy little bridges, before your final ascent to the falls.

Several vantage points offer superb views and picnic opportunities. The trail does not approach the falls, although many have obviously tried. Respect the fragile ecosystem around the falls and enjoy them from a distance—the photo angle couldn't be better. And, speaking of restraint, this is a good place to refrain from feeding wildlife, too. The chipmunks are friendly to the point of being aggressive. They do not need your lunch; it only teaches them dependence.

On the return trip, turn left at the TAMAWANAS FALLS TIE 650B, 0.4 mile back the way you came. Climb relentlessly up the side of the ridge—about 400 feet in 0.4 mile—to the junction of Trail 645, at which you turn right (east), then stroll along the ridgetop.

The viewpoint spur trail at about 3.75 miles forks off to your left to view the damage of a 1980 flood in the Pollalie Creek valley. Nature has done such a fine repair job that this overlook is really not worth the time today. Proceed on the main trail to return to the trailhead in 0.25 mile.

Nearest Lodgings: Inn at Cooper Spur, Mt. Hood B&B, Mt. Hood Hamlet.

LOST LAKE BUTTE
Bird's eye views of Lost Lake and Mt. Hood.

Map:	Green Trails #461, "Government Camp"
Distance:	4.0 miles round trip
Elevation Gain:	1268´
Estimated Time:	2 hours

This steep, scenic trail romps up the side of a 4440-foot butte above Lost Lake, a 240-acre trout lake northeast of Mt. Hood and southeast of Hood River. As Lost Lake is located in a campground/fishing resort privately operated by agreement with the forest service, a day use fee of $4.00 is charged for each carload.

A number of other trails around Lost Lake make this a great place to spend the day. See *Other Hike Notes* for more information.

Getting There
Many sources make finding Lost Lake needlessly complicated. It is really quite easy, especially from Hood River or points along Highway 35, such as Mt. Hood Hamlet or Mt. Hood B&B. All you have to do is get to the community of Dee, then follow Lost Lake Road to the lake.

To get to Dee from Hood River, go south out of town on a road known variously as Tucker, Highway 281, Hood River Highway, or Hood River-Parkdale. Any route to Dee will do. From points south of Hood River on Highway 35, find Woodworth Road, about a mile north of the village of Mt. Hood Corner (also known as just "Mt. Hood"), and turn west. Follow the signs northwest to Dee.

From Dee, simply follow the signs to Lost Lake via Lost Lake Road. It's paved all the way.

The route to Lost Lake from the south (Highway 26) corridor is a bit more difficult, but still very do-able. Road 18 is washed out more often than not, so this description should get you there. (Of course, check with the ranger station at Zigzag for current conditions.) Take E. Lolo Pass Road (Forest Service Road 18) north off Highway 26. You will find this road's junction with Highway 26 1.1 miles east of the Welches Road/Highway 26 stoplight junction, and just west of the Zigzag Ranger Station. Drive 10.5 miles to a junction with Forest Service Road 1810, which is conveniently signed LOST LAKE. Turn right on this gravel road, which is the washout bypass. Rejoin Road 18 after about 7.0 miles. Proceed another 6.5 miles to Road 13. Turn left and drive a short distance to the resort/campground.

Once you've paid your entry fee, get a free hiking map and ask the attendant for directions through the campground to the Lost Lake Butte trailhead. Alternately, you can park near the resort store and ask there.

The Hike

The trail climbs steeply from the get-go, intersecting another trail within the first 0.1 mile. Continue straight ahead at that intersection.

Just after 0.1 mile, you will intersect and cross a road, then continue ascending on a rocky, dirt-and-needle trail through the campground. Beargrass, rhododendron, and huckleberry line the trail.

Intersect the Old Skyline Trail at an angle at 0.3 mile. Proceed straight ahead, slightly to the right, and uphill, rather than taking a hard left or right at this unsigned junction.

The climb is switchbacking and persistent, but not horrendous. There's plenty of tree cover to keep you shaded, but bottles of water are in order. On the way

Lost Lake Butte's summit offers great views

up, you'll see occasional spur trails forking off to the left for view
is always to the right.

Just before you reach the summit, you'll come upon the remains of a ~~
tower. Bear right to reach the summit.

From the nice, flat, "sittin' rocks" on top, you get a smashing head-on look at
the northwest slopes of Mt. Hood, an angle different from any other hike in this
book. To the north, you can see the Columbia Gorge and Mt. Adams; to the
south, Mt. Jefferson. And below, due west, is Lost Lake. Linger atop for lunch
and unbeatable views, or charge back down the wooded slope and take a walk
around the lake.

Nearest Lodgings: Mt. Hood Hamlet, Mt. Hood B&B, all lodgings in this section and Hood River (see *Section 4*, "Columbia Gorge").

RAMONA FALLS LOOP

Beautiful, though popular, loop to a waterfall.

Map:	Green Trails #461, "Government Camp;" US Forest Service "Mt. Hood Wilderness" or "Mt. Hood National Forest"
Distance:	7.3 miles round-trip
Elevation Gain:	1000'
Estimated Time:	3 hours, 30 minutes

Hike this popular loop when the throngs aren't out—early in the morning, late
in the afternoon, or late in the season. Definitely try to come on a weekday. In
fact, if you really want to beat the crowds, Ramona Falls makes a dandy loop on
a rainy day, if you have the gear for it.

Begin with a walk up the Sandy River, then intersect with the Timberline
Trail/Pacific Crest Trail before you reach the falls. Return via a breathtakingly
beautiful, deep-forest walk along a creek.

Getting There

Ramona Falls Loop used to have two trailheads: an upper and a lower. Other
sources may give directions to both, or just to Upper Ramona Falls, as it was the
shorter trail. This trailhead is no longer an option due to a road washout, so follow these directions carefully.

Take E. Lolo Pass Road (Forest Service Road 18) north off Highway 26. You
will find this road 1.1 miles east of the Welches Road/Highway 26 stoplight
junction, and just west of the Zigzag Ranger Station. Drive 4.2 miles on Road 18,
then turn right on Road 1825, a paved two-lane. After 0.6 miles on Road 1825,
you will reach a fork. Stay right, crossing the Sandy River. Stay on Road 1825 as
it narrows and passes several turn-offs. Come to a signed fork after a total of 2.4
miles. Go left, onto Road 1825/100. In about 0.3 mile, arrive at a small parking
area, where a now-closed road used to lead to the Upper Ramona Falls parking
area, now inaccessible. Turn left here, and drive another 0.2 mile to a large gravel parking area and the signed trailhead.

e *Hike*

The trail begins relatively flat, following the course of the Sandy River east through Old Maid Flat. The first part of the loop is open to mountain bikers, equestrians, and hikers. After walking through young forest for 0.2 mile, you intersect the Sandy River Trail, which goes left toward Riley Horse Camp. Go straight ahead. As you continue through the flat, up the route of the Sandy River, the tread becomes sandy, and you can see Mt. Hood ahead on a clear day.

After walking through the woods for the better part of the first mile, you will drop down onto a former roadbed. This rough, rocky surface takes you to the former upper trailhead at about 1.25 miles. Here, following the sign RAMONA FALLS TR. 797, turn left and cross the Sandy River. (Mountain bikes must stop at this point; horses and hikers may continue.)

Across the river, climb up the bank and veer right. Continue at a moderate incline. At 1.4 miles, reach the beginning of the Ramona Falls Loop. You will return on the trail which forks left here. For now, stay to the right (essentially straight ahead). This is also the point where you enter the Mt. Hood Wilderness and fill out your free, self-issuing wilderness permit.

Continue ascending, walking along a ridge above a draw created by the Sandy River. At 2.9 miles, arrive at a junction with Timberline Trail 600, which is contiguous with the Pacific Crest Trail 2000 at this point. Turn left.

The climb continues gently to moderately until you reach a horse tie-up area just before 3.4 miles. From here, descend about 100 feet to the many-fingered cascade of Ramona Falls. Had Mondrian designed a waterfall, this would have been it—a wide, glistening cascade down chunky, pixilated rock blocks.

To complete the loop, cross the bridge at the base of the falls. The trail forks here, with the PCT/Timberline going to the right and uphill. Take the left fork, staying down alongside the creek.

Ramona Falls is a nice rainy-day hike

The next 1.9 miles are drop-dead gorgeous, and hiker-only. A playful creek meanders through a forest more lush and thick than the terrain on the first half of the loop. Thick pads of moss overhang the creekbanks. The trail follows the creek, crossing it a couple of times as both you and the water gradually descend.

At 5.3 miles, intersect Bald Mountain Trail 784. Turn left. Pass through a log gate designed to keep horses off the 1.9-mile segment you have just finished.

At 5.9 miles, you reach the junction with the trail on which you began your ascent to the falls. Turn right, retracing your steps down to and across the Sandy River.

Return back up the roadbed. Watch for a sign marked SANDY RIVER TRAIL 770 on your right; take this back up into the trees. When the Sandy River trail turns right (signed RILEY HORSE CAMP), stay straight ahead to reach the parking lot.

Nearest Lodgings: Brightwood Guest House, Resort at the Mountain, Old Welches Inn, Falcon's Crest Inn, Mt. Hood Inn.

ELK MEADOWS
High mountain meadow with view of Hood.

Map:	Green Trails #462, "Mt. Hood" (first mile of route described here does not show as a hiking trail)
Distance:	6.9 miles round-trip
Elevation Gain:	1000′
Estimated Time:	4 hours

There are many ways to reach Elk Meadows—every local hiker has his favorite. But they all agree on one thing: go there. This high meadow (around 5100 foot elevation) is full of flowers and has a spectacular view of Mt. Hood, especially early in the day, when the sun is coming from the east. I like this version because it starts and ends at a sno-park pullout, where there's plenty of parking and a toilet. Another popular access point is Mt. Hood Meadows ski area. Bring a huckleberry bucket if you plan to hike in late August—this route is full of them.

Getting There
From Highway 35, 7.5 miles east of the Highway 35/Highway 26 junction, turn north on a road signed MT. HOOD NATIONAL FOREST CLARK CREEK SNO-PARK. It's also signed ELK MEADOWS TRAIL 645. Go about 0.2 mile to a long sno-park parking pull-out alongside the road, where there is room for about 15–20 cars. You'll see a pit toilet on the north side of the road, and blue signs leading to a trail. This is a snow recreation trail and, while it will get you there, it's not the best hiker route. The hiker trailhead, which may be unsigned, is up the road about 80 feet west of the toilet.

The Hike
Enter the woods on a flat, dirt singletrack. Huckleberries and pipsissewa are all around you. After 0.4 mile, you are strolling adjacent to Clark Creek, gaining altitude very gradually.

At 1.0 mile, you reach a junction. Go right across a bridge over Clark Creek. (Going left would take you toward Umbrella Falls and Sahalie Falls trails.) This is also where you enter the Mt. Hood Wilderness and fill out your self-issuing permit.

Across the creek, the trail continues to climb gently through mature, semi-open forest, fording a few streams. Lots of beargrass here, and more huckleberries. Trail 646 intersects on your left just before 1.6 miles (may be unsigned). About 0.2 mile later, cross Newton Creek.

Upon crossing this second creek, go left briefly, then turn right and ascend the hill, which may be unsigned. (Ignore blue snow-recreation signs for ELK MEADOWS and NEWTON CREEK trails.)

Here's where the hike gains most of its altitude—some 700 feet in less than 0.8 mile. It is a switchbacking climb up a semi-open hillside dotted with flowers. The paintbrush, columbine, and pearly everlasting you see here are harbingers of the meadow beauty ahead.

Junction with Bluegrass Ridge Trail 647 and Gnarl Ridge Trail 652 just before 2.6 miles. The former goes to the right, to Elk Mountain (a neat side trip, about a mile each way, if you have time). To get to Elk Meadows, continue straight ahead.

Very shortly after that junction, at about 2.7 miles, you arrive at a T junction. This is the beginning of the perimeter loop of Elk Meadows. A sign tells you that ELK MEADOWS TRAIL 645 goes to the right, but you can make the perimeter loop in either direction. I find it's more dramatic to circle clockwise, so turn left here.

At first, you only glimpse the clearing of the meadow to your right. At 3.1 miles, come to another T junction. Go right. You are treading through the

Vast, flower-filled Elk Meadows

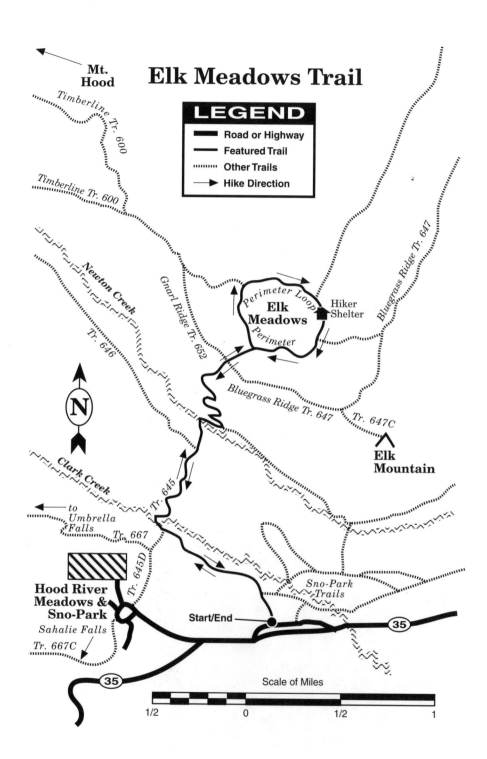

Elk Meadows Trail

Mt. Hood

LEGEND

━━━ Road or Highway
── Featured Trail
········· Other Trails
→ Hike Direction

Timberline Tr. 600

Timberline Tr. 600

Newton Creek

Tr. 646

Gnarl Ridge Tr. 652

Bluegrass Ridge Tr. 647

Perimeter Loop

Elk Meadows

Hiker Shelter

Perimeter

Bluegrass Ridge Tr. 647

Tr. 647C

N

∧ Elk Mountain

Clark Creek

Tr. 645

to Umbrella Falls

Tr. 667

Tr. 645D

Hood River Meadows & Sno-Park

Sahalie Falls
Tr. 667C

Sno-Park Trails

Start/End ●

35

35

Scale of Miles

1/2   0   1/2   1

meadow's periphery here. A sometimes-mushy trail is carved out of the loamy ground—try to stay on it. At 3.4 miles, reach another junction. Turn right to go to the hiker shelter.

Arrive at the hiker shelter at 3.5 miles. Woe to you if you didn't come on a clear day—this is the view you've been waiting for. The shelter is nestled on the east side of the vast, open meadow. Before you is a sea of color, and above it, Mt. Hood rises majestically, directly across the clearing to the northwest. Take off your daypack and rest awhile on the sitting logs provided in front of the shelter.

To complete the perimeter loop, return 0.1 mile the way you came, but instead of turning left and crossing the creek, stay straight. Watch for a sign to indicate you are on ELK MEADOWS PERIMETER TRAIL. Reach another junction in 100 feet. The trail straight ahead leads to Polallie Campground; turn right to stay on Perimeter Trail.

Reach an unsigned but distinct junction at 3.8 miles. Go right to complete the loop on ELK MEADOWS TRAIL 645. The trail to the left leads to another approach to Elk Mountain.

At 4.2 miles, reach the junction at which you began the perimeter loop. Turn left and retrace your steps.

Nearest Lodgings: Timberline Lodge, Summit Meadow Cabins, Falcon's Crest Inn, Mt. Hood Inn, Inn at Cooper Spur.

COOPER SPUR
Top o' the world view between two glaciers.

Map:	Green Trails #462, "Mt. Hood"
Distance:	6.0 miles round-trip
Elevation Gain:	2600´
Estimated Time:	4 hours, 30 minutes

An amazing alpine experience is yours for a mere 6.0-mile round trip effort when you hike up Mt. Hood's Cooper Spur. Have lunch at the hike's apex, perched between Eliot and Newton Clark glaciers, and know what it is to be a mountain goat. The summit of Mt. Hood looms a mere 2700 feet above you, appearing close enough to touch. You'll want a clear day to experience the exhilaration of Cooper Spur, but remember—they call part of the mountain "Cloud Cap" for a reason. Clouds seem to drift and float around up here more often than not. If you're patient, you can sometimes wait them out.

Getting There
You can start this hike from one of two campgrounds: Tilly Jane or Cloud Cap. Both are fine starting points and can, in fact, be linked for a sort of mini-loop via a segment of Trail 600A between the two campgrounds. These directions start and end at Cloud Camp Campground, a popular access point for Timberline Trail 600. (For more information on the Timberline Trail, Mt. Hood's round-the-mountain trail, see *Other Hike Notes*, below.)

From Hood River, drive 24 miles south on Highway 35 to Cooper Spur Road; turn right (west). From Government Camp, drive east on Highway 26 to the junction of Highway 35, then continue northeast on Highway 35, for a total of 19 miles, to Cooper Spur Road; turn left (west).

Proceed 2.3 miles on Cooper Spur Road to Forest Service Road 3512, also known as Cloud Cap Road. Turn left. Proceed on this road, following CLOUD CAP CAMPGROUND signs, a total of 10.2 miles to the trailhead. The road is gravel after the first 1.4 miles. A T-intersection at 9.5 miles gives you the choice of turning left for Tilly Jane Campground or right for Cloud Cap; turn right.

Parking for some 15 vehicles is provided at the campground trailhead. Pit toilets are available.

Cooper Spur Trail takes you to within 2700' of Hood's summit

Cooper Spur Trail

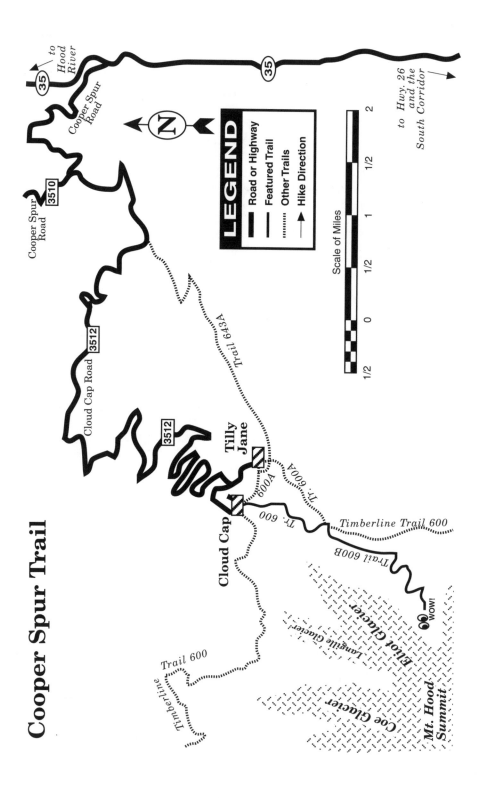

LEGEND

Road or Highway
Featured Trail
Other Trails
Hike Direction

Scale of Miles

1/2   0   1/2   1   1/2   2

to Hood River

35

Cooper Spur Road

3510

Cooper Spur Road

N

35

to Hwy. 26 and the South Corridor

3512

Cloud Cap Road

3512

Trail 643A

Tilly Jane

600A

Tr. 600A

Cloud Cap

Tr. 600

Timberline Trail 600

Trail 600B

Timberline Trail 600

Langille Glacier

Eliot Glacier

Coe Glacier

Mt. Hood Summit

WOW!

The Hike

Facing west from the parking lot (uphill; the side where the A-frame outhouse is located), you will see the trailhead sign to your right, a few dozen feet back into the campground. From the trailhead, you will go straight ahead onto Timberline Trail 600. (Going left on Tilly Jane Trail 600A would take you to the campground of the same name in 0.5 mile; going right on the continuation of Timberline Trail would take you toward Elk Cove.)

As part of the Mt. Hood Wilderness, this trail allows no bicycles, pets must be leashed, and you must fill out a self-issuing wilderness permit at the box just up the trail from the trailhead.

The trail forks just past the permit box; stay left on Timberline Trail. The sandy, rocky, rooty path meanders through the forest, climbing moderately, with a creeklet running off to your left. After 0.5 mile, emerge into open area, where lupine and heather are the predominant foliage. A huge ridge of glacial debris rises in front of you, between you and the mountain. Skirt along the foot of this sandy hill, where little creeklets flow, creating oasis-like draws filled with greenery.

The path across this basin leads toward a thick little stand of subalpine forest. You will cross one of the creeklets at about 0.7 mile, just before reaching the scrubby trees. At this creek crossing, some hikers will turn right, taking a steep, switchbacking ascent up the side of the debris hill. This alternate route follows vertical post markers to the crest of the hill, then goes left (southwest) along the ridge, eventually working its way up to the arm of Cooper Spur and intersecting with the Cooper Spur trail. The problem with this route is the lack of distinguishable trail after about 0.5 mile from the top, and several steep, treacherous scrambles over loose rock. I can't recommend it.

You'll know you are on the recommended path if your ascent is only moderate between 0.5 and 0.7 mile, and if you enter a thick little stand of subalpine forest at 0.75 mile. Gnarled, tough little trees line the path like scrappy gnomes, creating a final quarter-mile patch of greenery just below the treeline.

At 1.0 mile, you reach a 3-way junction. Timberline Trail 600, which you are on, continues straight ahead. Tilly Jane Trail 600A goes to your left. Cooper Spur Trail 600B goes to your right; turn right. Leave the last of the scrubby fir and other subalpine flora behind as you head up Cooper Spur, beyond the treeline.

After another 0.1 mile, arrive at a stone shelter, a good spot to take a water break and chat with other hikers, as this is a popular backpacker stopover for those doing the whole Timberline Trail (see *Other Hike Notes*, below).

The next 1.9 miles take you switchbacking up a well-defined trail through a landscape reminiscent of high desert. Snow patches may linger late in the season, but you will likely be able to follow boot-beaten routes across them, as this is a popular dayhike. The ascent is steady, gaining nearly 2000 feet between the hiker shelter and the trail's end at 3.0 miles. The exhilaration of wide-open spaces, thin air, and ever-better views urges you on.

Walk out until the trail ends and a mountain climb would begin. At 8500 feet, you've never seen Mt. Hood like this. Fingers of glaciers are all around you, and the tip of the mountain rises directly above you, seemingly close enough to touch. Linger here as long as you can, drinking in the singular scenery. As you face the mountain, crevasses in the snowfields below and to your right create shimmering patterns of blue at the base of Eliot Glacier. When you can tear your gaze away from the mountain, you'll see that the entire Hood River Valley lies open behind you. Vistas extend into the flat desert lands of eastern Oregon, north to the Columbia Gorge, and beyond to the other central Cascade peaks.

Nearest Lodgings: Inn at Cooper Spur, Mt. Hood B&B, Mt. Hood Hamlet.

OTHER HIKE NOTES
These hikes not personally reviewed or not as highly recommended as the above hikes.

Lost Lake Trails
Lost Lake is a 240-acre trout lake in the Mt. Hood National Forest. A private concessionaire operates the Lost Lake Resort Campground that controls access to the lake. Those who are not camping or staying in one of the resort's cabins must pay a $4.00 per carload day use fee. Besides Lost Lake Butte trail (featured above), dayhikes here include flat, easy 3.2-mile Lakeshore Trail (part of which is a short, barrier-free, self-guiding nature trail), a 1.0-mile Old Growth Trail, and a longer, 2.5-miles each way, climb called Huckleberry Mountain Trail, leading to the PCT. Pick up a free map and more information as you enter the campground.

Mirror Lake
This 3.2-mile round-trip hike, with its trailhead right on Highway 26 just west of Government Camp, is the most popular trail on the south corridor. So popular, in fact, it feels more like a stroll in an urban park on a summer Sunday than a wilderness experience. Rangers don't like to recommend it, and I can see why. It's badly overused.

Surveyor's Ridge
This popular multi-use trail (hikers, horses, hunters, mountain bikers) runs north-south, roughly paralleling Highway 35 down the Hood River valley. It's a dry, east-side-of-the-mountains trail with many access points. In its entirety, it's almost 17 miles long, but can be dayhiked in segments (see *Bald Butte*, above). The best feature of Surveyor's Ridge Trail 688 is its views of Mt. Hood and the Hood River valley.

Timberline Trail
The Timberline Trail is a 40.7-mile round-the-mountain trail constructed in part by the Civilian Conservation Corps (CCC) in the 1930s. It ranges from a low elevation of 3200 feet to a high of 7320 feet, and is generally hiked mid-July through October. Its west and south segments are contiguous with the Pacific Crest Trail. The most popular access is at Timberline Lodge. For more information and

current conditions, contact a Mt. Hood National Forest office. A neat little book by Sonia Buist and Emily Keller, published by LOLITS ("Little Old Ladies In Tennis Shoes") Press, 7276 SW Beaverton-Hillsdale Hwy. #333, Portland, OR, 97225, breaks the Timberline Trail down into dayhike-length segments.

Table 8.
Lodgings in the Mt. Hood vicinity

	BRIGHTWOOD GUEST HOUSE	BROOKSIDE B&B	FALCON'S CREST INN	INN AT COOPER SPUR	MT. HOOD B&B	MT. HOOD HAMLET
PRICE (1997 SUMMER RATES, PRE-TAX, 2 PERSON)	$95–$125	$35–$65	$95–$179	$65–$129	$85–$145	$95–$125
EXTRA PERSON	$15	included	$15–$25	$10	$15	$15
PAYMENT METHODS	Checks, cash	Checks, Cash	VISA, MC, AmEx, Disc, Checks	VISA, MC, AmEx, Disc, Checks, Cash	VISA, MC, Checks, Cash	VISA, MC, Checks
# OF UNITS	1	5	5	16	4	3
PRIVATE BATH	Yes	Yes, 1 room No, 4 rooms	Yes	Yes	Yes, 2 rooms No, 2 rooms	Yes
BREAKFAST INCLUDED	Yes	Yes	Yes	No	Yes	Yes
COOKING FACILITIES	Yes	Yes	No	Yes, some units	Kitchenette in 1 unit	No
POOL	No	No	No	No	No	No
HOT TUB	No	Yes	1 w/private hot tub; 1 w/ jacuzzi bath	Yes	Yes	Jacuzzi bath tub in 1 unit
CHILDREN	OK over 13	OK	Older child. by arrange.	OK	OK	By arrangement
PETS	No	OK	No	No	No	Negotiable
HANDICAPPED ACCESSIBLE	No	No	No	Call	No	Call

Table 9.
Lodgings in the Mt. Hood vicinity (cont.)

	MT. HOOD INN	OLD WELCHES INN (B&B)	OLD WELCHES INN (COTTAGE)	RESORT AT THE MOUNTAIN	SUMMIT MEADOW CABINS	TIMBERLINE LODGE
PRICE (1997 SUMMER RATES, PRE-TAX, 2 PERSON)	$105–$145	$75–$110	$130	$109–$240	$90–$130 S–Th, (2 nite min.); $200–$325 full weekend	$65–$170
EXTRA PERSON	$10 (over 12)	N/A	$20	$20 over 17	included	$15 over 11
PAYMENT METHODS	VISA, MC, AmEx, Disc, Cash	VISA, MC, AmEx, Disc, Checks, Cash	VISA, MC, AmEx, Disc, Checks, Cash	VISA, MC, AmEx, Disc, Checks, Cash	Checks, Cash	VISA, MC, AmEx, Disc., Checks, Cash
# OF UNITS	56	4	1	160	5	71
PRIVATE BATH	Yes	1 Yes, 3 No	Yes	Yes	Yes	60 Yes, 11 No
BREAKFAST INCLUDED	Yes, continental	Yes	No	No	No	No
COOKING FACILITIES	No	No	Yes	Yes	Yes	No
POOL	No	No	No	Yes	No	Yes
HOT TUB	Yes	No	No	Yes	Jacuzzi in 3	Yes
CHILDREN	OK	OK over 12	OK	OK	OK	OK
PETS	OK, $5 fee	No	OK by arrangement	No	OK	No
HANDICAPPED ACCESSIBLE	Yes	No	No	Yes	Call	Yes

Section 6—Central Oregon

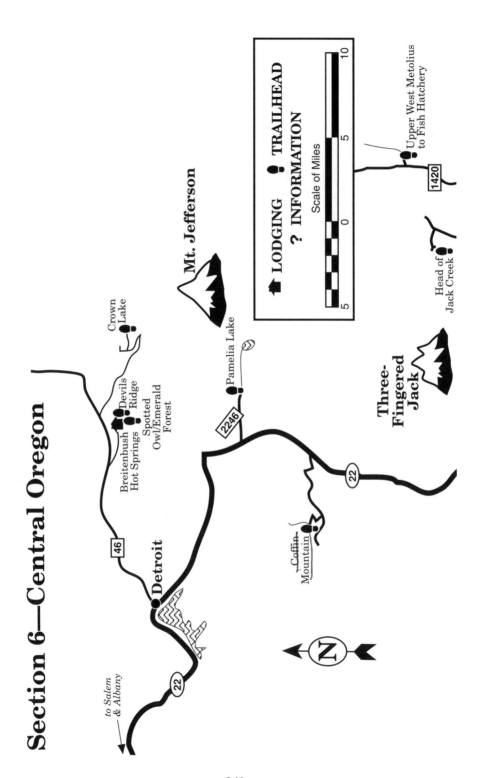

LODGING ▲ TRAILHEAD ● ? INFORMATION

Scale of Miles

Mt. Jefferson

Crown Lake

Devils Ridge

Breitenbush Hot Springs

Spotted Owl/Emerald Forest

Pamelia Lake

Detroit

46

22

to Salem & Albany

Coffin Mountain

2246

Three-Fingered Jack

Head of Jack Creek

Upper West Metolius to Fish Hatchery

1420

22

N

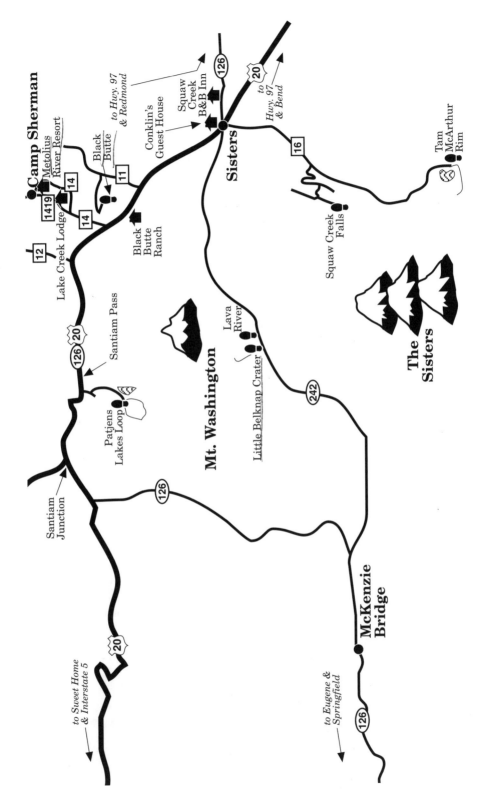

Camp Sherman

Metolius River Resort

Black Butte

to Hwy. 97 & Redmond

Conklin's Guest House

Squaw Creek B&B Inn

Sisters

Lake Creek Lodge

Black Butte Ranch

to Hwy. 97 & Bend

Tam McArthur Rim

Squaw Creek Falls

Santiam Pass

Patjens Lakes Loop

Mt. Washington

Lava River

Little Belknap Crater

The Sisters

Santiam Junction

McKenzie Bridge

to Sweet Home & Interstate 5

to Eugene & Springfield

Central Oregon

OVERVIEW

Allow me to begin with an apology.

"Central Oregon" is a broad area, an area absolutely packed with scenic beauty and hiking trails. Indeed, one could spend an entire summer hiking the trails of central Oregon and not begin to scratch the surface. It is an area of mountains—Mt. Jefferson, Mt. Washington, Three Fingered Jack, the Sisters—of lakes, of meadows, and of designated wilderness areas, including one of our nation's newest, pristine Opal Creek Wilderness and Scenic Recreation Area, near Detroit. It is an area criss-crossed by well-maintained little two-lane highways, creating a web of possibility for the dayhiker.

My apology is this: I cannot possibly "cover" central Oregon completely in one section of this book, so I don't pretend to. This is a book of highlights, of samples, of representative dayhikes and of interesting lodgings from which these hikes are accessible. Since I can't do it all, I selected a corridor upon which to concentrate. This corridor runs, with a minor exception or two, from just north of Detroit, down Highway 22 south to Santiam Junction, then east on Highway 20/126 to Sisters. I chose this area primarily because of the quality of its lodgings. From the unique retreat of Breitenbush Hot Springs on the north end, through the homey cabins of Camp Sherman and the isolated elegance of Black Butte Ranch, to the tourist-friendly B&Bs and motels of Sisters, there is something for everyone. I left out several charming small towns just to the west, a few rustic resorts in the high country, and the entire town of Bend, which is replete with lodgings. The places I included offer a range of accommodation, a friendly attitude, and great access to trails.

The town of Sisters has a population of only 820, but the soul of a major tourist destination. It nestles in the eastern foothills of the Cascades, where the sagebrush desert meets the forest. Nature endowed Sisters with crisp air, sunny skies, and views of the three Sisters mountains, and the forward-thinking residents took it from there. The cute little downtown, where building codes mandate "Old West" storefronts, is chockablock with ice cream stands, gift shops, and antique stores. Several outstanding B&Bs are located in and around Sisters, two of which are featured below, and visitors will find several dining options along its boardwalk-lined streets. The larger, more commercially developed city of Bend is just 20 miles down the road, southeast of Sisters on Highway 20. Sisters provides excellent access to Deschutes National Forest, Three Sisters Wilderness, Mt. Washington Wilderness, and McKenzie Pass hikes; to Black Butte; and, of course, to hikes on and near the Three Sisters themselves.

Just west of Sisters, Black Butte Ranch is a singular lodging; actually more of a total recreational experience.

Beyond Black Butte Ranch is the turnoff to Camp Sherman, a collection of cabins and support facilities along the fishing paradise of the Metolius River. Nearby are hiking trails along the lakes, rivers, and canyons of the Metolius River valley and the Santiam Pass area.

North of Santiam Junction, Highway 22 passes forest roads and trailheads of the Willamette National Forest and Mt. Jefferson Wilderness before reaching Detroit. A typical small, high-country vacation town, Detroit has a few eateries, motels, and services, most of which center around the vast fishing and boating reservoir of Detroit Lake.

Excellent hiking continues north of Detroit, in the forest and wilderness areas surrounding Breitenbush Hot Springs Resort and Conference Center, one of this book's most unusual featured lodgings.

This section includes a few short hikes of less than 2.0 miles, and several in the 4.0-mile to 5.5-mile range. Terrain ranges from shaded streambeds to open ridgetops, from nearly level strolls to steep climbs. Even after limiting this section's territory to the corridors described, I had a difficult time selecting hikes representative of this area. With two national forests, three designated wilderness areas, six mountains, and countless lakes and rivers from which to choose, it was a head-spinning smorgasbord.

Central Oregon's forests have been the subject of a great deal of struggle and controversy, with environmental groups, logging interests, the US Forest Service, and other parties battling for control of the precious resources. Progress has been made, but many areas show the scars of unchecked plundering. Others are exceptionally pristine and unspoiled.

I want to thank the people of central Oregon for their honesty and assistance as I did my field work in their complex region. Nowhere in the Cascades did I find people friendlier, more helpful, or more opinionated, than those I found in and around Detroit, Camp Sherman, and Sisters. Their love for the forest service is not universal, but their love for the forest is. Innkeepers, shopkeepers, and folks I met on the trails were always willing to stop and share a trail tip or a story about their beloved woods.

LODGINGS

BLACK BUTTE RANCH
P.O. Box 8000 • 13653 Hawksbeard (Main Office) • Black Butte Ranch, OR 97759
(800) 452-7455 • (541) 595-6211
www.blackbutteranch.com

Nothing compares with the experience of staying in your own 1800-acre gated community at the foot of Black Butte. Choose a low-maintenance deluxe hotel-type room, a condominium, or a private vacation home. Drive, walk, or bicycle on roads lined with delicate aspen and stalwart Ponderosa pine. Awaken to the brilliant pink sunrise kissing the snowcapped peaks of the Three Sisters over meadows draped in morning mist. Watch Canadian geese congregate on the

BUTTE
CH

Hotel-style rooms, condos, and private homes in an exclusive community

grounds. Prepare meals in your private, well-equipped kitchen, or dine at the full-service restaurant in the lodge. At dusk, you are likely to see as many deer in a casual walk around the ranch as you would see in a week of trail hiking.

The only "problem" with staying at Black Butte Ranch is there is so much to do on the premises, you might forget to leave for hiking! The property includes miles of walking, jogging, and cycling trails (bikes available to rent), two 18-hole golf courses, 19 tennis courts, four swimming pools, horse stables, an indoor recreation center, and a fishing/canoeing lake.

Prices start at $85 for two people in a standard lodge bedroom with bath. A deluxe lodge room, including a fireplace and bath with tub, is $105 for two. One-bedroom condominiums near the lodge are $137 for two people. Condominiums on the golf course are $163 for up to four people; two-bedroom, two-bath "country houses" are also $163. A golf course condominium or a three-bedroom, two-bath "country house" that sleeps six people is $178. Private homes, with capacities from four to eight people, range from $126 to $295/night. Minimum stays are required in some units. Children are welcome at Black Butte Ranch (cribs and rollaways available for a fee); pets are not.

Black Butte has a view of Mt. Washington

Interiors of the units vary (each is privately owned) but most are tasteful, contemporary, and surprisingly well-stocked with amenities.

Black Butte Ranch is located just off Highway 20/126, 7.3 miles west of Sisters and 12 miles east of Santiam Pass. Turn south into the driveway at the large, vertical BLACK BUTTE RANCH sign, pass the guard shack, and bear right. Continue for 0.7 mile, passing a meadow and several condominium buildings, until you reach the main lodge/guest registration building.

Hikes and Walks Nearby: Black Butte, Head of Jack Creek, Upper West Metolius to Fish Hatchery, Patjens Lakes Loop.

BREITENBUSH HOT SPRINGS
P.O. Box 578 • Detroit, OR 97342
(503) 854-3314

Devotees of Breitenbush Hot Springs were concerned when I said I was writing a book. "Don't *tell* people!" they begged. This 86-acre retreat, conference center, and wildlife sanctuary has been the secret favorite getaway for back-to-the-land types for years, and they guard its precious uniqueness as if it were their own second home. (It is, in fact, home for some—Breitenbush is a self-sufficient community run by a cooperative of socially, spiritually, politically, and environmentally responsible residents as a retreat and conference center.)

But, in truth, Breitenbush is not for everyone. Its rustic lodgings, wholefood vegetarian cuisine, and clothing-optional bathing are not everyone's cup of herb tea.

Lodgings consist of 42 clean, simple cabins, some with toilets and sinks. Men's and women's bathhouses are located near the cabins. Rates, based on double occupancy, are $65/person weeknights and $70/person weekends for a unit with toilet and sink; $55/person week nights and $60/person weekends for units without toilet or sink (facilities nearby). Rates for singles wishing a private cabin are slightly higher and limited to availability. A 10% discount is offered to those staying more than a week and to seniors 60+; children 5 and under are free, ages 6–10 $20/night, ages 11–15 $30/night. (Children are welcome at Breitenbush, except during certain times such as silent retreats and certain conferences. Pets are not allowed.)

> **BREITENBUSH HOT SPRINGS**
>
> Rustic cabins, natural hot springs, abundant vegetarian meals

The price of your stay includes use of the grounds and facilities, participation (if you wish) in Daily Well Being programs (which may include meditation, yoga, dancing, drumming, hiking, and other spirit-renewing activities) and three plentiful vegetarian meals daily. Guests should bring warm bedding (available for a fee if you forget), towel, pillow, and flashlight; other useful items include raingear, snacks, plastic water bottle, and coffee, if you drink it. Please do not bring electrical appliances, as the community is very thrifty in its use of electricity.

The property includes a dining hall/lodge, a sanctuary, meeting spaces, a healing arts center (where bodywork and other therapies are available by appointment), an office/gift shop, a steam sauna, soaking tubs, and natural

Breitenbush is a spiritual retreat

bathing pools. The hot spring waters of Breitenbush, in addition to providing geo-thermal heat for the cabins, are said to have healing and spiritual properties.

Meals at Breitenbush are healthy, filling, and delicious, served cafeteria-style in the communal dining room at specified times each day. All offerings are vegetarian; some are vegan (no egg, dairy, or other animal products); special diets such as wheat-free can be accommodated with advance notice. Organic foods are used extensively, and herb tea is provided with each meal. If you need a sack lunch while staying at Breitenbush, simply sign up the day before; it's all included in the price of your stay.

Creating a safe environment is a priority at Breitenbush. Residents manage a 24-hour security watch, and cabins have no locks (except privacy locks for use when you're in the cabin). Rules of conduct imposed by the communal government include a strictly enforced "no alcohol/no drugs" policy.

Guests at Breitenbush will want to hike the Breitenbush loop trail, about a 5.5-mile trek through a sacred old-growth forest zealously protected by Breitenbush community members and fans (including pop diva Bette Midler, who has contributed generously to its maintenance). Most of this trail is open to the public (see parts of it under Devils Ridge Loop and Spotted Owl/Emerald Forest, below), but the complete loop requires crossing Breitenbush property, a privilege accorded only to residents and guests.

Getting There

To find Breitenbush Hot Springs, find Detroit, on Highway 22. Turn north at the gas station onto Road 46. Drive 10 miles, until you pass Cleator Bend

Campground; just past the campground, turn right and cross a the signs, taking a left turn after every bridge, until you reach security gate and parking lot.

Hikes and Walks Nearby: Breitenbush Loop (see *Other Hike Notes*), Devil's Ridge; Spotted Owl/Emerald Forest; Crown Lake.

CONKLIN'S GUEST HOUSE
69013 Camp Polk Road • Sisters, OR 97759
(800) 549-4262 • (541) 549-0123
www.informat.com/bz/conklins

A top-of-the-line bed and breakfast experience awaits you at Conklin's Guest House. From the moment I saw the sprawling white farmhouse with its blue roof and trim, peering over a tumbling berm of wildflowers, I knew this was a special place. Coming closer, I saw the wrap-around porch, the commodious deck, the rambling lawn. A hammock suspended between two mature shade trees seemed to invite me to stay awhile.

CONKLIN'S GUEST HOUSE
Exceptional property and top-notch service

When I checked in at Frank and Marie Conklin's, I discovered the property was even more wonderful than I had at first suspected. A footpath winds through that hill of flowers, overlooking peaceful trout ponds, a gazebo, and a sparkling swimming pool. Over it all, an unobscured view of the Sisters.

Inside, refreshments await arriving guests. Dual sitting rooms are elegantly appointed in rich, deep tones, and graced with a baby grand piano. Adjacent to

Conklin's Guest House

.ese, an airy, inviting sunroom, has a coffee/tea bar, is filled with plants, and looks out on the pool, the grounds, and the view of the mountains. A full breakfast (in our case, crispy, thick French toast, barbecued sausages, and a fruit-and-yogurt parfait) is served in the sunroom each morning.

The Conklins offer five rooms, each with an elegant, well-stocked private bath. The Lattice Room, at $90/night for two, has a queen bed, a single bed, and is handicapped accessible. The Columbine, Forget-Me-Not, and Morning Glory rooms each have a queen and a single bed also, and their bathrooms have clawfoot tubs as well as showers. Columbine has a sitting room with a skylight, and Forget-Me-Not has a fireplace and outdoor deck; these rooms are $110/night for two. The Morning Glory suite has a balcony, outstanding view, and a bathroom that's a work of art; it's $120/night for two. Extra persons in these rooms are $20 each, and the room price includes breakfast. Children 12 and over are permitted. Pets are not allowed inside the guest house, but are welcome, leashed, on the grounds.

The fifth room at Conklin's, known as Heather, is a dormitory-style room, ideal for small groups. It has a queen bed and five single beds, and goes for $30/person/night, with a 3-person minimum.

The building that has become Conklin's Guest House started out as a one-room schoolhouse sometime before 1910. Later, it was converted to a private home, beginning the series of remodels and expansions that led to today's gracious establishment. Frank and Marie Conklin purchased the property in 1987, and have continued updating and remodeling, including the addition of the solarium. They have operated as a B&B since 1988.

Getting There
From Highway 126/20 at the east end of Sisters, turn onto N. Locust, which is also County Road 2610, and becomes Camp Polk Road. Go 0.6 mile, and watch for the sign, the flowers, and the striking home on the left.

Hikes and Walks Nearby: Squaw Creek Falls, Tam McArthur Rim, Black Butte, Lava River, Little Belknap Crater.

LAKE CREEK LODGE
13173 SW Forest Service Road 1419 • Camp Sherman, OR 97730
(800) 797-6331 • (541) 595-6331

A selection of cabins nestles on the edge of the woods around a trout pond and central lodge building at Lake Creek Lodge, an ideal retreat for couples, families, or groups near Camp Sherman. In addition to the pond, the beautiful grounds offer a swimming pool and two tennis courts. The lodge contains a rec room with two pool tables, ping pong, piano, comfortable couches, a fireplace, and a big screen TV.

> **LAKE CREEK LODGE**
>
> Comfortable cabins, friendly hosts, and park-like grounds

The campus includes 15 units: 14 complete cabins and a cottage with two bedrooms and a bath (no kitchen or living room). Some of the buildings date back to the 30s, but all have been modernized to a comfortable standard. The cabins are paneled with knotty pine, and include living rooms, bedrooms, complete kitchens, decks, and central heat. Some units have fireplaces, and a few have screened porches.

Summertime rates at Lake Creek Lodge (late June through early September) include dinner: two people sharing a cabin pay $160/night, and each extra person over the age of 8 is $50 (most cabins sleep 4–9 people); children 3–8 are $35. The kitchenless cottage unit is less: two people pay $110; single occupancy is $60; each extra person over the age of 8 is $40; children 3–8 are $28. Children 2 and under are free in any unit; bring your own crib. Early and late season rates run $70 and up, without meals. Breakfast available for purchase.

Getting There
To find Lake Creek Lodge, turn north off Highway 126/20 onto Road 14, signed CAMP SHERMAN/METOLIUS RIVER. You'll find this road 9.0 miles west of Sisters and 16.7 miles east of Santiam Junction (where Highways 126/20 and Highway 22 intersect). After 2.6 miles, stay left at a Y, following the arrow to RESORTS (the right-forking road is signed CAMPGROUNDS). This becomes Road 1419. Lake Creek Lodge is on the right, 1.4 miles past the Y.

Hikes and Walks Nearby: Head of Jack Creek, Upper West Metolius to Fish Hatchery, Black Butte, Patjens Lakes Loop.

Lake Creek Lodge cabins and trout pond

METOLIUS RIVER RESORT
25551 SW Forest Service Road 1419 • Camp Sherman, OR 97730
(800) 81-TROUT

These exceptionally well-crafted, privately owned vacation cabins offer the comforts of a deluxe, modern condominium in a rustic, backwoods setting on one of Oregon's premiere trout-fishing streams.

METOLIUS RIVER RESORT
Upscale cabins on the Metolius River

Rooms are large and airy, with vaulted ceilings and pale pine decor. Kitchens are very nice, with full-sized appliances, cooking and eating utensils, dishwashers, coffee makers, and microwaves. No smoking in any of the cabins. Most units have a TV/VCR, and each has its own telephone, deck, and river view. Barbecues are available for guest use, and the Kokanee Café (see *Dining*, below) is open for dinner during the hiking season.

Most hikers will come to the resort during the high season, May 1 through October 31. During that time, rates for two people are $120/night Sunday–Thursday, and $160/night weekends and holidays. Cabins must be rented for a minimum of two nights; three during holiday periods. The weekly rate is $850. Ten dollars is charged per night for each extra person over the age of 6.

Getting There
To reach Camp Sherman and the Metolius River Resort, turn north off Highway 126/20 onto Road 14, signed CAMP SHERMAN/METOLIUS RIVER. You'll find this road 9.0 miles west of Sisters and 16.7 miles east of Santiam Junction (where Highways 126/20 and Highway 22 intersect). After 2.6 miles, stay left at a Y, following the arrow to RESORTS (the right-forking road is signed CAMPGROUNDS). This becomes Road 1419. Pass Twin View Resort and Lake Creek Lodge. After 2.3 miles past the Y, you reach a stop sign. In order to stay on 1419, you need to

Metolius Resort cabin interior

turn right at the stop sign, following the CAMP SHERMAN sign. After another 0.5 mile, watch for the METOLIUS RIVER RESORT and KOKANEE CAFÉ sign on the right.

Hikes and Walks Nearby: Head of Jack Creek, Upper West Metolius to Fish Hatchery, Black Butte, Patjens Lakes Loop.

SQUAW CREEK BED & BREAKFAST INN
P.O. Box 1993 • 68733 Junapine Lane • Sisters, OR 97759
(800) 930-0055 • (541) 549-4312

If you can't get comfortable at Susie Johnson's bed and breakfast, you're just not trying. If ever a place makes you feel welcome, it's this unpretentious, yet clean and modern, B&B. Susie, her husband, Keith, and son, Joel, are friendly as can be, with a knack for being accommodating and available without being intrusive. You'll feel at home kicking back in the family living room in a robe and slippers, or you can withdraw to your own space for your entire stay—each of the four guest rooms has its own entrance.

The Johnson's have operated Squaw Creek B&B Inn out of their home since 1996. It's located in the woods 1.5 miles east of Sisters—close enough to be convenient, yet far enough that deer and other wildlife routinely wander their 8.5 acres.

> **SQUAW CREEK BED & BREAKFAST INN**
>
> Charming, unpretentious in-home B&B

Rooms at Squaw Creek rent for $75–$85/night for two people; $5 for an extra person sharing the room. Children are welcome (rollaway bed available), and pets can be accommodated with advance arrangements (a kennel is also available). Each guest room has a private bath, TV/VCR, in-room

Squaw Creek Bed & Breakfast Inn

coffee, and robes (handy for the hot tub!). Beds are made with sun-dried sheets, and decor is casual country. Fit For A King has a king bed, queen futon, and lots of room; Fireside Room has a queen sleigh bed and gas fireplace; The Twins has two twin beds (can convert to a king) and barnwood decor; Grandma's Beach House, just off the hot tub, has a queen bed and beach-theme decor.

The price of your room includes a full breakfast, which may range from strawberry waffles to an omelette, eggs and sausage, or biscuits and gravy.

Squaw Creek B&B Inn's hallmark is flexibility. They love to accommodate groups, and have slept up to 25. They even have RV hook-ups on site. Guests are welcome to use the kitchen, laundry, gas barbecue, spacious wrap-around deck, living room, hot tub, and other facilities. The Johnsons will gladly prepare something special for your party or group—barbecue dinners, retreats, family reunion picnics. Special diets graciously accommodated. Bring your recreation equipment—the Johnson's big pole barn offers safe, covered storage for bikes, snowmobiles, or whatever you enjoy.

Getting There
Take Highway 126 east out of Sisters toward Redmond. Turn north on Junapine Lane, 1.5 miles east of Sisters. Watch for the sign on the left, 0.1 mile off the highway.

Hikes and Walks Nearby: Squaw Creek Falls, Tam McArthur Rim, Black Butte, Lava River, Little Belknap Crater.

ADDITIONAL LODGINGS

Because the recommended lodgings above comprise a small total number of rooms, contact information for the following lodgings is provided here. These premises were not thoroughly reviewed by the author.

ALL SEASONS MOTEL   **(503) 854-3421**
P.O. Box 565; 130 Breitenbush Road • Detroit, OR 97342

15 motel rooms with private baths, baseboard heat, cable TV; 4 with kitchenettes. VISA, MC, AmEx, Disc, checks, cash accepted; kids and pets OK. ("No snakes, no forest service employees!") $40–$80/night.

COMFORT INN   **(800) 228-5150**
525 Highway 20 West   **(541) 549- 7829**
Sisters, OR 97759

Just west of Sisters. 50 large rooms, pool, spa, cable TV, continental breakfast. Some kitchenette units, some handicapped-accessible units. VISA, MC, AmEx, Disc, checks, cash accepted. King bed $74; 2 queen beds $69.

KOKANEE CAFÉ GUEST ROOMS   (541) 595-6420
25545 SW Forest Road 1419 • Camp Sherman, OR 97730

Two small, comfortable rooms above the Kokanee Café (see Dining, below). Queen bed, refrigerator, coffee bar, private bath with skylight. Cute and modern, each $60/night for two. Heat, fans (no a/c).

LAKESIDE MOTEL   (503) 854-3376
P.O. Box 519; 110 Santiam Ave. • Detroit, OR 97342

Right on Detroit Lake, 10 units with private baths & TVs, 4 with full kitchens. Children OK; no pets. Two persons $55/night; $65 for kitchen room. $5 each extra person. Picnic area w/BBQ.

SISTERS MOTOR LODGE   (541) 549-2551
P.O. Box 28 • Sisters, OR 97759

11 units, 4 with kitchens, 5 with 2 bedrooms, all with cable TV, in-room coffee, & phone. West end of Sisters. Afternoon tea & cookies, morning continental breakfast in lobby. Rooms $59–$75 for two; $69 & up for 3–4; kitchen adds $5. Kids OK (rollaway $8); pets by arrangement ($5 fee).

DINING

ALI'S TOWN SQUARE DELI
P.O. Box 1054 • 141 E. Cascade/Town Square • Sisters, OR 97759
(541) 549-2547

Ali's is a super spot for a light bite or midday meal in downtown Sisters. Whether you're out visiting the surrounding gift shops and antique stores, or taking a break between hikes, you'll enjoy a pick-me-up from their fresh, fun menu.

Specialty sandwiches, served in pita bread, include curry chicken, turkey-apple, dilly tuna, and lemon-ginger chicken with grapes, each $4.75. Ten different turkey sandwiches are offered, most at $4.25, and five vegetarian sandwiches, each $2.95. Standard deli sandwiches, with your choice of meat, cheese, and bread, are $4.75; $2.95 for a half. Ali's also features a variety of fresh bagels (served with or without spreads), a few hot sandwiches, homemade soup, ice cream, and espresso drinks.

BLACK BUTTE RANCH RESTAURANT
P.O. Box 8000 • Black Butte Ranch, OR 97759
(541) 595-1260/595-6211

Whether you're staying at Black Butte Ranch or not, the restaurant in the main lodge might be a good place to start, end, or break up the middle of your hiking day. Serving breakfast, lunch, and dinner, it is located at Black Butte Ranch, 7.3 miles west of Sisters, off Highway 126/20. (See Black Butte Ranch under *Lodgings,* above, and Black Butte under *Walks and Hikes,* below.)

Breakfasts at the ranch (which, to be fair, is more like a resort than a ranch) include the standard egg and griddle fare, plus Belgian waffles (from $4.50), house-made granola ($2.75), and a hearty "Cascade scramble": three eggs with mushrooms, peppers, onions, Tillamook (Oregon) cheddar cheese, and rosemary potatoes ($6.95). Morning gourmets can order their whole wheat buttermilk pancakes with hazelnuts or blueberries (from $4.25), or try the herb-parmesan polenta with poached eggs, served with fresh fruit compote ($6.95).

For lunch, choose from burgers, salads, and sandwiches starting at $5.95, or a few specialty entrées from $7.95.

Dinners at Black Butte Ranch are fresh and fashionable, but tend to come in "ranch-sized" portions, so come with an appetite! Specialties include Roasted Duck Cascade (with huckleberry sauce and hazelnuts), $18.95; Northwest oysters, $15.95; and slow-roasted prime rib, from $14.95. A daily fresh sheet rounds out a dinner selection suitable for a celebration meal. Take your time, enjoying the sunset over the Sisters and Mt. Washington, and try to leave room for one of their decadent desserts, or at least a cappuccino.

While Black Butte Ranch is a private resort, the restaurant is open to the public. From the guard station as you enter the ranch, stay right, curving around past a meadow, then several condominium buildings. The restaurant is in the same building as the guest registration office.

COYOTE CREEK CAFE
**Three Winds Shopping Center • 497 Highway 20 West • Sisters, OR 97759
(541) 549-9514**

When you're one of just a few restaurants serving a tiny town with a big heart (and a bustling tourism industry) like Sisters, Oregon, you're bound to attempt to be All Things To All People. Coyote Creek Café could be accused of that, but the fact is that they pull it off pretty well. The result is a family-friendly restaurant that switch-hits from fairly simple and reasonable breakfasts and lunches to moderately upscale dinners.

The main "hook" at Coyote Creek is the mesquite grilling fire, the subtlety of which is best showcased on a plain cut of beef or fish, such as the halibut ($8.95 at lunch, $9.95 on the Petite Dinners menu), or the 16-ounce T-bone steak ($16.95). Other dinner entrées, which come complete with soup or salad, bread, vegetable, and choice of potato or rice, include cream-cheese-spinach-and-bacon-stuffed Chicken Albuquerque ($12.95), baby back BBQ pork ribs ($15.95), or gulf prawns sautéed with mushrooms, tomatoes, zucchini, and garlic ($13.50). Pasta dishes ($10.50–$13.50), entrée salads ($7.95), burgers and sandwiches ($5.95–$7.25) are also available at dinner.

Luncheon fare focuses on hot and cold sandwiches, salads, and mesquite-broiled burgers, reasonably priced.

Breakfast can be a hiker's most important meal, and Coyote Creek is a good place to stoke up for an active day. Choose from eight different three-egg omelettes, several "scrambles," and traditional favorites including huevos rancheros, corned beef hash with eggs, and eggs benedict. Most any large breakfast runs $5.50–$6.50.

Coyote Creek Café also serves pizza, desserts, and has a full bar, including 13 microbrews on tap.

HOTEL SISTERS
105 West Cascade Street • Sisters, OR 97759
(541) 549-RIBS

It's hard to miss this big old hotel, situated on the northwest corner of the intersection of Cascade (the "main drag" of historic downtown Sisters) and Fir. Inside, you'll find the color and kitsch of the Old West, but you'll also find a pretty decent restaurant, open for breakfast, lunch, and dinner.

Breakfasts and lunch are standard fare, reasonably priced and generously proportioned: omelettes and French toast in the A.M., salads, burgers, and sandwiches in the P.M.

Dinner at Hotel Sisters is tasty and filling, with an emphasis on home-style Mexican and American fare and good beef. The restaurant features locally raised Corriente beef, a flavorful, lean breed raised without growth enhancers. A variety of cuts is available, starting at $16.95 for a New York strip.

The hotel's Mexican specialties are excellent, including enchiladas, tostadas, burritos, chimichangas, and chile rellenos, each priced at $8.95. Barbecue is another specialty, starting at $10.95 for pork hot links, up to $14.95 for ribs and a chicken breast. A Tex/Mex combo($15.95) includes ribs, chicken, *and* a taco or enchilada, plus sides of rice, beans, tortillas, and chile verde—that's a LOT of hiking!

Watch the daily specials board at Hotel Sisters, too, for some of the best offerings, like the Sunday chicken-and-dumplings—it's great!

KOKANEE CAFÉ
25545 SW Road 1419 • Camp Sherman, OR 97730
(541) 595-6420

This excellent restaurant, located on Forest Service Road 1419 at the Metolius River Resort, is open seasonally, serving families, fishing enthusiasts, and hikers who visit the Camp Sherman area from April to October. During the peak of summer, you'll find them open 7 nights a week; during "shoulder season," Thursday through Sunday only. Kokanee Café serves dinner only.

The atmosphere at Kokanee Café is bustling and convivial; the cuisine fresh and carefully prepared. The "kokanee" is a land-locked salmon or trout that inhabits the nearby Metolius River; brushed with olive oil and sautéed, it is one of the restaurant's specialties, at $14.95. Other entrées include broiled quail at $17.95; grilled Pendleton pork with herb-apple glaze at $16.95, and seared wild venison medallions with red currant sauce at $24.95. Dinners include soup or salad (with homemade salad dressing), fresh bread, and accompaniments. Lighter choices include pastas starting at $11.95, vegetarian black bean cakes at $9.95, hamburgers and garden burgers at $9.50, and a couple of children's items from $5.95.

WALKS AND HIKES
Listed in approximate order of difficulty

Deschutes and Willamette national forests participate in the Trail Park Pass system. See *Trail Park Pass System* in the Introduction.

HEAD OF JACK CREEK INTERPRETIVE LOOP
Barrier-free stroll makes this creek accessible to all.

Map:	US Forest Service "Sisters Ranger District Deschutes National Forest" (approach only; new trail does not show accurately)
Distance:	About a mile round-trip
Elevation Gain:	none
Estimated Time:	1 hour

This work-in-progress may, when completed, be one of the premier interpretive walks in the Cascades. It features a unique and very delicate riparian environment: the springs that feed Jack Creek.

Locals and visitors have known about the Head of Jack Creek for years—old ranger district handouts and trail descriptions provided by lodgings list a quarter-mile loop here. Due to overuse and misuse of the sensitive environment, the old loop has been modified. Access is now via a trail which begins less than half a mile downstream, and the loop itself—a portion of the old loop—is quite short but very impressive. Where the original loop had numbered signposts keyed to an interpretive pamphlet, the new trail, when finished, will have interpretive plaques in-situ to explain the creek's origins and what we can do to steward fragile landscapes like this one. The completed trail will be native-surfaced but barrier-free.

The trail as described below is now open to the public, but the amenities may be incomplete. As with many important forest service projects, the dollars and worker hours necessary to complete the vision are in short supply. Eventually, along with the addition of interpretive signs, the tread will be built up to protect root systems, and some form of curbing will be installed to help keep hikers on the trail. In the meantime, we can all do our part by staying on the trail and away from the sensitive edges of the springs.

Getting There
Drive west about 12 miles from Sisters, or east about 13.5 miles from Santiam Junction, to where Road 12 intersects Highway 126/20. (Road 12 is also signed JACK LAKE ROAD and MT. JEFFERSON WILDERNESS TRAILHEADS.) Go north on 12 for 4.3 miles, then turn left on paved, one-lane Road 1230. Follow Road 1230 for 0.5 mile, cross a one-lane bridge, then turn left onto Road 1232, which is dirt. You will pass Jack Creek Campground. Stay left when you come to a forking junction with Road 260. After about 1.0 mile on Road 1232, you come to another junction, where Road 1232 goes off to the right, and Road 400 goes straight. Go straight, onto Road 400. Cross a cattle guard. After 0.2 mile on Road 400, stay left at a fork with Road 470. Reach a gate at 0.3 mile, where a sign points left to HEAD

OF JACK CREEK PICNIC AREA & NATURE TRAIL. Proceed another 0.1 mile to the trail-head, where you'll find picnic tables, parking for about ten cars, and, thanks to the Youth Conservation Corps, a pit toilet.

The Walk

From the trailhead, stroll a wide, flat path for about 800 feet to a bench at the bank of Jack Creek. Turn right at the creek, and stroll upstream along a creekside path supposed, according to local lore, to be part of an old carriage route.

Before you have gone 0.5 mile, you will come to a bridge. Cross the bridge to begin the short loop trail at the head of the creek.

What you will find at the head of Jack Creek is a veritable oasis—a wet west Cascades habitat on the dry eastern slopes. It is cooler here than the surrounding area, and the humidity is higher, supporting Western hemlock and a number of other typically west-side plants. The sound of the gurgling springs will impress you as much as the sight. Whether curbs and signs mark the path or not, please stay on the trail and refrain from walking near or touching the springs themselves. This moist ecosystem, one of the dwindling number of spawning areas for the bull trout, is very fragile.

Upon completing the loop, return to the trailhead via the same path on which you entered.

Nearest Lodgings: Black Butte Ranch, Lake Creek Lodge, Metolius River Resort.

LAVA RIVER

Barrier-free stroll amidst geologic wonders.

Map:	US Forest Service "Willamette National Forest" or "Sisters Ranger District Deschutes National Forest"
Distance:	0.5 mile loop
Elevation Gain:	Slight
Estimated Time:	30 minutes

Bring everyone, hiker or not, out to the Dee Wright Observatory at McKenzie Pass. Nearly anyone can climb the short, paved walk to the cylindrical stone observatory, and most can stroll the short Lava River Trail. Even from the car, you can't miss the geologic wonders of these young lava flows.

Getting There

At the west end of Sisters, take the left-hand fork onto Highway 242. This narrow, well-paved highway is a scenic corridor, first through thick Ponderosa pine forest, then through the Belknap and Yapoah lavalands. Walls of chunky red and black rock line the road as you near your destination.

Reach McKenzie Pass after 14.6 miles. Watch for the cylindrical, stone Dee Wright Observatory on the north side of the road. Park on the south side of the road, across from the observatory, or just past the observatory in a parking area on the road's north side. There are restrooms at the parking area to the west of the observatory.

On the side of the road at the base of the observatory is an interpretive plaque. Standing at the plaque, the Lava River trailhead is just to your right.

From the west, take Highway 126 east from Eugene/Springfield through McKenzie Bridge, then approximately 5 more miles to the Highway 242 junction. Take 242 about 22 more miles, to McKenzie Pass. Parking is on the left, just before you reach the observatory.

The Hike

A smooth, paved walkway takes you out amidst fields of black, chunky "aa" lava (pronounced "ah-ah," an excellent Scrabble® word) from the Yapoah Crater. Interpretive plaques explain features such as lava levees, tubes, ridges, and gutters, and point out an area where early settlers crossed McKenzie Pass in their wagons.

The route is a keyhole loop—follow the path east from the trailhead a few hundred feet before reaching the loop. Take the loop in either direction. It goes up onto a lava levee, passing columnar joints, cooling cracks, and other features.

Bring the kids—this short stroll will be a good energy-burner for toddlers and the natural wonders should hold the interest of even the most jaded teen. The paved path will accommodate strollers. While the trail is classified barrier-free, wheelchair users may find the grades and some of the narrow passageways at the east end of the loop a bit challenging.

Before or after your walk, be sure to go up to the Dee Wright Observatory. Named for an old-time forest guide and packer, this chunky, rock-walled cylinder blends nicely with its surrounding landscape. Stand atop the building for a 360° panorama. Inside, peer through signed slots in the walls strategically placed to help you unmistakably identify all the surrounding geographic features.

Nearest Lodgings: Black Butte Ranch, Conklin's Guest House, Squaw Creek B&B Inn

CROWN LAKE
Easy, pretty walk to a mountain lake.

Map:	Green Trails #525, "Breitenbush"
Distance:	1.0 mile round-trip
Elevation Gain:	200´
Estimated Time:	45 minutes

The shorter of two trails leading to Crown Lake, Trail 3362 is brief and rewarding. The drive to the trailhead is spectacular in itself—if you don't mind heights and rough roads. It takes you from 2400 feet to 4700 feet elevation, with stunning views of Mt. Jefferson.

The trail alternates between forest shade and open subalpine meadows. Come early in the season to enjoy the beargrass and wildflowers in bloom, and the creek still swollen with water. Bring mosquito repellent. The fall offers seasonal color, fewer bugs, and berries ripe for the picking. It's just a 15-minute walk to the lake, but you'll want to linger a bit, and perhaps dip your toes.

Getting There

From Highway 22 in Detroit, go north on Road 46. At 10 miles, pass Cleator Bend Campground, then the right-hand turn over the bridge toward Breitenbush Hot Springs; reset your odometer at this junction, but continue straight ahead on Road 46. Those coming from Breitenbush will drive out to Road 46 and turn right, resetting their odometers as they turn onto Road 46.

Pass Breitenbush Campground at 0.4 mile and the two ends of loop Road 050 at 0.5 and 2.2 miles. At 2.6 miles, turn right onto a signed junction for Road 4685, known locally as South Breitenbush Road. Immediately cross the North Fork Breitenbush River and the road goes to gravel.

Pass several trailheads for South Breitenbush Gorge Trail 3366 on Road 4685; the first is at 0.6 mile, the second at 2.2 miles, the final at 2.7 miles. Each has a wide spot for a few cars to pull out.

Continue on Road 4685, gaining some serious altitude between miles 5.0 and 6.0, until you are up into a sad scar of old clearcut. At 7.6 miles, turn right onto Road 330. Drive directly toward Mt. Jefferson, looming large in the near distance, ignoring Road 029 as it forks to your left. This road is narrow, rough, and not for the faint of heart, with a dramatic drop-off on your right. Mercifully, it's only 1.1 miles long. Park at road's end, making sure you leave room for other cars to turn around.

The Hike

This hiker-only trail plunges from its sunny trailhead into deep forest shade, immediately losing the view of Mt. Jefferson you have enjoyed on the drive and

Crown Lake with view of Mt. Jefferson

from the trailhead. It is a rocky, primitive trail, beginning with a gentle ascent, dipping down into a creekbed (likely to be dry by midseason), then rising to a rocky, subalpine meadow. Pass through another stand of trees and into a second meadow, all within the first 0.25 mile. Beargrass, penstemon, lupine, and other grasses and flowers lend these meadows the air of a planned rock garden.

At 0.4 miles, plunge again into cool forest. You can hear the sound of water to your right. A fork just past 0.4 offers a short spur trail to the right to view the creek; the main path goes left. Descend the final 0.1 mile on the main path, through thick, low berry bushes, until you arrive at the lake. From the water's edge, you can see the top of Mt. Jefferson peeking over the trees to your right.

Nearest Lodgings: Breitenbush Hot Springs, Detroit motels (see *Additional Lodgings*).

SQUAW CREEK FALLS
Short, shady hike to a waterfall overlook.

Map:	US Forest Service "Sisters Ranger District Deschutes National Forest"
Distance:	1.7 miles round-trip
Elevation Gain:	300´
Estimated Time:	1 hour

This shady, pleasant walk takes you through a mixed coniferous forest in the Three Sisters Wilderness and ends at a waterfall overlook. You will encounter a few stream crossings and one short but steep uphill near the falls. Most of the route undulates gently up and down. Road surfaces can be rough en route to the trailhead.

Getting There
Find Village Green City Park, two blocks south of Cascade on Elm, in Sisters. From the park, continue south on Elm Street. Elm turns into Forest Service Road 16 as you enter the Deschutes National Forest, just outside of town. This is a two-lane, paved, shoulderless road. After 7.0 miles from the park, turn right on Road 1514, a gravel road with a cattle guard.

Many dirt or gravel forest service roads intersect with 1514; you want to stay on 1514 for almost 5.0 miles. (After 2.9 miles on 1514, you will come to a pronounced fork. The left road is 1516; stay right to remain on 1514.) At 4.9 miles, just after a sign warning NARROW BRIDGE, turn left onto road 1514/600, following the sign SQUAW CREEK FALLS. (Road 1514 continues straight ahead, crossing the narrow bridge over Squaw Creek.)

Stay on rutted, rough, single-lane 1514/600 for 2.0 miles, until you reach a T. The trailhead is 0.4 miles downhill to your left, but if the road has been about as rough as your vehicle can take so far, or if you have non-hiking passengers, you may want to park at a wide spot just to your right at this T and walk the 0.4 mile to the trailhead. The road downhill to the trailhead is pretty nasty, and the parking spot at the top of the hill is a nicer place to leave non-hikers than the trailhead, as it overlooks Squaw Creek (far below and inaccessible, but pretty), and has a bit of a view of the Sisters. Neither of these views is available at the trailhead.

Most of us will turn left and drive the additional 0.4 mile to the signed trailhead. A parking loop at road's end provides room for a dozen cars.

The Hike

This trail is part of the Three Sisters Wilderness; self-issuing permits are required and are available at the trailhead. The trail begins to the left of the permit box. As you start off up the hill, it feels as though you are going the wrong way, since the creek is behind you, but the trail veers right shortly. From here, your route roughly parallels Squaw Creek, but you cannot see it until trail's end at the falls.

The trail has a soft duff surface, covered in the characteristic extra-long needle bunches of the predominant Ponderosa pine. Other conifers include the grand fir and whitebark pine, creating a loose canopy with a rather open understory. In the fall, enormous mushrooms can be seen alongside the trail, looking for all the world like abandoned flapjacks.

Cross your first creek at 0.15; another at 0.6. When runoff is in full swing, smaller creeklets may be present just before 0.3 and just before 0.6. None of the creeks are bridged, but the fording should be easy.

Just after 0.7, tuck into a steep little climb that, mercifully, lasts only about a hundred feet. Let the kiddies tear ahead if you wish—there's a flat segment at the top before the trail reaches the falls overlook, so they won't plunge off the edge as soon as they reach the top of the climb.

The trail ends at 0.85 mile. Squaw Creek Falls is a frothy, spreading veil below you. The falls are neither accessible (due to the steep embankment) nor particularly photogenic (due to the trees in front of them), but are sufficiently rewarding to make this a recommended family hike. It's also an appropriate trail for foul-weather or overcast days, as it offers no panoramic vistas.

Nearest Lodgings: Squaw Creek B&B Inn, Conklin's Guest House.

SPOTTED OWL/EMERALD FOREST

Magnificent old-growth forest.

Map:	Green Trails #524 & #525, "Battle Ax" & "Breitenbush" (access only)
Distance:	3.4 miles round-trip (or longer; can extend up to 10 miles round-trip)
Elevation Gain:	400′
Estimated Time:	1 hour, 45 minutes

Experience a magnificent old-growth forest walk near Breitenbush Hot Springs. As you walk under a canopy of giants, you'll find a forest teeming with life: robins hop from branch to branch, rhododendrons and Oregon grape crowd the path, evidence of deer is everywhere. Trees along the way include cedar, yew (a less-common species with spectacular, dark reddish-purple bark), Douglas-fir,

Western hemlock, and alder. This little piece of land has been the subject of much controversy. It is only through efforts of fans, friends, and residents of

Spotted Owl/Emerald Forest

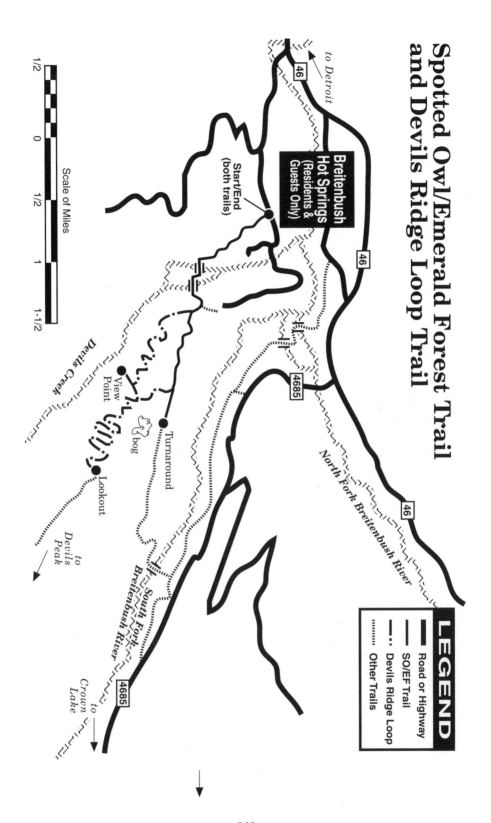

Spotted Owl/Emerald Forest Trail
and Devils Ridge Loop Trail

to Detroit

46

Breitenbush
Hot Springs
(Residents &
Guests Only)

Start/End
(both trails)

46

4685

North Fork Breitenbush River

46

Devils Creek

View
Point

bog

Turnaround

Lookout

to
Devils
Peak

South Fork
Breitenbush River

4685

to
Crown
Lake

LEGEND

— Road or Highway

— SO/EF Trail

–·· Devils Ridge Loop

······ Other Trails

Scale of Miles

1/2   0   1/2   1   1-1/2

263

Breitenbush that it remains for us to enjoy. (See Breitenbush Hot Springs under *Lodgings*, above.)

This trail is open to the general public. See also Devil's Ridge trail, below, which also begins and ends on the Spotted Owl Trail, but adds a steep hill climb to a ridgetop and former lookout site. Guests at Breitenbush Hot Springs can turn this hike into a 5.5-mile loop; see Breitenbush Loop under *Other Hike Notes*.

Getting There

If you are staying at Breitenbush, walk out to the parking area, out past the guard shack, and bear left onto the signed trail. This path will take you a few dozen feet through the woods to a road. Cross the road to the trailhead.

From the Detroit area, take Road 46 north. Pass Cleator Bend Campground at 10 miles, then turn right, crossing the river. From here, follow the signs toward Breitenbush Hot Springs, taking all the left turns until you reach the fork at the entrance to Breitenbush. Here, the left fork will take you into Breitenbush Hot Springs & Conference Center, and the right fork is a gated stub. Bear right and park alongside the road at the fork. Do not block either road.

Walk about 80 feet up the right fork (the gated stub road) to a trailhead on your right.

The Hike

The route begins on a trail called the Spotted Owl. You will pass through recovering clearcuts within the first half mile, but the old-growth forest is just ahead. The route is marked with unobtrusive arrow signs that help keep you on track.

Pass through a grove of alders at about 0.7 mile, just before reaching Devil's Creek. Pick your way through the deadfall to the first of two bridges across the creek, separated by an island in the middle. Bear left on the island to find the second bridge, and cross to the other side.

Follow the path to the left, through a horsetail fern marsh. Arrive at a fork at 0.8. A tract of summer homes is to your left; stay right. The trail begins to ascend.

At 0.9, reach a signed fork. Technically, this is where Spotted Owl ends. Stay left, following a sign for TREE TRAIL.

Aptly named Tree Trail is a rooty, gently undulating, needle-strewn half-mile path amidst giant Douglas-fir and Western hemlock. Nurse logs abound in this pristine old-growth ecosystem, which has been declared a permanent monitoring area for the US Forest Service's neotropical migratory bird conservation program.

At 1.4 miles, you'll reach another signed junction; this is the end of Tree Trail. To the right is Devils Ridge Trail, and straight ahead is Emerald Forest Trail. Continue on Emerald Forest Trail another 0.3 miles to a bog on your right. This is a good place to turn around, resulting in a 1.7-mile hike, 3.4 miles round-trip, that gives you a good look at the forest so many Oregonians and friends of Breitenbush are trying to protect. If you wish to continue farther, you will follow Emerald Forest Trail to a log bridge over the South Fork Breitenbush River. The trail then junctions with South Breitenbush Gorge trail, on which you can walk to the left or to the right, for a total of up to about 5.0 miles each way before you run out of trail and return the way you came.

Nearest Lodgings: Breitenbush Hot Springs, Detroit motels (see *Additional Lodgings*).

PAMELIA LAKE
Picture-perfect lake, easy hike.

Map:	Green Trails #557, "Mt. Jefferson"
Distance:	4.4 miles round-trip
Elevation Gain:	500′
Estimated Time:	2 hours, 30 minutes

Stroll a wide, needle-carpeted path through the loveliest of forests to a jewel of a mountain lake in the Willamette National Forest's Mt. Jefferson Wilderness. The path rises gently under a cathedral-like canopy of trees, with organ music courtesy of Pamelia Creek, which flows alongside.

This extremely popular trail requires, in addition to the Trail Park Pass (see *Trail Park Pass System* in Introduction), a special Limited Entry Permit that must be obtained in advance from the Detroit ranger station, located on the highway 1.6 miles west of Detroit. The permit is free, but only 20 groups are allowed on the trail each day (a "group" is from one to twelve persons). You may obtain the permit the same day you hike, or up to 30 days in advance of your planned hike date. Self-issuing Mt. Jefferson Wilderness permits are also available at the trailhead; these do not substitute for the Limited Entry Permit. This system, a bit cumbersome at present, is subject to change; please check with the Detroit ranger station at (503) 854-3366 before heading out.

Pamelia Lake

Getting There

From Detroit, drive 12.5 miles east on Highway 22 (which runs north-south at this point; you're going south). Turn left (east) onto Road 2246, also signed PAMELIA ROAD.

Heading west (north) on Highway 22, you'll turn right onto Pamelia Road 2.0 miles past the Willamette National Forest's Riverside Campground.

Pamelia Road is a paved, one-lane road. After 2.9 miles, Red Creek Road forks to the left; continue straight. Pavement ends. A stunning view of Mt. Jefferson reveals itself as you drive the final mile to the parking area.

At 3.8 miles, a large trailhead parking area provides toilets and room for about 20 cars.

The Hike

The trailhead for Pamelia Lake Trail 3439 is just to the right of the large information sign. Make sure you have all necessary permits (Trail Park Pass, Limited Entry Permit, self-issuing Wilderness Permit). Pets on leashes are allowed. The wide path proceeds at the gentlest of inclines through a gorgeous forest of stalwart Douglas-fir. The understory is thick with nurse logs and the fragrance of things dying and being reborn, among them coral root, bunchberry, and rhododendron. Pamelia Creek flows to your right.

Officially enter Mt. Jefferson Wilderness at 0.25 mile. After 1.5 miles, the ascent steepens slightly and the path becomes a tad rockier. When you see the warning signs about camping and fires, at 2.1 miles, you know you're almost there. You arrive at 2.2 miles.

Pamelia Lake is a popular destination, and it's easy to see why. It's a picture-perfect lake nestled in the bottom of a steep-walled, forested draw. The forest service's limited entry permit system may be a good thing, for this trail is so pretty, so easy, and so accessible, it could be a real crowd scene on a summer weekend if access weren't limited.

Nearest Lodgings: Breitenbush Hot Springs, Detroit motels (see *Additional Lodgings*).

UPPER WEST METOLIUS TO FISH HATCHERY

Riverbank walk to a fish hatchery.

Map:	US Forest Service "Sisters Ranger District Deschutes National Forest"
Distance:	4.5 miles round-trip
Elevation Gain:	Negligible
Estimated Time:	2 hours, 30 minutes

This anytime, all-weather hike is a treat whenever the roads and trail are open. In sunshine, it's sparkling; in misty overcast, it's ethereal; in rain, it's raw and powerfully beautiful. Whether you walk the banks of the boiling, black Metolius River during the high runoff of spring, the lazy green days of summer, or the multi-colored spectacle of fall, it's a soul-satisfying experience.

The trail leads from an easily accessed campground parking area to a well-kept fish hatchery, complete with informative Oregon Fish & Wildlife officers and public restrooms. The entire route follows the banks of the Metolius—at times, merging into its mucky margins. It's a beautiful walk for most any hiker, but footing can be difficult due to rocky surfaces, and the proximity to fast-moving water could be a hazard for small children.

Getting There

From Highway 20/126, turn north on Forest Service Road 14. This turn, signed CAMP SHERMAN and METOLIUS RIVER, is 1.9 miles west of Black Butte Ranch and 9.2 miles west of Sisters. Immediately after turning, you'll see a pull-out with information kiosks about the Metolius River area on your right—worth a stop.

Proceed on paved, two-lane Road 14. At 2.5 miles, stay left at the Y, following the sign for RESORTS rather than the sign for CAMPGROUNDS. You are now on Road 1419.

After 2.3 miles on 1419 (4.8 miles from Highway 20/126), the main, paved road turns sharply to the right. Yielding to any oncoming traffic, go straight here, onto Road 1420, a rougher paved road.

After 0.6 miles on Road 1420 (5.4 miles from Highway 20/126), the road turns to gravel. Cross Canyon Creek after 3.2 miles on Road 1420 (8.0 miles from the highway). In another 0.1 mile, turn right onto Road 1420/400, following the sign for CANYON CREEK CG and W. METOLIUS TR. HD. (I have given cumulative distances from Highway 20/126 as well an incremental distances for each road because, although you travel on three separately-numbered roads, it is essentially a straight shot to this point.)

Follow one-lane, gravel Road 1420/400 along the path of Canyon Creek to the campground, which sits at the confluence of Canyon Creek and the Metolius River. At 0.6 miles, the road forks to loop through the campground. Either fork will get you to the trailhead, which is just ahead and to the left, on the bank of the Metolius.

The Hike

Begin at the sign WEST METOLIUS TRAIL. The trail drops down immediately to the bank of the river and heads north, away from the campground. The trail surface is rocky-dusty and very irregular; wear good ankle support or plan to pick your way along slowly.

Tucked close along the bank of the seething, onyx-green Metolius, the path is surrounded by brush and berry bushes, shielded by pine, fir, and the occasional incense cedar. A lively array of birds, squirrels, and butterflies (or, depending upon the season, caterpillars) shares the path.

Central Oregonians know the Metolius River best for its underwater inhabitants, and you can see why any trout worth his scales would want to live here. The river is clear and cold, fed by numerous creeklets cascading down the banks in miniature waterfalls. (Those on the opposite bank are particularly lovely; those on your side make for muddy walking.)

ər the first mile, where the river's banks are steep and the foliage is thick around the trail, things open up. The banks slope more gently, the surrounding greenery thins out, and more sun (or more rain…) falls on the path.

At 2.0 miles, you can see a bridge ahead. This foot and one-lane auto bridge is adjacent to your destination, the Wizard Falls Fish Hatchery. After you catch sight of the bridge, the trail veers left into the woods and away from the river. Two bridged stream-crossings later, you emerge at the hatchery, at 2.25 miles.

Take a few minutes to wander around the park-like grounds of the fish hatchery before returning the way you came. Six species of fish are reared here: rainbow trout, brown trout, kokanee, mountain whitefish, dolly varden, and brook trout. The hatchery, built in 1947, hatches up to 5,000,000 eggs annually, some of which are transferred to other hatcheries.

Hikers wishing a longer hike can continue north (downstream) from the hatchery on the Lower West Metolius trail.

Nearest Lodgings: Lake Creek Lodge, Metolius River Resort.

COFFIN MOUNTAIN
Lush meadow, great view.

Map:	Green Trails #556, "Detroit," also access roads on #557, "Mt. Jefferson"
Distance:	3.2 miles
Elevation Gain:	1100′
Estimated Time:	2 hours

This wide-open hike charges up a meadowed hillside to a working (and inaccessible) lookout tower. If you don't like steep trails, you won't like this one. But if you like lush meadows, great views, and big panoramic payoffs for minimal mileage, check it out.

Getting There
From Highway 22, designated West Cascades Oregon Scenic Byway, turn west on Road 11, also marked STRAIGHT CREEK ROAD. From points north and west such as Detroit, this turn is about 3.0 miles south of Marion Forks. From points south and east such as Sisters, the turn is 12.2 miles north of Santiam Junction (the junction of Highway 22 with Highway 20/126).

Follow Road 11, a well-paved, two-lane road, 4.1 miles to a Y. Take the right fork onto gravel Road 1168, signed COFFIN MTN. TR. 4, BACHELOR MTN. TR. 5. (Do not be confused by an initial junction with Road 1168 1.3 miles from the highway; it's a long loop road, and you want the second junction.)

As you ascend through the clearcuts, say a little prayer for all the dear departed trees. Be prepared for loose gravel and steep drop-offs—concentrate on all the altitude you're gaining by car and won't have to gain on foot. Passengers will enjoy views of Mt. Jefferson and Mt. Hood to the north, Three-Fingered Jack to the east, and the Sisters to the south.

Stay left when you pass forks at 1.1 and 1.3 miles. At 3.8 miles, turn le a short spur signed COFFIN MTN. Almost immediately after turning, pull off a signed trailhead, COFFIN LOOKOUT TRAIL 3392. Room for 3 or 4 cars.

The Hike

Ascend a rocky dirt singletrack through pearly everlasting, fireweed, mountain daisy, lupine, and fern. This steep, open trail offers views from the start, beginning with the pointy snowcap of Mt. Jefferson to your right from the trailhead. After about 0.25 mile, Three-Fingered Jack can be seen back behind you to the southeast.

Continue ascending through an old burn, where the meadow has re-asserted itself with purple thistles, red-orange paintbrush, and creamy-headed beargrass. Near the 0.5-mile point, a view of Mt. Washington opens up to the south, followed shortly by views of Broken Top and the Sisters.

At 0.75 mile, you crest a ridge and get your first views to the west; Detroit Lake lies below. (From Detroit, this mountain looks formidable indeed; it is from that angle that it takes its name, appearing box-like.) The higher you climb, the more obvious is the contrast between the clearcut and mature-growth areas below, resulting in a disconcerting patchwork.

At 0.8 mile, the switchbacks relent, and the grade lessens as the path contours around the east side of the mountain, heading northeast. Kodak moments abound, as Mt. Jefferson looms across the open meadows.

At 1.1 miles, double back to your left (southwest) to ascend more steeply again. This must have been the angle from which the Three Sisters were named—they look more like three equal peaks from here than from any other vantage point in this book.

Enter a stand of trees at 1.3 miles. A spur trail joins you on the left after 200 feet; it heads out across a meadow (a good alternate picnic spot) toward some

Coffin Mountain with lookout tower

.dons equipment, as the main trail continues straight ahead. In 200–300 feet, at 1.4 miles, you reach a signed junction. A trail to your left toward Road 137 and an alternate Coffin Mountain trailhead; the trailhead om which you came is alleged to be 2.0 miles back (it isn't). Continue straight ahead on the trail to the lookout.

Emerge from the trees almost immediately after the junction; the lookout building is clearly visible on a rocky outcropping ahead. Reach the top at 1.6 miles, where you'll find the lookout tower (please respect the occupant and stay away from it, on the main paths), a helicopter pad, and a 360° view of the central Cascades: Mt. Hood's graceful symmetry to the north, Mt. Jefferson's snowy bulk to the east, Three-Fingered Jack's irregular crags just south of Jefferson. The slender finger of Mt. Washington is south of Three-Fingered Jack, the Three Sisters are due south, and the snaggletoothed ridge of Broken Top appears in a visual saddle between Washington and the Sisters. Walking around the helicopter pad to the west side of the summit, you can see Detroit Lake below. Watch out for the edge—this could be why they named it "Coffin" Mountain. It's a five-screamer to the bottom.

Nearest Lodgings: Any in this section.

BLACK BUTTE
Perfect panoramic views; 3 lookout towers.

Map:	US Forest Service "Sisters Ranger District Deschutes National Forest"
Distance:	4.0 miles round-trip
Elevation Gain:	1556′
Estimated Time:	2 hours, 30 minutes

Here's a chance to apply that geometry you learned in school. To look at the Black Butte trail on a map, it doesn't look like it could be 2.0 miles to the summit. Compared to other trails, or to the mileage grid, it looks like a scant 1.5 miles—1.7, tops. Well, remember how the hypotenuse is always the longest leg of a right triangle? It's 2.0 miles, all right.

Black Butte is a wonder. Not only is the view from the top a veritable central Oregon geography lesson, but the buildings on top provide a slice of history, too. You'll find three mostly intact fire lookouts of varying vintages plus a deluxe cabin to house the current lookout. If you're especially lucky, the on-duty lookout will invite you up to the tower. (Don't count on it, though. All three towers, while interesting to look at, are strictly off-limits to the public except by invitation of the lookout.)

The hike is steep and partially exposed, which can be a killer combination on a hot day. Bring water, take your time, and go on the clearest day you can—the views will knock your socks off. For the most comfortable experience and the best photos, go early in the day, when the trail is shadiest and the light on the numerous visible peaks is coming from the east.

Getting There

From Highway 20/126, turn north on Forest Service Road 11. This turn, signed INDIAN FORD CAMPGROUND and BLACK BUTTE STABLES, is 2.0 miles east of Black Butte Ranch and 5.3 miles west of Sisters. After 3.7 miles on paved, two-lane Road 11, reach a Y. Road 11 continues, paved, to the right; you should fork left onto gravel Road 1110, which is signed BLACK BUTTE TR. HD. This road, which warns NARROW ROAD NOT SUITED FOR TRAILER TRAFFIC, lives up to its promise. It's a rough, washboard, one-lane affair with turnouts.

Watch for two hairpin turns, the first at 3.6 miles, the second at 4.0 miles. At the second one, a primitive road continues straight ahead, but it should be pretty obvious that the Black Butte trailhead route continues uphill and to your right.

At road's end (a total of 5.1 miles on Road 1110), you'll find a signed trailhead and room for half a dozen cars. Should this area be full, another potential parking pullout is just a few dozen feet back down the road. No toilets or water are available at the trailhead or anywhere on the route.

The Hike

This is a hiker-only trail. Dogs are allowed, but leashes are required, and are especially important at the summit, where chipmunks, grouse, and other critters abound. The trail begins to the right of the information sign; follow the split-rail fence uphill.

Black Butte ranger cabin, cupola lookout, and 85' tower

The rocky-dusty trail ascends steeply through sparse Ponderosa pine, grand fir, and whitebark pine forest. Manzanita, snowbrush, and hardy clumps of ferns line the dry trail.

Views begin near the end of the first mile. At 0.9 mile, just after an interpretive sign identifies a whitebark pine on your left, look to the right for a tree-framed view of Mt. Washington—it's the one with the absurd little nodule of rock poking up on top, sort of like Dr. Suess might have drawn it. At this point, you will notice many aspens around the trail; their clean, white bark and dainty, heart-shaped leaves provide a pretty contrast to the conifers.

The canopy all but disappears after a mile; berry-bearing shrubs appear in profusion: serviceberry, squaw currant, bitter cherry. Heading southeast, the Sisters and Broken Top are straight ahead of you. The clearing of Black Butte Ranch lies below. Behind you is Three-Fingered Jack (which makes you wonder—why don't they call Mt. Washington "One-Fingered George?")

At 1.75, as you trudge through bitterbrush and other low-growing plants that signal subalpine summits, you mercifully and finally contour around the east end of the summit. For the first time, you can see to the north. Still ascending, the first peak you will see (looking through the skeletal remains of a 1980s burn) is Mt. Hood. As you ascend farther, you see three snowcapped giants: Mt. Jefferson in the foreground on the left, Mt. Hood in the middle distance in the center, and the tip of Mt. Adams in the far distance on the right.

Once on top, stay on the designated paths. The first tower you encounter is the 1995 lookout, 65 feet tall, currently in use, and off-limits to the public except by invitation of the lookout. Follow the paths across the butte's summit to the historic 1934 tower. Used until 1990, this 85-foot tower was constructed by the CCCs. Continue down the path to a small structure most of us would not recognize as an early fire lookout. This 1924, "cupola-style" tower, once common, is one of the few remaining such structures in our national forests. Around this little tower are signs helping you identify the peaks and geographic features surrounding you. Behind the tower is a forest service cabin which serves as sleeping quarters for the lookout on duty; please respect its privacy.

Black Butte has been a lookout site since 1910, and you can see why. It provides an amazing 360° panorama.

On the way back down, watch your step. Those steep surfaces you battled all the way up are covered with loose rock that can be slippery.

Nearest Lodgings: Black Butte Ranch; any Sisters or Camp Sherman lodging.

DEVILS RIDGE LOOP
Challenging climb; serene old-growth.

Map:	Green Trails #524 & #525, "Battle Ax" & "Breitenbush" (access only)
Distance:	4.8 mile loop
Elevation Gain:	1300'
Estimated Time:	3 hours, 15 minutes

This trail patches together pieces of several trails near the Breitenbush Hot Springs area for a walk through magnificent old-growth forest and a steep climb to a former lookout site. Those who want to experience the old-growth walk without the climb can do so, resulting in the 3.4-mile out-and-back hike called Spotted Owl/Emerald Forest (see above).

Whichever route you choose, you'll get to experience a forest teeming with life. Nurse logs nourish rhododendrons and Oregon grape; dozens of species of birds congregate (this is a monitoring area for the US Forest Service's neotropical migratory bird conservation program), and trees along the way include cedar, yew, Douglas-fir, Western hemlock, and alder.

Getting There

If you are staying at Breitenbush, walk out to the parking area, out past the guard shack, and bear left onto the signed trail. This path will take you a few dozen feet through the woods to a road. Cross the road to the trailhead.

From the Detroit area, take Road 46 north. Pass Cleator Bend Campground at 10 miles, then turn right, crossing the river. From here, follow the signs toward Breitenbush Hot Springs, taking all the left turns until you reach the fork at the entrance to Breitenbush. Here, the left fork will take you into Breitenbush Hot Springs & Conference Center, and the right fork is a gated stub. Bear right and park alongside the road at the fork. Do not block either road.

Walk about 80 feet up the right fork (the gated stub road) to a trailhead on your right.

The Hike

The route begins on a trail called the Spotted Owl. You will pass through recovering clearcuts within the first half mile, but the old-growth forest is just ahead. The route is marked with unobtrusive arrow signs that help keep you on track. (Also see map: "Spotted Owl/Emerald Forest Trail and Devils Ridge Loop Trail," in this section.)

Pass through a grove of alders at about 0.7 mile, just before reaching Devil's Creek. Pick your way through the deadfall to the first of two bridges across the creek, separated by an island in the middle. Bear left on the island to find the second bridge, and cross to the other side.

Follow the path to the left, through a horsetail fern marsh. Arrive at a fork at 0.8. A tract of summer homes is to your left; stay right. The trail begins to ascend.

At 0.9, reach a signed fork. Technically, this is where Spotted Owl ends. Stay left, following a sign for DEVILS RIDGE TRAIL via TREE TRAIL. This is also the way to reach EMERALD FOREST TRAIL. The right fork leads uphill to CLIFF TRAIL; this is the way you will return from Devils Ridge.

Aptly named Tree Trail is a rooty, gently undulating, needle-strewn half-mile path amidst giant Douglas-fir and Western hemlock.

At 1.4 miles, you'll reach another signed junction; this is the end of Tree Trail. To the right is Devils Ridge Trail; turn right and head uphill. This junction is signed DEVILS RIDGE 2 MI, but it's actually just over a mile (granted, a killer-steep

e top) to the turnaround. The climb begins on a trail that's just mod-
p, on a path surrounded by thick deadfall.

Just past 1.7 miles, arrive at another junction, signed JUNCTION CLIFF TR. & DEV-
ILS RIDGE TR. Cliff Trail, on which you will return, is a hard right. Turn left, following a sign toward DEVILS LOOKOUT.

Climb along the ridgeline, moderately at first, then steeper and steeper. The
canopy thins, and the understory becomes sparse and dusty. By the time you
pass 2.0 miles, you're getting a real "top of the world" feeling. Just when you
think things couldn't get much steeper, they do. Log stairsteps just after 2.3 miles
(more like a ladder at this angle) help you ascend.

At 2.5 miles, you reach the former lookout site, an exposed ridge with views
both to the southwest into the Devils Creek valley, and northeast into the
Breitenbush River valley. This is the best viewpoint, and a logical place to turn
around. If you continue past this point, you'll slope downhill a bit, then continue climbing along the ridge, eventually reaching Devils Peak. But the trail is
unmaintained and, some 0.4 miles past the lookout site, it can really be a bush-
whacking trek.

Descend the same way you came up, reaching the junction with Cliff Trail
and Devil's Ridge Trail just before 3.2 miles. To descend via Cliff Trail, go
straight (as opposed to right). As you descend, watch for a short spur trail on
your left in the elbow of a switchback at about 3.3 miles. It leads a short distance out on a rocky ledge to a viewpoint overlooking the Devils Creek
drainage.

Continue descending on Cliff Trail, a rocky, rooty, difficult trail that switchbacks steeply down to the junction with Spotted Owl and Tree Trail at 3.9 miles.
Turn left and return via Spotted Owl, re-crossing Devils Creek and retracing
your steps back past the recovering clearcuts to the trailhead.

Nearest Lodgings: Breitenbush Hot Springs, Detroit motels (see *Additional
Lodgings*).

PATJENS LAKES LOOP
Three backwoods lakelets and one Big Lake.

Map:	US Forest Service "Mt. Washington Wilderness," "Willamette National Forest," or "Sisters Ranger District Deschutes National Forest"
Distance:	5.6 mile loop or 4.4 miles round trip out-and-back to Middle Patjens Lake
Elevation Gain:	450′ on loop, 300′ on out-and-back
Estimated Time:	2 hours, 45 minutes

If you want to get away from the more-popular Square Lake and Suttle Lake
crowds (see *Other Hike Notes*, below), try this loop. It takes you from a large, popular recreational lake to three backwoods lakelets known collectively as Patjens
Lakes. The loop is the longer version, utilizing a narrow, sometimes mucky trail

up and over a ridge northeast of the lakes, then returning via a shorter, more popular route to the Big Lake trailhead. The loop route is more likely to provide solitude, but the first 3.0 miles are more difficult and yield no great payoffs in terms of views or features. This part of the trail is narrower and a bit overgrown; long pants and/or gaiters are recommended, especially in wet conditions.

The alternate route is an out-and-back, utilizing only the wider and more popular path from Big Lake (the second part of the loop route). This route takes you to Patjens Lakes more quickly, with less elevation change. It travels along the shore of Big Lake, then a short distance through the woods to the lakes.

Take the loop if you have the time and the inclination for a good leg-stretch and a bit of solitude; take the out-and-back if you have kids or less hardy hikers along.

Getting There

From Highway 20/126, take the turnoff south toward Hoodoo Ski Bowl. This turnoff is located 0.7 miles west of Santiam Pass, which makes it 20.0 miles west of Sisters, 12.7 miles west of Black Butte Ranch, and about 5.0 miles east of the Santiam Junction, which is where Highway 22 from Detroit junctions with Highway 20/126.

Head south on this paved, two-lane road 0.8 miles to a fork. Take the left fork, Road 2690, following the sign for Big Lake. This road, though narrower, is also paved. Stay on it as it curves around Hayrick Butte, then goes straight south toward Mt. Washington—this is the closest you will get to Mt. Washington's north side on any of the hikes in this book. Enjoy the view en route; you don't see Mt. Washington on the trail. (For a hike that brings you good close-up views of Mt. Washington's south side, see *Little Belknap Crater*, below.)

After 2.9 miles from the fork, just before a gate, pull into the wide spot on the right side of the road signed PATJENS LAKES TRAILHEAD, TR. 3395. Space is provided for about 15 cars.

The Hike

This hiker and equestrian trail is part of the Willamette National Forest's Mt. Washington Wilderness; fill out your self-issuing wilderness permit at the trailhead.

Begin on a little dirt singletrack carved from the meadowed ground behind the trailhead marker. A partial canopy of slender pine and fir shades an understory thick with grasses, including beargrass.

Just past 0.1 mile, you come to a Y. To do the loop trail (counterclockwise is recommended, saving the easy part and the Big Lake views for the end of the hike), take the right fork. To do the shorter, out-and-back trail, take the left fork. (The loop trail will return that way.) The balance of the detailed description pertains to the loop trail.

Continue on a nearly flat, narrow path southwest through the woods, ignoring any trails that junction on your right. A long, narrow, open meadow parallels your route for much of the first mile, visible on your left through the trees. Keep an eye peeled for deer.

After 1.3 miles, begin a steady ascent. Still ascending, you will officially pass into the Mt. Washington Wilderness at 1.6 miles. Shortly thereafter, top out at 4800 feet; this is the highest point on the hike. After barely a glimpse of the peaks to the south, your descent begins all too soon.

The next mile is where you'll wish you had long pants—waterproof ones or gaiters on a wet day or dewey morning. The path is a trench through thick meadow, the sides often overgrown with ferns, wildflowers, and grasses that rub your legs with each step. Down, down, down you go, losing nearly 400 feet gradually to moderately over most of the mile.

At 2.5 miles, you may notice a small pond through the trees to your right. There is no good access to it, and it is not one of the Patjens Lakes. At this point, the path levels off.

At about 2.8 miles, the path curves to the east (your left), and goes uphill a bit. At 2.9, it flattens out again. Here, too, the quality of the trail improves. You have a sense that you have arrived somewhere, and, indeed, you have. Just after 2.9, you come to a horse tie-up area, and the westernmost Patjens Lake is down a short slope to your left. Like the other two, this little blue-brown lake is slightly marshy, tranquil, and without any particular view features. It is a nice place to be still and watch the wildlife. After visiting its banks, return to the main path.

Continuing past the first lake, ignore a fork at 3.1 miles (i.e., stay right, the left fork leads down to a meadow that you will be able to see from the second lake). Shortly, at about 3.2 miles, you will see the second and largest of the lakes to your left. At 3.4 miles, a backwards-forking Y leads to your left to the meadowed margins of the lake.

This second and largest lake is also the best choice for a picnic stop. It even has bathing potential, though you may want to save yourself for Big Lake. Be respectful of the shoreline and meadows; these are fragile areas.

Upon returning to the main path, continue east. A path to the third and smallest lake junctions on your left at 3.5 miles.

From here, the wide, forested path takes you back, at a slight to moderate grade, toward Big Lake. You will pass out of the designated wilderness area after about a mile. At this point, a few narrow trails lead off to your right; stay left until you reach the lake.

At 4.7 miles, Big Lake comes into full view. Living up to its name, it's a vast body of water with ample room to recreate. Directly across the lake looms the flat-topped bulk of Hayrick Butte. Choose any one of several short trails down to Big Lake's rocky-sandy banks for a celebration dip.

Walk along the lake's southeast shore for nearly half a mile. Your last chance to access the lake comes at a fork at 5.1 miles. The right fork is a spur leading to the lake. The left fork is the main trail, which heads west, away from the lake, around a low hill, and eventually intersects the trail on which you began, just before 5.5 miles. Turn right at this familiar junction and continue to the parking area.

Nearest Lodgings: Black Butte Ranch, Lake Creek Lodge, Metolius River Resort.

TAM MCARTHUR RIM
Breathtaking high-altitude views of the Three Sisters and Broken Top.

Map:	US Forest Service "Sisters Ranger District Deschutes National Forest"
Distance:	5.2 miles round-trip
Elevation Gain:	1200´
Estimated Time:	3 hours, 30 minutes

Stupendous views await you on this intensely beautiful volcanic ridge. This hike begins at altitude (over 6500 feet elevation) and keeps on climbing. Snow patches remain late in the season, so you'll want to make sure the trail is open before making the sixteen-mile drive south from Sisters. From the top, an in-your-face look at the Sisters dominates a panorama that includes Three Fingered Jack, Mt. Washington, Black Butte, Belknap Crater, Black Crater, Three Creek Lake, and Little Three Creek Lake.

Getting There
Find Village Green City Park, two blocks south of Cascade on Elm, in Sisters. From the park, continue south on Elm Street. Elm turns into Forest Service Road 16 as you enter the Deschutes National Forest, just outside of town. This is a two-lane, paved, shoulderless road with the high-desert character typical of the foothills of the eastern Oregon Cascades. Ponderosa pines dot a dry landscape, becoming thicker as you ascend and head south.

Tam McArthur Rim

The road turns to gravel after 14 miles. Various roads fork off of Road 16, the most pronounced of which is just past milepost 15. In each case, take the road that is most nearly straight ahead, following the signs for THREE CREEK LAKE.

At about 16 miles, a road intersects on your right, leading to Driftwood Campground. Just after that, you can pull off pretty much anywhere along the side of the road. You will see the TAM MCARTHUR RIM TRAILHEAD sign on the left. Three Creek Lake and Three Creek Lake Campground are just ahead at the end of the road.

The Hike

From your parking area along the road near the signed trailhead, if you look up and to the southwest, you will see a sheer rock shelf curving up and westward. The rocky outcropping at its top west edge is your final destination.

This trail passes into the Three Sisters Wilderness, so you will need a wilderness permit; these are self-issuing at the trailhead. The multi-use trail is popular with equestrians, hence its surface is rocky and dusty. You, too, may wish you had a horse as you attack most of the climb in the first three-quarters of a mile. Give yourself a break if you're feeling winded—a 1200-foot climb is tough enough, but this one starts higher than most, and tops out at over 7700 feet elevation.

Climb steadily through sparse forest dotted with hardy lupine until you reach the official boundary of the Three Sisters Wilderness at about 0.8 mile.

From here on, the hike is quite open. Enjoy a flat quarter mile through an open meadow from which you can once again see the outcropping of your final destination, due west. Climb a short, steep rise at the end of the meadow, at about 1.1 miles. In the second mile, your uphill progress comes in a series of long benches with inclines between—a sort of geologic staircase. These benches can hold snow patches quite late into the season.

Deep red and black volcanic rock dominates the landscape by the 2.0 mile point. Between the rockiness and the snow patches, you may have trouble discerning the path from time to time. Just stay right, following the ridgeline, and you'll be fine.

Climb a short, steep rise at 2.2 miles, then a final gradual one from 2.4 to 2.5 miles. (Watch for Mt. Bachelor to the south during this stretch.) At 2.5 miles, the path forks. Take the right fork up to the knoll. Watch your footing along the edge of the rim and at the viewpoint—it's a long way down.

On top is the view you've been waiting for. Standing with South Sister directly in front of you, you'll see the aptly-named, jagged Broken Top on your left. Middle and North Sister, appearing connected by massive Hayden Glacier from this angle, are to the right of South Sister. To the right of the Sisters is Mt. Jefferson, which, along with Three Creek and Little Three Creek lakes, has been your constant companion for most of the ascent. On a clear day, you can see Mt. Adams, clear across the border in Washington state.

Nearest Lodgings: Squaw Creek B&B Inn, Conklin's Guest House.

LITTLE BELKNAP CRATER

Eerie lava field and small crater.

Map:	US Forest Service "Mt. Washington Wilderness," "Willamette National Forest," or "Sisters Ranger District Deschutes National Forest"
Distance:	5.0 miles round-trip
Elevation Gain:	1000′
Estimated Time:	3 hours, 15 minutes

If you've never seen a lava field up close, you must make the trip to the area around McKenzie Pass. Here, some of our nation's most recent lava flows (about 1500 to 3000 years old) cover some 65 square miles. An observatory at McKenzie Pass offers a good roadside look at it, and the 0.5-mile Lava River Trail (see above) provides an easy interpretive stroll through it. But if you want to get out into the midst of it, and experience the remains of a small crater first-hand, Little Belknap is the dayhike for you.

Hike a 2.5-mile segment of the Pacific Crest Trail off Highway 242 to a spur trail leading up to the crater itself. You'll pass through islands untouched by lava rivers, then hike on the chunky lava itself. Wear good shoes with ankle support and hard-nubbed soles, as these surfaces are irregular, sharp, and abrasive. Carry water, too—the hike is very exposed.

Getting There

At the west end of Sisters, take the left-hand fork onto Highway 242. This narrow, well-paved highway is a scenic corridor, first through thick Ponderosa pine forest, then through the Belknap and Yapoah lavalands. Stop and get your bearings at an interpretive viewpoint as you enter the lava flow zone, nearly 12 miles out of Sisters. From here, you can see Belknap Crater as well as Little Belknap, your destination.

Reach McKenzie Pass after 14.6 miles, and the cylindrical, stone Dee Wright Observatory. This area is definitely worth a stop en route or on your way back toward Sisters. (See Lava River Trail, above.)

Go 0.4 mile west past the observatory to a right-hand gravel turnoff for the Pacific Crest Trail. Parking for 8 or 10 cars is available at the trailhead.

Traveling from the west, take Highway 126 east from Eugene/Springfield to McKenzie Bridge, then approximately 5 more miles to the Highway 242 junction. Take 242 about 21.5 miles. Turn left at the PCT marker to the parking area. If you reach the Dee Wright Observatory at McKenzie Pass, you've gone 0.4 mile too far.

The Hike

You will be following the Pacific Crest Trail (PCT) 2.3 miles north. Fill out a self-issuing permit for the Mt. Washington Wilderness at the trailhead. The hike begins at a moderate incline, on a duff surface shaded by forest and flanked with huckleberries and ferns.

ile, you break out into a the first open lava flow area. A boot-beat- osed of smaller lava chunks is easily discernible through the larg- ocks of lava. This is actually a narrow "river" of lava stretching alongside an "island" of forest that was untouched by the 1500–3000-year-old lava flow. Cross the lava and step onto the forested island.

The path skirts around south, then west edges of forest island, finally curving around to its north side and heading east. Just before 0.7 mile, you turn left (north), back onto lava, where you will remain for the remainder of the hike. The only "trees" on the rest of the trail are occasional bleached-white snags, sticking from the rubble like ghostly sentinels.

As you walk through the lava rubble, you can see various geological phenomena such as lava tubes that have collapsed to form gullies, caves, and tunnels, as well as places where plates of cooling lava have shifted against one another to create dramatic folds and contrasts. Most of the lava through which you are walking is black; Little Belknap is the sharp point of red rock to the north.

At 2.3 miles, with the rounded, tan bulk of Belknap Crater to your left, the ragged, red point of Little Belknap Crater to your right, and the scrawny pyramid of Mt. Washington dead ahead, you come to a junction. Turn right, leaving the PCT, to ascend Little Belknap.

As you ascend, you can see Mt. Jefferson to your left. The lava caves and tubes along this little 0.2-mile spur trail are the most dramatic on the route; watch for an especially well-formed cave after 2.4 miles, where the path makes an abrupt jag to the right. Reach a false summit just before 2.5 miles, after which you must drop down a bit, to the right, and climb a little dirt trail to reach the actual summit.

From the top, views of Jefferson, Washington, the Sisters, Belknap and Black craters are yours as you rest and refuel for the walk back. Don't be surprised to find that the rough, uneven surfaces have taken their toll—the level of effort to get here is more than your average 2.5-mile hike.

Enjoy the wide-open views to the south of the Sisters as you return the way you came.

Nearest Lodgings: Black Butte Ranch, Conklin's Guest House, Squaw Creek B&B Inn.

OTHER HIKE NOTES

These hikes not personally reviewed or not as highly recommended as the above hikes.

South Breitenbush Gorge

Access this beautiful river-gorge trail from Forest Service Road 4686, as described under the Crown Lake hike, above. The trail is 2.0 miles each way, but has car access points at each end, and at 1.5 miles, so you could do anything from a 0.5-mile one-way shuttle to a 4.0-mile round-trip. Also accessible on foot from Breitenbush Hot Springs.

Breitenbush Loop

Guests at Breitenbush Hot Springs have excellent access to seve
be combined to result in a 5.5-mile loop trail that begins and
ings. The loop combines the Spotted Owl, Tree, Emerald Forest (see above),
South Breitenbush Gorge trails, all of which are open to the public, and connects
them via a 0.5-mile trail segment that runs through the Breitenbush property
(closed to non-guests). Obtain a map from the Breitenbush Hot Springs office.

Iron Mountain

A major wildflower destination, Iron Mountain boasts hundreds of species of
plants and flowers, many of them rare. Take Highway 126/20 west or Highway
22 east (south) to Santiam Junction, then proceed west on 126/20. After 3 miles,
stay right on Highway 20, toward Corvallis. Continue 8 miles on Highway 20;
watch for the signed trailhead parking on the left. The trailhead is on the other
side of the road. It's about 3.2 miles round trip, and it's steep, but worth it when
the flowers are in bloom.

Suttle Lake

This popular round-the-lake path is a flat 3.5-mile loop around a fishing and
boating lake. Find the Suttle Lake turnoff on Highway 126/20 about 13 miles
west of Sisters and 6 miles east of Santiam Pass. Good walk for families. The
loop trail can be accessed in several places.

Square Lake

This gem of a lake is the victim of overuse because of its proximity to the highway. Still, it can be a nice walk on a weekday or if it's open in the shoulder season. Near Santiam Pass on Highway 126/20, watch for a turnoff on the north
side of the road for Pacific Crest Trail. Drive up a short spur to a parking loop
and the trailhead. Walk a few hundred feet to the PCT and turn left. After about
0.5 mile, watch for a right turn to Square Lake. The round trip is about 5.0 miles.
If you're up for a longer walk, leave the crowds behind and go the additional
(and a bit more difficult) 1.5 miles to Booth Lake, for a total hike of 8.0 miles.

Table 9.
Lodgings in the Central Oregon vicinity

	BLACK BUTTE RANCH	BREITENBUSH HOT SPRINGS	CONKLIN'S GUEST HOUSE	LAKE CREEK LODGE	METOLIUS RIVER RESORT	Sꞯ CREꞇ INN
PRICE (1997 SUMMER RATES, PRE-TAX, 2 PERSON)	$85–$295	$110–$140	$90–$120	$110–$160	$120–$160	$75–$85
EXTRA PERSON	Included	adult $55–$70; age 11–15 $30; age 6–10 $20; age 0–5 free	$20 (see also dormitory description)	$50	$10 over 6	$5
PAYMENT METHODS	VISA, MC, AmEx, Disc, Checks, Cash	VISA, MC, Checks, Cash	VISA, Checks, Cash	Checks, Cash	VISA, MC, Cash	VISA, MC, Checks, Cash
# OF UNITS	100	42	5	15	11	4
PRIVATE BATH	Yes	yes and no	Yes	Yes	Yes	Yes
BREAKFAST INCLUDED	No	Yes, 3 meals daily included	Yes	Yes, plus dinner	No	Yes
COOKING FACILITIES	Yes	No	No	Yes	Yes	Yes
POOL	Yes	No	Yes	Yes	No	No
HOT TUB	Yes	Yes	No	No	No	Yes
CHILDREN	OK	OK; except during certain times (call)	OK, 12 & over	OK	OK	OK
PETS	No	No	Not inside; outside on leash only	By arrangement; $8 fee.	No	By arrangement; deposit required.
HANDICAPPED ACCESSIBLE	Yes	Yes	Yes	Yes	No	Call

Contact Information

Bureau of Indian Affairs (Mt. Adams' east side)

Glenwood, WA
(509) 364-3327
(this location mostly resource management)

Toppenish, WA
(509) 865-2255
(this location farther from trails, but more likely to have answers)

Chambers of Commerce/Tourist Information

Hood River County Chamber of Commerce
405 Portway Ave., Port Marina Park
Hood River, OR 97031
(541) 386-2000
(800) 366-3530

Klickitat County Tourism Office
P.O. Box 1220
Goldendale, WA 98620
(509) 773-3466

Mt. Adams Chamber of Commerce
P.O. Box 449
White Salmon, WA 98672
(509) 493-3630

Sisters Area Chamber of Commerce
231 E. Hood St., Suite D
P.O. Box 430
Sisters, OR 97759
(541) 549-0251

Skamania County Chamber
of Commerce
P.O. Box 1037
Stevenson, WA 98648
(509) 427-8911
(800) 989-9178

Columbia Gorge National Scenic Area

Waucoma Center,
902 Wasco Ave., Suite 200
Hood River, OR 97031
(541) 386-2333

Deschutes National Forest

Headquarters/Supervisor's Office
1645 Highway 20 East
Bend, OR 97701
(541) 388-2715

Sisters Ranger District
P.O. Box 249
Sisters, OR 97759
(541) 549-2111

Emergency (most areas)

911

Gifford Pinchot National Forest

Forest Headquarters
10600 NE 51st Circle
Vancouver, WA 98682
(360) 891-5000
24-hour recording: (360) 891-5009
TTY: (360) 891-5003

Mt. Adams Ranger District
2455 Highway 141
Trout Lake, WA 98650
(509) 395-3400
24-hour recording: (509) 395-3420
TTY: (509) 395-3422

Packwood Ranger District
13068 US Highway 12
Packwood, WA 98361
(360) 494-0600
TTY: (360) 494-0601

Randle Ranger District
10024 US Highway 12
Randle, WA 98377
(360) 497-1100
TTY: (360) 497-1101

Recreation Report &
Other Information
www.fs.fed.us/gpnf

Wind River Ranger District
1262 Hemlock Road
Carson, WA 98610
(509) 427-3200
TTY: (509) 427-4541

Highway Information

AAA Pass Report
(425) 646-2190

Oregon Department
of Transportation
(503) 588-2941

Washington State Department
of Transportation
(888) SNO-INFO (766-4636)

Washington State Patrol
Highway Information
(360) 690-7100

Maps

Call or write the specific National Park, National Forest, or area you plan to visit, or contact:

MapLink
30 S. LaPatera Lane
Santa Barbara, CA 93117
(800) 962-1394

Outdoor Recreation
Information Center (ORIC)
(a joint Forest Service/
National Park Service venture)
R.E.I., 222 Yale Ave. N
Seattle, WA 98109
(206) 470-4060

Mount St. Helens National Volcanic Monument

Administrative Headquarters
42218 NE Yale Bridge Road
Amboy, WA 98601
(360) 247-3900
24-hour recording: (360) 247-3903
TTY: (360) 247-3902

Climbing Information Line
(360) 247-3961

Visitor Centers
3029 Spirit Lake Highway
Castle Rock, WA 98611
24-hour recording: (360) 274-2103
TTY: 274-2102

Coldwater
(360) 274-2131
Johnston Ridge Observatory
(360) 274-2140
Silver Lake
(360) 274-2100

Mt. Hood National Forest

Please note that the Forest Headquarters and the Zigzag Ranger Station are primarily administrative numbers. For hiker information along the Hood River Valley, contact the Hood River Ranger District; along the south corridor, contact Mt. Hood Information Center.

Forest Headquarters
16400 Champion Way
Sandy, OR 97055
(503) 668-1771

Mt. Hood Information Center
65000 E. Highway 26
Welches, OR 97067
(503) 622-7674

Hood River Ranger District
6780 Hwy. 35
Mt. Hood-Parkdale, OR 97041
(541) 352-6002

Zigzag Ranger Station
70220 E. Hwy. 26
Zigzag, OR 97049
(503) 622-3191

Mt. Rainier National Park — (360) 569-2211

Longmire Museum and Hiker Info Center	ext. 3314
Paradise, Jackson Visitor Center	ext. 2328
Sunrise Visitor Center	ext. 2357
White River Ranger Station	ext. 2356
Wilderness Information	ext. 3317

Weather-Related Information

Avalanche Forecast Center	(206) 526-6677
National Weather Forecast, Seattle Office	(206) 526-6087 www.seawfo.noaa.gov
National Weather Forecast, Portland Office	(503) 261-9246 nimbo.wrh.noaa.gov/Portland
Portland Oregonian Inside Line	(503) 225-5555
Central Oregon Cascades Weather	x 8072
Columbia Gorge Weather	x 8053
General Oregon State Weather	x 8055
Northern Oregon Cascades Weather	x 8070

Southern Oregon Cascades Weather   x 8071
Portland Weatherline Forecast Service   (503) 243-7575
Seattle Times Information Line   (206) 464-2000
General Weather   x 9900
Cascades & Olympics Weather   x 9904
Mt. Rainier Weather   x 9915

Willamette National Forest

Headquarters
211 East 7th Ave./P.O. Box 10607
Eugene, OR 97440
(541) 465-6521

Detroit Ranger District
HC73 Box 320
Mill City, OR 97360
(503) 854-3366

Sally O'Neal Coates is a writer, musician, and outdoor enthusiast, and is the author of two other books from Wilderness Press: *Hot Showers, Soft Beds, and Dayhikes in the North Cascades* and *Great Bike Rides in Eastern Washington and Oregon.* She lives in Richland, Washington, with her husband, Doug, stepson, Mitchell, and an assortment of indoor livestock.

Index

Your safety is your responsibility

Hiking and camping in the wilderness can be dangerous. Experience and preparation reduce risk, but will never eliminate it. The unique details of your specific situation and the decisions you make at that time will determine the outcome. This book is not a substitute for common sense or sound judgment. If you doubt your ability to negotiate mountain terrain, respond to wild animals, or handle sudden, extreme weather changes, hike only in a group led by a competent guide. The authors and the publisher of this book disclaim liability for any loss or injury incurred by anyone using information in this book.